D1162989

How to Conduct and Analyze Real Estate Market and Feasibility Studies

How to Conduct and Analyze Real Estate Market and Feasibility Studies

Second Edition

G. Vincent Barrett

Professor and Director
Center for Real Estate and Land Use Research
New Mexico State University

John P. Blair

Professor
Department of Economics
Wright State University

VNR VAN NOSTRAND REINHOLD COMPANY
New York

332.6324
B27h2

Copyright © 1988 by Van Nostrand Reinhold Company Inc.
Library of Congress Catalog Card Number 87-18861
ISBN 0-442-21220-8

All rights reserved. No part of this work covered by the copyright hereon may be reproduced or used in any form or by any means—graphic, electronic, or mechanical, including photocopying, recording, taping, or information storage and retrieval systems—without written permission of the publisher.

Printed in the United States of America

Van Nostrand Reinhold Company Inc.
115 Fifth Avenue
New York, New York 10003

Van Nostrand Reinhold Company Limited
Molly Millars Lane
Wokingham, Berkshire RG11 2PY, England

Van Nostrand Reinhold
480 La Trobe Street
Melbourne, Victoria 3000, Australia

Macmillan of Canada
Division of Canada Publishing Corporation
164 Commander Boulevard
Agincourt, Ontario M1S 3C7, Canada

16 15 14 13 12 11 10 9 8 7 6 5 4 3 2 1

Library of Congress Cataloging-in-Publication Data

Barrett, G. Vincent.
  How to conduct and analyze real estate market and feasibility studies.

  Bibliography: p.
  Includes index.
    1. Real estate development. 2. Feasibility studies. I. Blair, John P., 1947–.
II. Title.
HD1390.B37 1987   332.63′24   87-18861
ISBN 0-442-21220-8

Preface

One reason a second edition of this book was needed is the short half-life of information in real estate. Thus the first edition required updating to reflect the many changes in the real estate environment. The most notable of these changes is the 1986 Tax Reform Act.

The changing nature of real estate has made market and feasibility studies more important tools for planning and development than ever before. The market study analyzes whether there is sufficient demand for a proposed development. The feasibility study examines a project's profit potential. Together these studies provide points of departure for judging a project's likely success.

The purpose of this book is to provide real estate developers, planners, loan officers, appraisers, investors, and other players in the development process with the tools to:

- Understand the nature and uses of market and profit feasibility studies.
- Undertake market studies.
- Effectively present market and feasibility studies to clients.
- Determine "weak links" where errors are most likely to be introduced in market studies.
- Forecast and understand forces that affect the future success of a property development.

This edition differs from the first edition in several important respects:

- There is a stronger orientation towards the uses of market and profit feasibility studies.
- The impacts of the 1986 Tax Reform Act on the profitability of real estate projects are discussed in detail.

University Libraries
Carnegie Mellon University
Pittsburgh, Pennsylvania 15213

- A major new section has been added explaining how to measure and forecast the demand for retail space.
- A discussion of "How to conduct a highest and best use study" is included.
- An important new section on real estate cycles has been included.
- The number of cases has been increased to include an office space example.

The book is intended primarily as a "how-to" book. Therefore, emphasis is placed on data sources, organization, and purposes to which the studies can be put. While the subject matter is by nature quantitative, a knowledge of difficult mathematics is not required.

Section I describes the fundamentals of the market and feasibility study. The role of the market and feasibility study in the land development and planning process is described first. The studies are then related to the architectural and engineering plans. The various elements of the studies are made consistent with one another through successive rounds of approximation. Chapters 2 and 3 sketch the market and feasibility study. They describe the basic information and discuss the process by which basic data are determined and meaningful information is derived. Because of the increasing importance of land use regulations, the environmental impact statement is a frequent appendage to the market study. Therefore, a special section describing the environmental impact statement is included in the description of market studies. The computerized cash flow model is the principal technique used to determine project profitability. Factors that users of market and feasibility studies should understand are highlighted in Chapter 4.

The market environment that shapes the prospects for profitably selling the developed property is described in Section II. Three perspectives are presented. Neighborhood influences encompass the immediate area in which the site is to be located and its relationship to other activities. Urban and regional growth affect citywide prospects for real property development and are therefore an important part of the market and feasibility study. National economic and social influences affect the demand for new development because the state of the national economy affects consumer demand and confidence.

The final section turns to practical applications of the market and feasibility study. Three cases involving different types of land use are presented: (1) a large industrial project, (2) a regional shopping center, (3) a high-rise residential development, and (4) an office development.

In order to include as complete a perspective as possible, the cases are, to a limited extent, stylized so that features of more than one actual study are combined in the examples. Two other considerations of market and feasibility studies are their interpretation and presentation. A developer, for instance, should be able to analyze critically the market study and effectively present the results to investors, lenders, public officials, and others interested in the project. Anyone who is expected to be persuaded by a formal study should be able to analyze the report critically.

G. Vincent Barrett
John P. Blair

Contents

SECTION II. NEIGHBORHOOD, REGIONAL, AND NATIONAL INFLUENCES ON LAND DEVELOPMENT

SECTION I

The Land Development Planning Process and Market and Economic Feasibility Studies

The following chapters describe the basic nature of the real estate development planning process and its component parts. One of the component parts is the market study. The requirements of market studies and the methodology necessary to carry them out are discussed in detail. The feasibility component is also reviewed, and the mechanics of a discounted cash flow analysis is modeled in a clear and straightforward manner. The 1986 Tax Reform Act and its major provisions affecting real estate are used in the examples. Finally, the shortcomings in market and feasibility studies are reviewed, and some partial solutions are offered.

1

An Overview of the Land Development Planning Process

Real estate development has become increasingly complex within the last two decades. Competition and regulatory influences are becoming greater than ever before. The result is a continuing challenge for developers, lenders, planners, and other participants in the real estate industry to approach real estate development with new awareness, attitudes, and technical skills.

Since the early 1950s, real estate projects have become increasingly broad in scope and highly sophisticated and have required massive amounts of capital investment. The largest and most well known examples of these new complex developments in the 1960s and 1970s were new towns. Although new towns certainly stand out as large-scale land uses, the vast majority of projects, though they may not approach the scale of new town development, involve many-faceted land use programs and major commitments of resources. Typical projects on the urban land development scene might include projects of less than an acre to several hundred acres combining single-family, townhouse, and high-rise residential units, as well as commercial activities, all in one land use plan. Other projects focus on industrial land development combining light industry, heavy industry, warehousing, commercial, and possibly buffered residential areas.

The principal factors responsible for the emergence of large-scale real estate projects—whether residential, commercial, or industrial—are:

1. Concentrated massive markets created by the growth of our urban fringe areas.
2. Increasing productivity and incomes.
3. The interstate highway system and the growth of the trucking industry.
4. Increased and better corporate communications, changing man-

agement philosophies, and distribution systems, all of which allow firms a larger range of locational choices.

5. Increasing concern with our urban environment and the efficient functioning of urban systems, which require planned and orderly development.
6. The emergence of comprehensive zoning and other regulatory ordinances.
7. Tighter restrictions on water and sewer treatment facilities, which have caused the costs of these systems to skyrocket, thereby eliminating many smaller projects from being economically feasible.
8. The creation of many federal, state, and local public grant, loan, and insurance programs, all of which lend support to many private enterprise development activities.
9. New financing techniques, the attraction of new capital resources to land development, and the creation of large publicly held development companies. These companies have the capability of amassing large quantities of capital and management ability to sustain extended sales programs.
10. More efficient secondary mortgage market operations.

As a result of these factors, the approach to development planning continues to change dramatically. New approaches for conducting market analysis, economic feasibility studies, financing techniques, and property management are being developed by both private and public developers. Many of the marketing, management, financial, and risk analysis systems being experimented with by large-scale developers and consulting firms today have long been used by industrial operations. But many of the problems and constraints in real estate development are different, in both concept and practice, from those in industrial production.

The objective of this chapter is to describe a comprehensive, analytical planning methodology for large-scale real estate developments from inception to the first phase of physical development. We will also discuss the role and nature of land development consulting firms, which are the principal organizations responsible for conducting the land development planning process. The focus of the planning process as described here is directed more toward applied techniques and procedures of real estate analysis and financing rather than the techniques of physical design planning.

THE LAND DEVELOPMENT PLANNING PROCESS

Market analysis, site planning, and economic feasibility studies are the key components of the planning process and are applicable to any scale and mix of real estate development. The project size, capital resource commitment, and community concern would determine the level of analytical detail required in each phase of the planning process. The discussion in this chapter does not cover the extensive detailed analysis which would normally underlie summary calculations and recommendations undertaken for large-scale developments. The intent is to indicate the basic nature of the comprehensive methodology that should be employed in the construction of market studies, development programming, and financial analysis. This general overview is essential to a clearer understanding of the detailed materials that follow in the text.

The methodology presented here integrates the analysis of market, financial, and physical factors which may influence any potential development, from small projects to new towns. The comprehensive nature of the process is essential to the overall effectiveness of the physical plan. No one element or step in the planning process should be viewed as static. Although presented in sequential steps for explanatory reasons, in reality each component of the process may be running parallel with others, one acting as an input to the other as the process unfolds. Each section is continually revised. Although certain segments of the process will be frozen into reports at some point in time, any socioeconomic or physical changes that occur after the report will be easier to perceive and would be incorporated into the knowledge base of the consultant company, the developer, and his management group. The final physical plan should reflect any changes that may have taken place after a report is printed.

Figure 1–1 is a schematic presentation of the planning process and details the various steps involved.

THE PLANNING PROCESS AND CONSULTING FIRMS' RESPONSIBILITIES

Due to the complex nature of the planning process and the necessity for objective analysis, a developer will typically employ a consulting firm to carry out the predevelopment planning process. These consult-

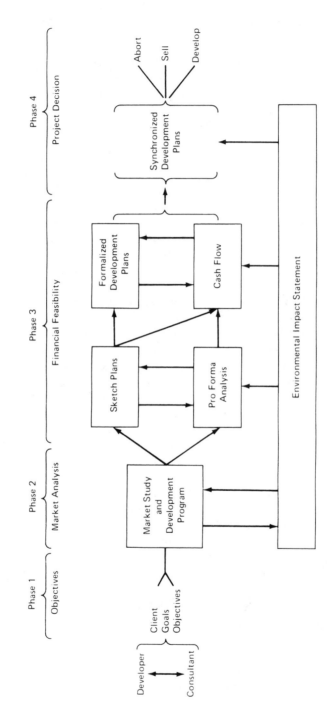

Figure 1-1. Land development planning process.

ing firms are referred to generally as *architectural, engineering, and planning firms* (AE&P), and their role in the real estate industry is one of the most important, yet least understood, aspects of land development planning. These companies are at the very vortex of urban growth. It is estimated that AE&P firms conduct the planning for and make recommendations about the size, type, timing, and design for approximately 80% of all land development in the United States. The top 500 AE&P firms in recent years have had over $6 billion in billings and directly affect the development of approximately 600,000 acres of land annually. The quality of their recommendations, planning, and design efforts determines the environment within which we all must live. The quality of development planning can be no better than the ability of those who administer it on all levels, and it is within this country's AE&P firms that the design of much of our urban environment is decided upon. Because of their importance, the process by which AE&P firms become involved in real estate development and the practices that they follow deserve careful consideration.

Typically, after initial contact, the developer will visit the main office of the consulting firm to tour the facilities and meet the principals involved. The discussions are very general at this stage since normally the developer will be investigating the potential of other firms. At the same time, the firm will be analyzing the client, his capabilities, and the scope of the proposed project, and determining whether or not it has the in-house talent to handle the project and if the project can fit into the present work load. Once developers decide to move on a project, they generally want market studies and planning work to begin immediately.

Consulting firms are becoming increasingly aware of the importance of offering a full line of quality services to both private and public developers. The communication and coordination of work among several firms such as a marketing and economic research firm, a land planning firm, an architecture firm, and an engineering firm is beyond the capabilities and patience level of most developers involved in large-scale projects. Developers are inclined to go with one or possibly two firms that offer a full line of development services.

In the initial planning stages of real estate development, the personnel and methodology employed are extremely important both to the ultimate physical development and to the professional position of the firm doing the work. Recently, traditional architecture and engineering firms have found it necessary to expand their services to include market research and land planning capabilities. In many instances, this has proved to be a disastrous move. Being generally unfamiliar with the technical aspects of the planning process, firms have hired incompetent persons or left the planning and market research departments understaffed and underbudgeted, which has resulted in slow and poor-quality reports. The clients, seeing poor-quality work in the initial stages of the development process, may lose confidence in the firm as a whole and take their engineering and architectural work elsewhere. Any relationship between a developer and a consultant should be based on mutual respect and trust.

Once the developer has decided on a particular consulting firm, he or she will present the idea of the project in as much detail as possible and ask the company to submit a work proposal. Initial proposals generally contain an outline of the scope of the work the company feels is necessary to get the project to a point where physical development will begin, a time schedule for the proposed work, and the fee.

A developer who is familiar with the firm and has confidence in its ability and judgment may accept the entire proposal at the outset and sign an agreement contract. On the other hand, a developer who is not familiar with the company may request that it do only preliminary investigation and some market analysis at a set fee. If satisfied with the preliminary work, the client may then sign a full scope of services contract and eventually contract with the company for all engineering and architectural work. These later contracts are the most sought after by AE&P firms, being, percentage-wise, the most lucrative.

Phase 1: Developer's Goals and Objectives

After a developer has selected a firm, the firm's first step is to define the developer's goals and objectives. This is generally done in discussions before proposal development and shortly after the firm has been selected to do the work. Whatever the developer's objectives may be regarding the project, they must be clearly established before considering specific uses for the site. In these discussions, the developer's motivation, business capacities, and financial situation should be openly discussed. These discussions should also provide fundamental reference points for evaluating land uses for the subject site. Increasingly complex objectives underlie developing entities' goals. It is a fair assumption, however, that the private developer is motivated by financial considerations rather than the characteristics of the project, although the latter should be of supreme concern to government agencies because of their public responsibility. Even though developers are motivated primarily by financial considerations, their objectives may still vary substantially. Developers may have nothing more than an idea that a certain type of project may be profitably developed. They may or may not have a particular site in mind. Alternatively, they may have a site and be searching for the most profitable use. Regardless of the circumstances that may exist, it is imperative that the consultant determine as specifically as possible the client's developmental goals and objectives.

A few development groups, such as local housing authorities or city and state agencies, may be socially motivated. These groups tend to be nonprofit-motivated and are concerned primarily with social costs vs. social benefits. However, they must still operate within financial and market constraints that must be clearly defined at the outset. Private-sector developers who state their goals to be socially motivated are generally held suspect by consulting firms. Society's needs, as opposed to effective demand, cannot be met by the limited resources of individual real estate developers. To plan, design, and build outside the constraints of market-determined supply and demand forces is to court disappointment and financial disaster, for both the developer and consultant.

The developer and consultant must define their capabilities—technical, financial, and managerial—relative to the scope of the proposed project. In the event that the proposed project should come up against community or political resistance, it is very important to review the developer's social and political influence within the impact area of the proposed project. Whatever the developer's objectives—financial or otherwise—they will affect the resultant land use pattern. Also, during these initial discussions, the scope of the planning work to be done by the consultant will be established and a service contract signed. As soon as preliminary client objectives have been established, a detailed market analysis should be undertaken.

Phase 2: Analysis of General Market Conditions

Once the client's goals and objectives have been established and a service contract has been signed, the consultant will begin the market analysis. A comprehensive market study should incorporate the analysis of both direct and indirect economic forces. In general, along with the direct market forces of supply and demand, all social, political, environmental, and other regulatory influences applicable to the project should be investigated.

The principal purpose underlying the market analysis is to establish the range of specific land uses and the rate of physical development that can be supported within constraints imposed by supply and demand conditions, local public policy, and environmental considerations. The determination of land use possibilities and the estimated absorption rate, i.e., the number of units of land, housing, or other types of space which can be sold or rented annually, set the basis for development programming, master planning, and economic feasibility analysis. For this reason, the market study is perhaps the most important single element in the planning process.

The market study is also the most difficult planning element to undertake. Among the problems that may face a market analyst, to name just a few, are: old and noncomparable data, lack of data, little or no historical precedent to serve as a guidepost, and lack of cooperation from officials, other developers, and managers of competing projects. Most of the time, the developer wishes to keep the project from becoming general public knowledge, and this also puts the analyst in a difficult position. People are generally reluctant to give out information unless they know why they are being interviewed. This may be especially true when an individual feels a project is a competitive one.

Analysts may face other problems generated within the consulting firm. Often the analysts will be working within a budget that is too small to allow for a good market study. Also, pressure is frequently exerted on analysts to come up with positive results, or at least to play down negative market factors, in an effort to increase the possibility of the project being built. The firms, of course, would like to obtain the more lucrative engineering and architectural contracts. The developer may have preconceived ideas about the project and attempt to influence the outcome of the study. A glowing market study generally guarantees an experienced developer financial backing. The lack of supporting facilities within the firm, such as competent people and computer capability, may also hinder the study.[1]

One major weakness of most market studies is the general inability to quantify with any degree of accuracy major elements of local supply and demand and, consequently, the questions a market study sets out to answer. One reason for this is incompetent analysis, but in the vast majority of studies the limited available data do not lend themselves to precise mathematical formulation. This is particularly true when trying to relate supply and demand data to a specific site. In the end, the core of most market studies consists of objective, educated estimates by the analyst. The analyst's estimates, however, should not be taken lightly.

If the market study has been handled properly, the researcher will know more about the project and its potential than any other individual. The inability to fit any given market study into a quantifiable framework does not necessarily detract from the validity of the results. The very nature of a comprehensive market analysis does not readily lend itself to formulization.

Indirect Economic Influences.   A comprehensive market analysis involves an investigation of both direct and indirect economic influences that may affect land use possibilities. The indirect economic factors are: public regulations, social impact, and environmental concerns.

Public Regulations.   Regulatory policies such as local zoning and building codes will affect the land use potential of any parcel within their jurisdiction. Zoning laws and other regulatory policies are constraints on land use possibilities and define the general framework within which a project may be built. An ever-increasing number of communities are including in their zoning regulations a "floating" planned unit development (PUD) category. This PUD category usually allows for a greater degree of flexibility and innovation in planning the project while working within an overall set of regulations. Regardless of the type or degree of public regulations, they impose basic guidelines for determining potential land use. These regulatory laws and policies must be carefully reviewed at the outset of any project.

Social Impact.   The impact on a community of a real estate development is becoming a vital factor in the project review and acceptability process. Local governments are becoming increasingly reluctant to accept large-scale developments that they feel may unfavorably affect their urban systems and fiscal positions. The question of growth, per se, is generally the crux of the matter. Many communities want no growth at all. They generally see no compensating factors for continued urban expansion and view growth as synonymous with a decline in the quality of their existing lifestyles.

These conflicting viewpoints of urban growth are not minor problems; confrontations between developers, consulting firms, and public agencies are rapidly increasing. In many instances, the developer and his consulting firm will have completed the entire planning process by following all community regulations to the letter and still not receive project approval. This resistance to change may take many forms:

outright disapproval for some minor or perceived irregularity or insurmountable regulatory delays often arbitrarily applied by local officials. In many instances, these problems could have been foreseen if the key public officials had been properly consulted at the outset of the planning process. But even this is no guarantee that the question of growth will not later be an issue or hindrance. Many public officials are reluctant to express their positions openly. The best safeguard against this problem is a thorough investigation by the market analyst or planner of the community's attitude toward growth.

The urban subsystems which are of most concern to a community are utilities, schools, fire protection, police protection, medical facilities, social services, and traffic. In large urban areas, any given project may have a small impact and may encounter little opposition. However, in smaller urban areas, an in-depth study of the project's potential impact is now advisable, even if not stipulated by local ordinances.

In general, a project's impact on a community may be assessed by determining the overall influx of new population that would result from construction of the project. A market analyst will, by estimating the future population of a project, be able to determine its potential impact on the various urban systems. Typically, this is done by comparing existing local ratios of police, teachers, firefighters and equipment, hospital beds, gallons of water used, and sewage produced with national averages. Increased traffic on local connector streets and additional parking requirements are also of major importance. One consideration most often put forward by growth advocates is that the property tax base will be increased, to the benefit of the entire community. A good market analyst should be prepared to argue this point quantitatively for a client. Many studies have found that industrial and commercial real estate contribute more in taxes than they cost the city, while residential properties have a differential impact. Apartments that are small enough to discourage families with children may contribute more than they cost. However, the "child ranch" tends to create a net fiscal burden for the municipality in which it is located.

Environmental Concerns. Transportation linkages and surrounding land uses, location of the property, utilities requirements, subsoil characteristics, topography, tree coverage, drainage, and natural amenities all affect land use possibilities. These items should be investigated promptly because they are fundamental to land use potential. The developer should anticipate providing a certain amount of the physical infrastructure for the project. This happens frequently with water and sewer systems. This shifts the incidence of partial infrastructure costs away from local government and the area tax base. When these developer-provided systems are paid for, and assuming they are constructed to meet all governmental standards, the community will generally assume the operation and maintenance functions.

Analysis of existing and projected, local and regional land use patterns and transportation systems is basic to the market today. Any improvements in, or additions to, existing transportation systems might give the project wider regional appeal. Conversely, limited transportation facilities will tend to isolate the project and reduce land use potential.

Regardless of zoning, existing land use within the proximity of the site may preclude certain types of development. For example, if a site is generally surrounded by industry, it is doubtful that any type of dwelling units would have much market appeal. As the surrounding land use pattern affects site potential, so does the regional pattern. A large-scale project will typically draw on a regional, as well as local, market, and it is the regional pattern and trends that provide the overall framework for its potential use. There is no one systematic approach to regional analysis, and the approach used will depend a great deal on the developer's objectives, local regulatory constraints, and the consulting firm's budget limitations.

Many local governments and projects involving federal funds require careful consideration of environmental impacts before they will approve a development. The impacts are frequently described in an environmental impact statement, which is dealt with in a later section of this chapter.

Direct Economic Influences.   The competitive position of the site itself must be evaluated in relation to the local and regional real estate markets. Competitive offerings in each land use category must be examined in detail to determine the relative market position for the proposed project. In evaluating the market potential for specific land uses, all the criteria used in site location analysis for that particular type of activity should be explored.

Detailed techniques of market analysis are covered in the following chapter. However, the principal direct economic market forces are those which are most easily quantified and are the basic source of all demand, i.e., population, employment, and income. It is necessary for the market researcher to review the historical trends in these variables, relate these trends to existing conditions, and make future projections.

The researcher must also be able to translate the movements of these variables into various components of effective land use demand—such as residential, industrial, and commercial. He or she must also determine what share of the projected demand the subject project will capture. In addition to analyzing the principal sources of demand, the competitive environment, i.e., similar projects or land uses, must be researched in detail. This is generally referred to as analyzing the existing and planned supply side of the market.

The Operational Development Program.   During the final stages of the market analysis, the consulting team's planning analyst should outline a functional development program that must be established within the scope of estimated market opportunities for the project. Large-scale projects may have multiple land use opportunities that require years to sell or lease. Any development program with extended time periods requires long-range planning for land use optimization. Optimizing land use is a matter of allocating the available land to the alternative uses so as to maximize the economic return, within the socio-economic constraints imposed by community regulations and market forces.

There are two basic factors AE&P firms must consider in land use optimization. First is the developer's business objective, which should include the total role the developer is to play in the various development activities and the economic opportunities of the project. Other profit centers are available to the developer in addition to profits from subdividing and improving land. Profit centers exist in the building and operating of improvements. Land developers may or may not choose to participate in this aspect of a development. Because of initial large capital requirements in the land development stage, they may not have enough equity for further investments.

Second, the total site holding capacity must be maximized by proper land planning and allocated among alternative uses according to market constraints and relative economic contribution to the developer's objectives. This is generally accomplished in the initial sketch plan of the project.

Site Holding Capacity.   The financial objectives of the developer are usually constraints on maximization. In addition to these, a second set of constraints needs to be considered—the physical holding capacity of the site as it relates to local zoning and other regulatory influences— and estimated absorption rates for each land use must be considered.

The physical holding capacity of the site is established relative to current or expected zoning or other land use ordinances during the initial stages of the market study. The market analyst must then work very closely with the engineers, architects, and public planners to allocate the amount of each land use based on estimated absorption rates. Site holding capacity is always a critical issue, and the degree to which land use ordinances modify this capacity is directly reflected in total potential revenue and profits from the project. The higher the holding capacity or density, the more important the accuracy of the estimated absorption rate, the location and capital expenditure related to individual buildings, and other site improvements. Combinations of planned land uses involve more rigorous computations and more refined market, planning, and design considerations. In lower-density developments, natural site characteristics typically become more important in accommodating various land uses which assure an attractive and marketable environment.

Results of the market analysis provide not only the basis for determining types of salable land use, but also annual absorption rates for each use. The overall program parameters will have been established in the process. Without sufficient identifiable effective demand, a given land use should not be considered and the overall pace of development should not proceed beyond estimated absorption rates. The final land use allocations will normally have different time frames for development. This could possibly include closing off lower value uses in early years, thus leaving the land for future development at higher value uses. Arriving at this allocation is part of the optimization process.

A complete market study will analyze the major sources of supply and demand and the strength of the underlying elements of each. The study should also identify all marketable land uses appropriate to the development concept, locations, and regulatory influences. Estimates of the total volume (and monthly or annual number) of units that may be marketed, i.e., the absorption rate, will also be included. The type, style, amenities, and price range that the units can be marketed within should be included. This information will set the stage for developmental programming.

A good residential market study should answer the following set of questions:

1. What percentage of the total market can the project hope to absorb and over what time period?
2. Within what price range will the units have to be marketed in order to remain competitive?

3. What basic type of structure or combination of types would be the most marketable on the subject site?
4. How large should the units be? (This is generally measured in square feet.)
5. What amenities should be provided to make the project competitive with existing supply? (For a residential development this would include such considerations as swimming pools, tennis courts, saunas, exercise rooms, a children's playground, and a general recreational area.)

One important question that a market analysis does not answer is: Can a profit be made? The gross revenue may be estimated from the projections of a market analysis—unit price times the estimated number of units to be sold or rented gives the developer an idea of gross revenue. However, in order to determine profit the developer must also know the cost. This requires additional analysis generally referred to as the feasibility study.

Phase 3: The Feasibility Study

Sketch Plan and Pro Forma Analysis.   A sketch plan is a rendering, generally to scale, of the anticipated physical layout of the project. The information and recommendations from the market study should provide the required input. The sketch plan should be laid out in accordance with the development program established in the market study. Once the project is properly sketched, then developmental cost estimates may be made. For example, the total required linear footage of road, lighting, water, sewage, wiring, and piping can be determined. Total grading and landscaping requirements can be determined and their costs estimated. By this method, a rough estimate of total project costs may be determined and serve as an input to the pro forma analysis.

The pro forma analysis is a static picture of the estimated cost/revenue projections of the project. The data are structured for a given point in time, generally assuming full development. A pro forma analysis will typically deal in constant dollars and present all estimated revenues and costs. This is considered to be a first rough cut of the project's financial picture. The sketch plan and pro forma analysis are actually planning tools and should undergo continual adjustment and revision in an attempt to optimize the economic benefits of the project. If, for example, the cost estimates developed in the sketch plan exceeded the revenue projections developed in the market study, then program adjustments would have to be made. All the variable cost elements in the sketch plan would have to be reviewed. Perhaps less costly road configurations could be designed. Less expensive water and sewage systems may have to be employed. Certain amenities may have to be forgone. The upper limits of the price range may have to be tested. Thus the market analyst may reestimate absorption rates at higher prices.

It is after the pro forma statement has been scrutinized that the quality of many projects begins to decline and the best designs of architects, engineers, and land planners are set aside because the costs of quality are more than the market can bear. The drive for extraordinary profits is also a contributing factor, but in today's real estate markets there are very few projects that generate higher than normal profits. For the most part, due to increasing costs, profits have been reduced to barely acceptable levels when compared with investment alternatives and levels of risk.

A number of important issues may be resolved in the pro forma analysis, particularly with regard to the developer's business objectives and the land use mix. Adjustments may be made to the development program accordingly. The principal purpose of the preliminary sketch development plan and pro forma analysis is to give some indication of the economic viability of the project, before expending more effort on in-depth planning and feasibility.

It is extremely important at this point for the AE&P firm's development team, especially the market and financial analyst, to work closely with the land planners. Relationships between market findings, financial objectives, and land planning principles must all be coordinated and directly reflected in the sketch plan.

Even after successively revising the sketch plan and varying the estimated absorption rates and price ranges within acceptable limits, it may be deemed that the project is not economically feasible and should be abandoned or set aside until some future date when market conditions may be more favorable. Assuming, however, that the pro forma analysis is roughly acceptable, then a dynamic cash flow model and formal development plan should be started.

Modeling the Project.   The cash flow analysis is the focal point for both profit and nonprofit development organizations. A total financial planning framework should be structured by the consulting firm within which any item of the planning process can be changed and the financial results reviewed. The development program and master plan components can thus be successively revised by the systematic varying of factors to achieve an optimal development strategy.

The key element of the project's economic model is the cash flow statement. The cash flow system incorporates the absorption rate, estimated price ranges, key results of the market study, projected capital costs, revenue, operating expenses, and financing terms. These items are then organized into a statement reflecting the project's potential financial results over the entire sell-out period. The final decision about the project's feasibility is based on the results of this analysis.

The cash flow model is basically a planning tool and is an integral part of the process of creating the optimal land use plan. The pro forma analysis is a static analysis generally incorporating rough cost and revenue estimates; it may or may not include financing variables. On the other hand, the cash flow model is a dynamic program; i.e., the timing of the cash inflows and cash outflows is considered while incorporating all financial variables and generally in discounted dollars. Once the original sketch plan and pro forma analysis establish a tentative "go" position, a cash flow model is generally begun. Successive revisions of the sketch plan and cash flow model are then undertaken until an optimal land use program is developed.

Cash flow programs for large projects are almost always computerized models. Once a computer model is developed, it is a relatively simple matter to change one or any number of variables and review the impact on the project's profit position. To do this by hand would, for all practical purposes, be impossible. The authors were involved in a $50 million project in Florida recently for which the cash flow model was computed over 300 times before an optimal plan was developed. Had this been done by hand (which is unlikely), it is estimated that it would have taken over 6,000 man-hours and nearly $180,000 to complete. Computer models, however, are not essential components of the planning process, but serve as valuable tools in analyzing alternatives and levels of risk. A model is no better than the basic input data, and the results must be tempered by the experienced judgment of the developer and the planning team's analyst.

The first step in the cash flow analysis is to consolidate the various development cost estimates, operating expenses, and revenue projections into a basic summary form. All development costs, including project infrastructure and amenities, are the result of preengineering cost estimates made on the basis of the successive sketch plans. Costs are generally grouped into basic categories including land purchase, planning, engineering, real estate taxes, interest and other land carrying costs, land development costs, developer overhead, and management and sales costs.

Cost estimates for infrastructure such as roads, lighting, water and sewer lines, sewer plant, and site preparation should be calculated by the consulting firm's engineers. These costs should be allocated to specific land uses where possible. Unallocable costs should be on a pro-rata basis per acre or other unit of measurement. These cost estimates can either make or break a project. Experienced planners and feasibility analysts will always review these cost estimates in detail with the engineers involved, since cost estimators have a tendency to be conservative or high in their estimates. In addition, there is generally a 10–15% contingency fee attached to these figures.

If utilities (sewer and water systems) are to be provided by the developer rather than by city-connected services or a special district, then the initial capital cost must be shared proportionately by each land use. This may be done by estimated gallonage requirements for each land use. The operations and maintenance costs must be projected on a pro-rata share by land use on an annual basis. All other community facilities and amenities provided must be costed out by using similar procedures. If the land developer is also involved in the building and operation of structures, then the cost revenue functions of these activities must also be included in the analysis.

Real estate taxes must be determined. This is generally done in discussions with the local tax assessor's office. An attempt must be made to project the rates as they would apply to the declining amount of acreage in project inventory. Tax assessment practices vary widely from community to community, but in all cases they represent a significant financial consideration and must be investigated thoroughly.

All project management costs must be projected. These figures include: predevelopment planning, management of land development activities, sales, and promotion. Predevelopment planning costs are fees paid for the initial planning process and estimated future expenditure of this nature, prior to actual land development.

Management of land development activities is generally projected as a percentage of planned site improvement costs or a percentage of projected gross revenue. These percentage rates will vary and should be established by an evaluation of the business standards and salary levels in the community. Start-up costs are generally high, then decline and stabilize during the middle years of the project—and possibly increase toward the end of the project as the less desirable sites are sold—although this need not be true in any specific case. The most valuable land may very well be the last piece sold. Selling and promotion costs of 5–10% of gross revenue are typical in most areas. The amount provided must support an effective sales staff, display facilities, advertising, and other sales supports.

After the cost figures have been organized, revenue estimates must be summarized and projected on an annual basis and entered in the cash flow statement. Potential revenues realized from projected land sales are established on an annual basis for each use. Revenues will increase or decline in relation to the development pace. Revenue projections may be either in inflated constant dollars, that is, projected in today's dollars not taking into account land appreciation, or in anticipated cost increases, or in an inflated cash flow system. The more sophisticated developers are using discounted cash flow systems.

Sales prices are generally developed for land uses set out in the program. These prices are established by the firm's analyst. These estimates should be based on market data. Typically, large-scale projects will also include "opportunity sites," the use of which cannot be fully defined in the initial plan but which are reserved for high-value future development. These sites generally have a unique location or physical features and allow for land sales flexibility. Although it is simple enough to establish a price level based on residential land values or a predetermined rate of return, in the final analysis the supply and demand conditions of the regional market determine the selling price. Each project must be compared with all other projects competing in the same market, with prices being a function of several factors. Revenue projections based on price schedules are the key element in determining project feasibility, but historically they have been the weakest link in highly quantified cash flow systems. In an effort to improve the method of predicting prices some analysts will employ a computerized economic model, generally regression analysis, developed to predict land values given certain market constraints.

Models are not intended to take the place of reasoned estimates by the analysts, but assist in adding some degree of quantification to an area which to date has relied solely on qualified judgments. In addition to pricing schedules, the absorption rate or estimated number of units to be sold annually is critical to projecting revenue flows.

If the land developer also functions as the structural builder, the transition from developed land to the final stages of parcels with erected improvements should appear as a distinct transaction in the cash flow. Although this integrated process may be presented in a consolidated statement, it would be necessary to at least evaluate the two different functions as separate profit centers. Initially, this may be done by a simple pro forma analysis.

In addition to cost and revenue summaries, the financing alternatives must be organized into a complete summary package for inclusion in the cash flow. Financing large projects is generally a very complex process and typically requires separate accounting for financing land purchase and development costs. Each parcel of land acquired in making a large developable tract may have been purchased under considerably different terms. In this case, each separate transaction should be accounted separately with only summary results used as inputs to the cash flow statement. In many cases, income-producing properties are already on the site when purchased for development. These will include individual financial arrangements which must be reflected in the cash flow.

Most successful developers have several alternative financing programs from which to choose. Typically, the developer will have made these decisions and will have given the terms as established to the analyst for the cash flow input. It may be required, however, that each alternative be evaluated in terms of its impact on overall project yield. The relationships between land purchase price, amortization schedules, release arrangements, and interest rates may be varied to test for combinations which will optimize the development situation.

The client developer may also require that the impact of income taxes upon project cash flow be considered. From a tax standpoint, there are critical differences in the type of yield which a project may generate. Generally, when developers wish an after-tax cash flow analysis, they will make available their accountants and tax attorneys to supply the required data. There are substantial differences between actual cash flow and taxable income. Various development organizations prefer different forms of earnings. Tax considerations in real estate investments will be considered in Chapter 3. In many cases the consulting firm will limit itself to a pretax cash flow analysis only, leaving all tax questions up to the development entity, i.e., the client's tax accountants and attorneys.

The comprehensive economic framework resulting from the above analysis has a great deal of utility well beyond the predevelopment phases. By inputting ongoing results of actual development—including cost data, rate of sales, and final prices—programming and financial objectives may be changed to achieve or exceed previously established targets. In addition, the same framework may be used to monitor performance and aid in budget control.

The items discussed above can be modeled and programmed for convenient and efficient computer calculations. Without the aid of computer facilities and programs, it is doubtful that a comprehensive financial analysis could be made on large projects without running into manpower and budget constraints.

The Formal Development Plan.   A formalized development plan is the final physical design that, once approved by a community's zoning and planning commission, must be adhered to by the developer. The plan, which exhibits how the physical development will take place, should optimize the development potential of the site. The plan may not maximize profits or site holding capacity, but it will optimize the alternative land uses within the economic, social, and political constraints imposed by the community.

Once a community's zoning and planning commission approves a developer's formal plan, it generally may not be changed without another hearing on the matter. Requests for changes may involve additional debates by commission members and concerned citizens; this costs a developer time and considerable expense and can result in the rejection of the new plan. For this reason, it is very important that the original plan submitted for approval be the optimal plan that the consultant, lender, and developer are willing to abide by for the development period.

Phase 4: The Project Decision

Once the final development plan has been completed, the developer, with the consultant's advice, must decide on the future of the project. There are three basic alternatives: (1) abort the project, (2) sell the plans along with the site, or (3) move ahead with the approval process, financing, and physical development of the site.

It is not unusual for a project to be aborted during the final stages of the planning process. The final determination of the economic benefits of an optimal plan may not be sufficient to warrant any further investment. The developer is, of course, out the consultant fees paid, but this is a small price to pay since in all likelihood a much larger financial disaster has been avoided. It may also be that the formal development plan is not acceptable to the community's zoning and planning commission. The commission members may believe that the social costs to the community are too great and may not want the project in any form, or they may insist on certain conditions which, if incorporated in the plan, would cause it to be suboptimal and not profitable to the developer. Numerous projects have been aborted for the latter reasons. However, many of these situations could have been avoided if the original market study had been properly conducted and if the commission and its technical experts had been consulted on all aspects of the development plans.

Often a developer, for a variety of reasons, may not wish to continue with the physical development of the site and will sell the plans and the site to another developer. It may be that the developer's financial conditions have changed since the outset of the planning process, or that the recommended land use is not the one which the developer expected and has experience in. There are also investors who do little development themselves but specialize in buying and selling land. They may buy or take an option to buy a particular parcel of land, have the planning process conducted, and meanwhile publicize the future development of the site. The public disclosure of future development and the planning process itself tend to increase investor interest in the site. The investor will then sell the plans and the site, generally at a handsome profit.

The third alternative is to proceed with the physical development. The developer in this case must seek financing for the project. The market study, cash flow model, and formal development plan, along with proof of control of the site, are the principal documents a developer will need when seeking financing. Increasing regulatory influences may in many cases add still another element to the land planning process: the environmental impact statement.

THE ENVIRONMENTAL IMPACT STATEMENT

Concern over the impact of economic development on the environment was expressed forcefully in the National Environment Policy Act of 1969 (NEPA). This Act and similar legislation at the state and local level have attempted to balance the need to develop or modify land for new uses with environmental concerns or externalities. The Act declared it a national policy to encourage a productive and enjoyable harmony between people and the environment and to prevent damage to the environment and biosphere. Expressed more positively, the Act is intended to stimulate the health and welfare of people by focusing attention on the environmental impacts of human activity. NEPA created the Council on Environmental Quality to appraise programs and activities of the federal government ". . . to be responsive to the scientific, economic, social, aesthetic, and cultural needs and interests of the Nation, and to promote the improvement of the quality of the environment."

Perhaps the most far-reaching aspect of NEPA is a requirement that an environmental impact statement (EIS) accompany major federal actions that affect environmental quality. "Federal actions" encompass not only direct federal projects such as a reservoir or highway construction, but also licensing activities. For instance, the Nuclear Regulatory Commission requires an EIS to accompany proposals for nuclear power plant construction. Since power plants must be licensed and that is a federal action which will affect the environment, an EIS must be part of the decision. The EIS is normally written by a government official, although private developers are sometimes charged with the task. In either case, it is important that the private developer understand the source and purpose of the EIS.

The concept of environmental impact has been interpreted broadly. In the words of the Act, the EIS should:

> utilize a systematic, interdisciplinary approach which will insure the integrated use of the natural and social sciences and the environmental design arts in planning and decision making which may have an impact on man's environment.

Thus the impact of a project on such factors as crime, poverty, and employment should be as much a part of the EIS as the effects on birds and water quality.

If the EIS were required only of projects involving the federal government, its impact on real estate development would be limited by the fact that most projects are local in nature and hence are regulated by state and local governments. However, since 1970 over 32 states and numerous localities have adopted EIS requirements, many of which follow the national model legislation. Consequently, preparation of EISs is an important step in the planning process. Environmental impact statements may be necessary to attain zoning and other land use permits.

How to Structure an Environmental Impact Statement

There is no single formula for constructing an EIS. The nature of the project and the area in which it will be located should dictate the questions that require the most attention. The EIS for a small subdivision will be significantly different than an EIS for a regional suburban shopping center. However, the Council on Environmental Quality has described an eight-step procedure that may serve as a skeleton around which an EIS may be structured.[2]

1. *A description of the present conditions* is an appropriate starting place and should include physical, social, and aesthetic features of the area. A detailed description of the entire environment would not be appropriate. Those features to be discussed later in the report and that may be controversial should receive the most attention at this stage.

2. *The description of the proposed project* should be adequate to allow a careful assessment of the environmental repercussions by agencies that will evaluate the project. Maps showing the project's relationship to the community and the region should be included.

3. *The probable impact* of the proposed action can be tied closely to the description of present conditions. Each type of impact categories may be subdivided into numerous other subcategories. Because so many factors conceivably can be included in an impact statement, a checklist might be useful simply as a reminder of what sorts of impacts might be important. The Department of Housing and Urban Development has suggested 14 areas that ought to be included: (1) geology, (2) soils, (3) special land features, (4) water, (5) biota, (6) climate and air, (7) energy, (8) services, (9) safety, (10) physiological well-being, (11) sense of community, (12) psychological well-being, (13) visual quality, and (14) historic and cultural resources.

4. *Probable adverse environmental impacts* that cannot be avoided or that would be adverse to the environmental goals of the nation or community should be described next. This step requires a value judgment concerning what impacts are *adverse*. Also, some distinction must be made between significant and insignificant adverse affects. For instance, would the filling of a mosquito-infested swamp be considered an adverse impact? Is the probable extinction of the snail darter (a small fish) significant? Real estate projects should be particularly sensitive to social impacts such as congestion, as well as solid and liquid waste disposals damage to ecosystems.

5. *The review of alternatives to the proposed project* requires the responsible party to "study, develop, and describe appropriate alterna-

tives to recommend courses of action in any proposal which involves unresolved conflicts concerning alternative uses of available resources'' [Sec. 102 (2) (D)]. Normally, reviewing agencies believe this step is critical because it serves to avoid premature foreclosure of options that might be less disruptive. Alternative real estate proposals include adjusting the size of the project and varying the mix of units (to decrease density), building designs, and landscape possibilities.

6. The sixth step should *distinguish between the short-term and long-term impacts*. This requires the analyst to assess the project from the perspective stated in the legislation. Each generation should act "as trustee of the environment for succeeding generations" [Sec. 101 (b)]. The time dimensions vary from very short-term construction disruption, to short-term effects (such as temporarily increased erosion), to permanent changes in the natural or social environment. The long-term impact forces policymakers to think beyond the projected economic life of a project.

7. *Irreversible impacts and irretrievable losses* are effects that will be very difficult to obviate once the project has been approved. Resources that are permanently lost are irretrievable. Topsoil that is destroyed, during development, on agricultural land is an irretrievable loss; the commitment of public resources to support a development— police, roads, etc.—is, for most practical purposes, an irreversible commitment. This section should not simply reiterate impacts discussed in previous sections. Rather, the focus should be on resource use.

8. Finally, a discussion of *problems and objections raised* by other governmental agencies as well as private organizations should be included. The Council suggests that this might best be developed near the end of the review.

Many analysts have objected to the basically linear presentation. Figure 1–2 represents an alternative report system suggested by Hopkins and his associates.

How well have environmental impact requirements succeeded in improving land use decisions? Perhaps they have encouraged thought about the direct and indirect repercussions of projects, and there are probably instances where they have led to clearly improved decisions. However, most studies contend that EISs are developed in such a manner that they contribute little to the decision-making process. One reason for the lack of influence is that the EIS is seen as "just another requirement" by private and public officials alike, and thus the EIS is

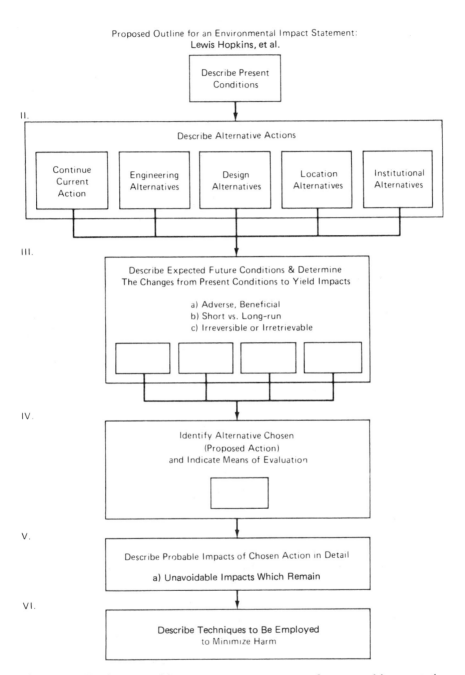

Proposed Outline for an Environmental Impact Statement:
Lewis Hopkins, et al.

Describe Present
Conditions

II.

Describe Alternative Actions

Continue
Current
Action

Engineering
Alternatives

Design
Alternatives

Location
Alternatives

Institutional
Alternatives

III.

Describe Expected Future Conditions & Determine
The Changes from Present Conditions to Yield Impacts

a) Adverse, Beneficial
b) Short vs. Long-run
c) Irreversible or Irretrievable

IV.

Identify Alternative Chosen
(Proposed Action)
and Indicate Means of Evaluation

V.

Describe Probable Impacts of Chosen Action in Detail

a) Unavoidable Impacts Which Remain

VI.

Describe Techniques to Be Employed
to Minimize Harm

Figure 1–2. Environmental impact statement—content, format, and interpretation.

Source: Lewis Hopkins, *et al., Environmental Impact Statements: A Handbook for Writers and Reviewers,* Chicago, Illinois, Institute for Environmental Quality, 1973, distributed by National Technical Information Service.

not taken seriously. Consultants often view the requirements as a new meal ticket. Furthermore, the state of the art is not sufficiently developed to satisfy the requirements of a good EIS. For instance, it is unrealistic to examine all of the impacts or alternative courses of action. In the future, improved methodology for determining the public interests in land use will enhance the efficiency of environmental impact statements.

Chapter 2 will explore the generally accepted methods and techniques that should be employed when conducting a comprehensive market analysis. Much of the information thus gathered will also be useful in an EIS.

SUMMARY

This chapter presents an overview of the land development planning process. The process evaluates, interprets, and translates the economic and social forces which are shaping our urban environment into a physical design plan commensurate with the highest and best land use and profit optimization. The development process for most large projects is carried out by architectural, engineering, and land planning consulting firms. The basic elements of the development process consist of four general phases. Phase 1 is the establishment of the developer's goals, objectives, financial strength, and experience. Developers have diverse reasons for investing, limited amounts of capital, and special areas of developmental expertise. These matters must be clearly defined at the outset since they will ultimately affect the nature of the land use plan. Phase 2 is the undertaking and completion of a comprehensive market study. The market study will analyze the social, economic, and political constraints impacting any proposed development. The study will also analyze the supply and demand conditions for alternative land uses in the local market area. The results of the market study will answer several essential questions for the developer. The questions which the market study answers relate to the type of improvements to build and the quantity, size, price range, and amount of units the market can absorb over the developmental period. With this information, gross revenues may be projected. The market study will not tell developers if they can make a profit; the determination of profitability requires the determination of costs.

Phase 3 is the analysis of financial feasibility. Cost information can be developed from the sketch plan. The cost figures, along with the revenue figures from the market study, are structured into a static pro forma analysis. This gives the developer a rough idea of potential profits. Financial feasibility may also include the development of a formalized development plan and a dynamic cash flow model. Phase 4 is the synchronization of the development plan and cash flow model so that the projected land uses optimize the potential profit.

The chapter also touches on the role of and the relationship between the developer and the consulting firm that is carrying out the planning process. There are weaknesses in the planning process that often result in poorly designed projects that are not properly integrated with the prevailing economic and social forces in a community. These weaknesses are not insurmountable ones and should be guarded against by all those involved in large-scale real estate development.

Environmental impact statements may also be required for some projects by local, state, or federal regulations. The EIS's requirements in some cases may be a by-product or extension of the market analysis. In others the EIS may have to be conducted as a separate effort. The results of an EIS may significantly affect the cost/revenue position and the finalized land use plan.

Chapter 2 will deal primarily with Phase 2 of the planning process. The chapter covers the methods and techniques that may be used to conduct a real estate market analysis and development program.

2

How to Analyze
Real Estate Markets

Because of the unique characteristics of real estate markets and their large variances from the perfectly competitive economic models, market analysis has become an essential part of the development process. As we saw in Chapter 1, real estate market analysis is one of the first steps in the planning process and is perhaps the most important element. Market studies attempt to analyze and predict the future demand for various types of real estate services and relate that demand to existing supply conditions. They may attempt to identify the highest and best economic use or the potential of a specific use on a specific site. The data developed in a market study form the basis for the economic feasibility and physical design stages of the planning process.[1]

WHAT QUESTIONS SHOULD
MARKET STUDIES ANSWER?

Before going into the techniques of analysis, it would be beneficial to look at the questions that a market analysis attempts to answer. There are various types of market studies, but a good comprehensive market analysis will direct itself to the solution of a basic set of questions generally similar for all types of development.

The Residential Market

The residential market analysis attempts to answer six basic questions.

1. What are the indirect economic constraints?

In our urban society there are many considerations that are related only indirectly to the market forces of supply and demand. Widespread concern by citizens over a development's potential impact on the quality of the physical, social, and political environment of a community has been increasingly apparent in recent years. Real estate development historically has been one of the most regulated industries in society; zoning laws, building codes, licensing requirements, and various permits and approvals will all impose certain constraints, which are intended to protect a community's interests, on a project. These requirements must be explored in depth, and the potential development constraints that they may present should be outlined in the market report.

There are also certain physical factors or characteristics of the land that may impose limitations on the nature and type of improvements that may be constructed. The land itself needs to be analyzed along with its linkages to the rest of the community.

2. What is the size of the future market, and what percentage of the overall market can be attracted to the subject site?

This question must be answered by making an analysis of the factors of demand. A determination must be made about what percentage of the estimated total future demand can be expected to locate in the new development. This segment of total demand must also be estimated by time periods. This is typically done on a monthly or annual basis. For example, it might be estimated that a specific project could expect to absorb 10% of the total market each year until the site holding capacity has been reached, which may take, for instance, 10 years. This is a critical estimate because it will be the basis for the project's projected gross revenues and for all other cash flow variables and, hence, the estimate of its market value. Many projects have been lost because the developer underestimated the length of time necessary to sell or rent the units and therefore failed to provide reserves for the first few years. From a financial point of view, the decision about whether or not the project is to be financed and built at all will depend to a very large extent on the answer to this question.

3. What is the market-determined price range?

The market analysis must also determine the price range within which the units can be sold or rented. This is largely determined by estimating the magnitude of effective demand. If the project's cost to construct plus economic profit exceeds the ability of the market to pay, then the project should be redesigned, or alternative land uses should be considered, or perhaps the project should be abandoned. A thorough analysis of future estimates of population and the distribution of community income is essential in the determination of effective demand and the unit price range. An analysis of the existing supply or competitive environment is also a crucial factor in this calculation. The projected annual absorption rate times the price will give estimates of the project's gross revenues. The importance of the accuracy of the answers to Questions 2 and 3 cannot be overstated.

4. What type of unit is justified by market demand?

Although a market analysis need not specify architectural styles or other design concepts, it should recommend certain broad categories. The categories recommended will depend to a large extent on that portion of market demand the developer is attempting to capture, such as upper-, middle-, or lower-income groupings. For example, a housing market analysis for the potential of Site A might indicate that 60% of the development should be single-family units and 40% three-story walk-up rental units. The price recommended for the single-family unit might be $55,000 and the maximum rent for the apartments $325 per month. The project divided in this way may attract the largest possible share of the market and have a high absorption rate. If the project were instead to be all single-family units or all rental units, then it would appeal to a smaller segment of market demand and have a lower absorption rate.

A good market analysis may also indicate more specific types, styles, or ownership patterns. For example, rather than make a single recommendation for condominiums, it may be expanded to single-family, ranch-style, zero lot line condominiums. The market study then provides the developer and the architects with the general type of units to design and the cost parameters within which they must design to have the broadest market appeal.

5. How large should the units be?

The market analysis will also recommend the size in square feet for the various recommended types of units. These recommendations are generally based on analysis of existing and planned future supply, i.e., the competitive environment. The size recommendations are critically important to the architectural design and the overall cost of the project.

Generally speaking, the larger the units, the higher the cost. However, the cost of construction would not necessarily decline proportionately with a decrease in size. In addition, the size will also affect the marketability of the project. If the size of the units is significantly smaller than competitive projects, then the absorption rate will decline and, consequently, so will gross revenues, and the project could very well find itself in financial danger.

The typical size of a unit will differ considerably from one part of the country to another. The market in Aspen, Colorado, for example, might absorb all of the rental units that could be built under existing zoning at a price of about $350 a month and 550 square feet of space. For the same price in Atlanta or Miami, on the other hand, the size would have to be 800–850 square feet to be competitive.

6. What amenities should be provided?

A market analysis must also indicate what amenities—such as swimming pools, golf courses, tennis courts, laundry facilities, party rooms, and playgrounds—are necessary to make a project competitive and increase its marketability. This information is typically developed by investigating the existing supply in that segment of the market to which the project is attempting to appeal.

The Commercial Market

A typical commercial market analysis, such as that for a shopping center, should answer basically the same questions as those for a residential study, with just a few variations.

1. What are the indirect economic constraints?

These are, for the most part, the same factors we would have to consider in a typical residential analysis.

2. How many square feet can be leased annually?

Rather than determining the potential number of dwelling units that could be sold on a yearly basis, the study estimates the square footage of commercial space that a community could absorb annually and the portion the subject could attract. This would depend on the community's projected population growth, income distribution, and purchasing power. Since demand for commercial space is derived from demand for the product or service being sold, the size of a commercial property depends on: (1) the overall size of the market and (2) the percentage of the overall market that the site attracts. If a clothing store requires $60 of revenue annually per square foot of leased space and the site can expect to attract $600,000 in clothing expenditures annually, then a market study could indicate a potential for 10,000 square feet ($600,000 ÷ $60 sq. ft.) devoted to such activity. A thorough analysis of the existing supply of commercial space would also have to be undertaken.

Since the 1950s, when the large suburban shopping centers began to capture large portions of the market, much data have been accumulated on the types of shops best suited for certain locations within these centers, space requirements for various activities, and commercial square footage requirements to population ratios. This information is published in various forms and may be generally found in such industry-related publications as *Shopping Center World* and *The Dollars and Cents of Shopping Centers*. These publications should certainly be consulted when conducting a major commercial market analysis.

3. What should the lease rate be per square foot?

A commercial market analysis must also include the competitive lease rate or price range that the commercial development must charge for its space. Generally, the various commercial activities located in a shopping center will pay different lease rates per square foot depending on the amount of space they require. For example, a key shop may pay $25 per square foot per year for 25 square feet of space while a major supermarket may pay only $3.50 per square foot for 20,000 square feet. In addition to a flat lease rate, most developers are now requiring a percentage of gross receipts from each business. A typical lease might be $6 per square foot of leasable space per year plus 5% of gross receipts. The amount, however, would depend on the prevailing market conditions that should be determined in the market analysis. The lease rate times the absorption would give the projected gross revenues for commercial developments.

4. What type of retail activities are most likely to locate on the site?

This is an extremely important consideration, since the size and design of a commercial shopping center will depend on the type of activities which will locate there. The market should be analyzed to determine what types of commercial activities are in short supply in the community and if there is sufficient demand to warrant the establishment of such activities. If the data indicate a positive potential for certain types of shops and stores, then efforts can be made to attract interested businesspeople into these activities and leases can be signed for the new space. Construction will generally begin after 30–50% of the projected required space is preleased.

5. What is the potential sales volume of each prospective tenant?

This information is required in order to estimate the possibility of success or failure of a given type of commercial activity. It is also an important element in the developer's cash flow analysis of the overall development. This is particularly true when the lease arrangements include a percentage of gross revenues from each store for the developer. The sales volume for each tenant depends upon the mix of stores that constitute the project and the overall market size. The modern mall-type shopping center is particularly dependent upon the linkages between stores for success. Estimates of sales may be obtained from talking with knowledgeable people, such as individuals presently operating similar establishments. National averages of sales per square foot of floor space for communities of various sizes may be obtained from related industry publications, such as *The Dollars and Cents of Shopping Centers*.

6. What amenities must be provided?

This part of the market analysis would be conceptually the same as that conducted in the residential market analysis, except the required amenities would of course differ. The concerns might be with indoor ice skating rinks, fountains, carpeting, trees and shrubs, a babysitting service, the provision of baby walkers, security, maintenance, and other items relating to the overall quality of a commercial shopping center.

The Industrial Market

A typical market analysis for industrial property, such as an industrial park, would address itself essentially to the same questions just reviewed for residential and commercial development. However, there are many special and technical considerations to be taken into account in this type of study which would require an analyst with a high level of education and experience in this field.

Although an economic base study is not an absolute necessity for this type of research, the analyst must have a thorough knowledge of economic base theory. However, if an economic base study did exist, the use of it in the market study would improve the overall quality and give more strength to the accuracy of economic projections. Knowledge of interindustry transactions as shown by an input-output table would also be helpful in making industrial projections.

1. What are the indirect economic factors?

Most of the indirect economic factors are the same as those discussed for commercial and residential properties. However, with industrial property, special emphasis should be placed on transportation linkages, topography, soil conditions, utilities, and environmental impact analysis. Manufacturing establishments with undesirable by-products need to be particularly sensitive to environmental issues.

2. How many acres can be sold annually and to what types of firms?

This requires the same type of analysis of the prevailing supply and demand conditions as was done for residential and commercial markets. There is, however, one significant difference: the demand for industrial land, unlike other real estate markets, may be national in scope. All industries expanding at the national level may be considered as potential candidates for the purchase or lease of local industrial acreage. When determining the potential for industrial land sales at the local level, national and regional growth trends need to be analyzed. The market analyst conducting such a study must be familiar with the site location criteria of the specific industries identified as having the most potential for locating in the area. This requires a sound knowledge of the availability of input supplies for specific industries as well as manufacturing space requirements and necessary transportation linkages. Once the potential demand is estimated, the required size of the industrial site and the number of acres expected to be sold annually may be determined. The annual absorption rate, together with the estimated price per acre, will establish the gross revenue projections to be used in the cash flow analysis.

3. At what price per acre could the improved land be sold?

This question primarily requires a thorough investigation of the sales prices of competing sites, not only in the local area but throughout the general region surrounding the site. Most localities in this country are constantly attempting to expand their industrial bases and are competing with other cities in trying to convince firms to locate in their areas. In some cases, cities may purchase land and provide it at a low cost to developers. The actual price of the land is only one of the competitive elements that need to be analyzed. Other items might include local tax inducement, special utility provision, union or nonunion labor supply, and state-insured industrial development bonds.

4. What amenities should be provided?

These amenities would be totally different from those for residential and commercial development. The executives of a firm may prefer community amenities—such as the availability and quality of schools, golf courses, country clubs, cultural activities, and shopping facilities—but they may also want site amenities such as landscaping, parking, and security.

WHO USES MARKET STUDIES?

Developers, architects, land planners, engineers, lending institutions, city planners, and city planning commissions will all, to some extent, rely on a market analysis when making their decisions concerning specific projects. The key individuals involved with the development process depend on the information provided by these studies, combined with their own professional judgment, for making their critical developmental decisions.

Developers will rely on a market analysis to tell them the extent of effective demand, the physical and social constraints the project may face, the number of units they can hope to sell or rent within a projected time period, the sort of competition they face, and the general price range they must operate within to remain competitive. They also use market studies to demonstrate the potential of their projects when attempting to obtain financing.

Architects will use a market study to tell them what type of units will best fit the prevailing market conditions, the size of the units, the maximum number of units that may be built on the site, and the general cost constraints that they must design within.

Land planners and engineers will use a market study to tell them the type and extent of water and sewer facilities to provide, road and parking requirements, and general land design constraints.

Lending institutions will review the market study and its recommendations to determine the project's potential for financial success. Loan officers are particularly concerned with the quality and accuracy of the quantitative materials developed in the report. They generally are quite familiar with their local market area and view with concern any overly optimistic projections of population, income, and effective demand. They also tend to view with skepticism any projected rate of sales that would indicate a particular project would be absorbing more than its normal share of the market. However, when a project being considered is outside of their local market, it becomes increasingly difficult for loan officers to judge the quality of the market study. In these cases, loans will often be made based primarily on the "salesmanship" of the developer, his or her past track record, personal financial strength, and established relationships. Any data presented may be taken at face value. During periods of generally rising income, growing national demand, and expanding money supply, real estate lending institutions operating in a highly competitive market are anxious to expand their portfolios. Large percentages of their lendable funds may go to areas of the country with which they have little familiarity, often with disastrous results. During the boom years of 1971–1973, many of the country's lending institutions, notably the Real Estate Investment Trust Companies (REITs), were making loans far removed from their home bases. Rapidly expanding areas, such as Florida, were becoming largely overbuilt, and the REITs had no adequate means for assessing faraway markets. They depended in many instances on developer-influenced market studies and past track records. The result in many cases, as the markets became overbuilt and inflationary forces caused a rapid decline in effective demand, was financial disaster. This situation again pointed out the importance and necessity of thorough and objective market studies conducted by competent consultants not connected with an equity position in the project, and rigorous data review and on-site observation by lending institutions.

City planners will use a market analysis to determine the impact of a fully developed project on existing transportation systems, water and sewer facilities, schools, and fire, police, and health facilities. They will tend to view the project from the perspective of its potential impact on the general safety, health, and welfare of the community. Among the key interests of city planners, in a market study, is the projected total population density per acre and general conformance of the project plans with zoning requirements and area-wide land use plans.

A City Planning Commission, which may be made up of local citizens appointed by a mayor, or, more typically, may be a subcommittee of the elected city officials, will have varying degrees of influence on whether or not a project will be allowed to be constructed. These commissions will seldom be made up of experts in the field of real estate development and so rely heavily upon the recommendations of the city planners and other technical experts. However, a conscientious commission should review any available market study in an attempt to weigh the social and environmental cost to the community against the long-run economic benefits which may occur as a result of the additional growth.

TYPES OF MARKET STUDIES

There are various types of market studies ranging from the very general to the very specific. An example of a general type of study would be one which determines the overall community demand for housing

Table 2–1. Types of Market Studies

I No Specific Site	II Specific Site
A. Community demand for housing.	A. Highest and best economic use for Site A.
B. Community demand for rental units.	B. Potential for housing on Site A.
C. Community demand for single-family units.	C. Potential for rental housing on Site A.
D. Community demand for commercial activities.	D. Potential for commercial usage on Site A.
E. Community demand for office space.	E. Potential for a shoe store on Site A.
F. Community demand for industrial land.	F. Industrial potential for Site A.
G. Community demand for light manufacturing space.	G. Potential for a mini steel mill on Site A.

and does not relate this demand to any specific parcel of land. A city or private real estate organization might commission this type of study to help determine future land requirements necessary to accommodate population growth and future housing needs. The most general type of analysis for a specific piece of property would be a *highest and best economic use* study. This type of study would necessitate an analysis of all potential uses for a particular parcel and a determination of which use would produce the maximum economic benefits to the developer. A more specific type of market analysis for a given site would be to assess the supply and demand relationships for a predetermined use, such as the potential for a shoe store at 405 East Main Street in Hartford, Wisconsin. Table 2–1 gives some general examples of market study types.

TECHNIQUES OF MARKET ANALYSIS

The format of a typical market study may be broken down into three general areas:

1. Indirect economic factors
2. Direct economic factors (supply and demand forces)
3. Data synthesis and recommendations

Indirect Economic Factors

Any real estate project, regardless of its physical size or the amount of money invested, will face a host of internal and external factors that could come together in such a fashion as to preclude development, regardless of the market forces of supply and demand. A comprehensive market analysis will attempt to identify and assess the importance and potential impact which these forces may have on the envisioned project. Any one of these indirect economic concerns could create an insurmountable obstacle and cause the project to be classified as nonfeasible. Consequently, they should be investigated at the very outset of the market study.

Some of these indirect economic factors which should be considered are:

1. Zoning
2. Soil conditions and topography

3. Utilities: sewage, water, electricity, and gas
4. Transportation linkages and traffic
5. Parking
6. Environmental impact
7. Impact on government services
8. Prevailing attitudes

Zoning.   Existing zoning is a critical consideration since it will establish certain physical constraints on any project from the outset. Land presently zoned for single-family residential housing may not be used for any other type of land use without zoning variance approval from local officials, which in many cases is exceedingly difficult—if not impossible—to obtain. It is not uncommon for a parcel of land to be zoned for some type of use that a developer feels is not the highest and best economic use. However, if zoning changes are considered difficult or impossible to obtain, then it would be a waste of time and money to conduct a market study directed toward determining the property's highest and best economic usage. The nature and direction of the market study in this case would be dictated by the existing zoning regulations. Zoning regulations may also dictate the allowable density, i.e., the maximum number of units per developable acre. Even though a market study may indicate that a site could absorb a significantly higher number of units than established by the zoning laws, a developer would be prevented from constructing them.

In some cases developers may feel that a market analysis is not necessary since the zoning laws set the type of land use and maximum site density. Consequently, they simply build to the maximum limits allowed. This type of speculative building could be unnecessarily risky since effective demand may not be sufficient to absorb the site if developed to full capacity. Zoning does not eliminate the need for market analysis but instead may determine the type of study required.

When studying zoning constraints, city and county planning and zoning commissions should be consulted. In some smaller communities the city engineer may be responsible for zoning regulations. The person who is responsible for a community's zoning regulations and enforcement should be interviewed, and the possibility of any future variances should be explored at that time.

Soil Conditions and Topography.   A comprehensive market analysis will also check soil conditions and the general topography of the land. These factors increase in importance with the size of the development and when raw land is brought into productive use. Soil condition is particularly important where septic tanks or aerated spray sewage systems are anticipated. Adequate analysis of the land's topography will also help determine the amount and cost of grading, road configuration, and the best location for such utilities as sewage treatment plants and water holding tanks. The slope of the land is critically important in the development of industrial parks where rail sidings are anticipated. Generally, rail lines will not be laid with slopes of 3° or more. A market analyst should consult with an experienced land planner, soil engineer, or geologist who is knowledgeable about the local area.

In many parts of the country, aerial photographs combined with topographical maps are necessary to determine subsoil conditions. Florida, for example, has a problem with sinkholes. Because of ground water action, the surface soil begins to sink in the holes. This leaves a depression in the earth which in many cases cannot be observed from ground level. It is illegal to build on these sinkholes since the additional weight of a structure may cause the earth to settle even more and possibly bring about the collapse of the building. Many novice land developers have purchased large tracts of land in these areas, only to find out later that large amounts could not be developed because of the poor subsoil conditions.

Utilities.   Utilities are becoming increasingly complex and are of considerable concern in the planning, design, and financing of a project. If city water and sewer facilities are presently available to a site, the problems become less severe. However, if a new development is being considered on a site not previously served by city utilities, the developmental problems could become so complex and costly to solve that the project would not be feasible. It is not uncommon for cities to impose moratoriums on all new developments within their boundaries because of overloaded and outdated sewage lines, pumping stations, and treatment facilities. Due to new federal regulations that upgrade the quality of effluent which sewage treatment plants may put back into the environment, the cost to construct new facilities has risen significantly. Newly planned projects that are required to build, operate, and bear the entire cost of independent water and sewage treatment facilities are often priced out of the market.

In some areas of the country, special water and sewer districts are formed that have taxing power over the new community. The special district is actually an independent political entity. Generally, the project developer and his associates will direct the activities of the special district's administrative duties until the project is near completion. There have been many reported cases of abuses under this system. At the outset, property taxes may be relatively low, but then the unaware home buyers often find themselves saddled with a much higher property tax levied by the special district to pay off the bonds issued to build the water and sewage systems.

In the absence of existing city-supplied utilities, sewage treatment facilities will generally take the form of either a standard central treatment plant that is very costly or septic tank systems that require certain spatial requirements and soil conditions that may not exist on a particular site. If space or soil conditions are not suitable for septic systems, earth mounds could be constructed—but their cost is high and their effectiveness is still questionable. Holding ponds and aerated spray systems are yet another alternative, but they require a great deal of space and are banned from certain parts of the country. Package plants, which are actually prefabricated sewage treatment facilities, may be used in some parts of the country. They are generally effective for small areas, but their operating costs are high and their economic life is relatively short. They are generally used as stopgap measures until permanent facilities can be constructed. Each of these systems has its own peculiar political, physical, and financial set of problems that must be dealt with.

Sewage treatment facilities become especially complex when planning for industrial development. Many types of manufacturing concerns produce effluent which requires considerably more and costlier treatment than would that from a residential development. In these cases the effluent should be treated before it leaves the manufacturing plant and enters the regular waste treatment system.

Independent water systems are also complex and costly. Not only must a sufficient amount of drinkable water be supplied, but fire protection must also be a consideration. Insurance companies are reluctant to insure homes, commercial operations, or factories in areas where there is limited or no fire protection. Water holding tanks must be constructed with sufficient capacity to produce a certain amount of water flow for a given amount of time and sizes of developments.

Generally, a market analyst does not have the engineering background required to make final recommendations about the provision of utilities. However, the market analyst can and should be able to point out the potential problems regarding utilities and indicate what obstacles may be encountered, physically, politically, and financially.

Frequently, a market analyst will recommend that an independent consulting engineer be brought in to conduct an in-depth analysis of the utilities' problems. A market analyst at least should provide the developer with enough data so that the developer may make an informed decision.

The first place a market analyst should consult when assessing the utilities' situation is the city and county planning groups. These planning groups will have all the current information on existing utility systems and future commitments. Another excellent source may be regional governmental advisory groups. These groups, referred to as Councils Organizations of Governments, generally serve as an advisory body to several surrounding counties. They are involved in the development of regionwide land use plans which incorporate, among other items, future transportation and utility requirements for the region and local communities. These groups are funded by federal, county, and local contributions with the aim of coordinating regional growth and assisting in correcting problems that overlap local political boundaries. These groups are inherently political and their interests are to serve the region as a whole, and their recommendations should be taken in that light. Therefore, their suggestions may not be in the best interest of an individual real estate investor. Their basic data, however, may be quite good.

The utilities should also be interviewed and will generally give a more technical assessment of the problems which the project may encounter. They will need to know generally what the projected population of the project will be at full development and the density per acre.

In addition to interviewing the water and sewage companies, the telephone, gas, and oil companies should be contacted and the project explained. These groups may face problems of construction, timing, and limited supplies. Some utility companies are also good sources of information for population projections. They must constantly collect data and often conduct their own studies which make excellent comparative bases. These firms are generally quite cooperative and very interested in new developments since they have a continuing interest in the nature and direction of community growth.

Transportation Linkages and Traffic.   Transportation linkages to a project should also be reviewed in the preliminary stages of the market analysis. Proximity to freeways, connecting streets, and the availability of public transportation are all important to a project's competitive posture. Time and distance to major sources of employment, commercial activities, schools, and health and recreational facilities should be plotted and compared with existing or planned competitive projects. In some cases, recommendations may have to be made about how to alter existing road configurations to accommodate the additional traffic burdens of a new development. Local and regional governmental planning bodies, and state transportation agencies because they are continually conducting traffic counts throughout a state, are good sources of information.

Parking.   Parking requirements may also be a major obstacle to a new development. This is particularly true in an urban area, where a combination of open space and parking requirements may severely limit the type of development that can take place. The population density of high-rise developments in urban areas, in conjunction with off-street city parking requirements, may necessitate underground parking facilities if sufficient land area is not available. Underground parking, in turn, results in significantly higher per unit costs, which may cause the units to be priced out of the market—resulting in no construction at all.

Table 2–2 lists data developed on nine sites in the city of Milwaukee, Wisconsin. The developers wished to explore the possibility of building a 200-unit high-rise apartment building with surface parking. They felt nine sites had good locational qualities. However, the zoning regulations required a certain amount of open space on each site, ranging

Table 2–2. Parking and Open Space Requirements

Site	Total Land Area, Approx. Sq. Ft.	Surface Parking Requirement, Sq. Ft.	Required Open Space, Sq. Ft.	Open Area and Parking, Sq. Ft.	Deficiency or Excess
1	75,360	65,000	47,520	112,520	−37,160
2	79,084	65,000	43,496	108,496	−29,412
3	76,200	65,000	41,910	106,910	−30,710
4	76,962	65,000	42,329	107,329	−30,367
5	122,742	65,000	67,508	132,508	− 9,766
6	248,899	65,000	136,894	201,894	+47,005
7	30,270	65,000	21,725	86,725	−56,455
8	178,178	65,000	97,997	162,997	+15,181
9	142,500	65,000	85,500	150,500	− 8,000

from 55–65% of the land area. When this requirement was combined with that of parking space per unit, it was found that only two sites could accommodate this type of development with surface parking. All other sites would require expensive underground parking. Parking requirements alone may cause a project to be economically infeasible or bring about a major redesign of the original concept.

Environmental Impact.   More and more citizens are becoming environmentally conscious, and even though no official policy or regulations may be established in a community with respect to the environmental impact of real estate development, a great deal of resistance may be encountered if a developer cannot adequately answer all questions brought up about this issue. A thorough market study will attempt to anticipate the concerns of environmentally conscious citizens and politicians, and attempt to provide satisfactory answers even though they may be quite qualitative in nature.

The principal concerns are generally with the project's impact on air, water, and noise pollution. For residential developments, these concerns are not quite as great as they are when dealing with commercial or industrial development. The amount and type of waste that a project will create should be calculated, and presentations which demonstrate that these wastes will be safely returned to the environment should be prepared. In many cases, the physical beauty of the site may be held by some to be of such a social value to the community that no development should be allowed. If this situation is anticipated, then special attention should be paid to the land planning and landscaping concepts in an effort to enhance rather than to detract from the physical qualities of the site. Many communities have established regulations to protect and maintain the natural beauty of their area. Tree ordinances, for example, have been established in many cities prohibiting the destruction of trees of a certain type and age grouping. For any tree that is destroyed another must be planted, within a reasonable distance, to take its place. Animal habitats are also of concern to many, and developers should be made aware of and plan around such sites.

Impact on Government Services.   The project's potential impact on essential government services such as police and fire protection, schools, health facilities, and rubbish removal should also be considered. If it is expected that the requirements of the new development may exceed the existing capacity of community services, then the developer, in anticipation of resistance to the project, should prepare alternative development concepts or in some manner demonstrate the compensating benefits to the community. Depending on the type of development, these benefits—such as increased employment and income, an expanded tax base, and possible slum removal—may take many forms. Generally, the smaller the community, the more important a project's impact becomes.

To determine a project's impact, it may be helpful to use certain national averages and prevailing local ratios of police officers and firefighters per capita, teacher-to-pupil ratios, and the number of doctors and hospital beds per capita. If the projected population of the project at full development does not appreciably alter prevailing ratios, then little justification can be made for opposing the development on the grounds that it would put a dangerous strain on the ability of government to provide essential services.

Prevailing Attitudes.   A good market study will also attempt to assess the attitude or attitudes of the local political structure toward the anticipated development. The elected officials who represent the citizens in the impacted area should be interviewed. They should be fully informed about the nature and extent of any proposed project. Also, any official who may be influential in the decision-making process concerning the project should be consulted. The concerns and possible objections of these individuals should be noted and included in the market study or, if appropriate, in a separate report. The developer should be made fully aware of the prevailing attitude of the local officials so that the planning process and final design may include and be sensitized to reflect their concerns.

In many communities there are citizens' groups that are concerned with the quality of their environment as well as the preservation of certain social values. These special-interest groups should not be ignored in the real estate investment decision-making process. Groups such as the Sierra Club, for example, are concerned with the quality of our physical environment, and their views regarding the project should be taken into consideration.

Even though social values may be difficult to measure and quantify, they should not be ignored, for it may be very costly to do so. The incidences of development plans going astray after substantial investments have been made, because of a failure to assess a particular group's or perhaps an entire community's social values, are increasing. In order to avoid this possibility, the market analyst should speak to as many community leaders as possible and qualitatively judge the prevailing attitudes and the strength of any antidevelopment forces. If the antidevelopment forces are financially and politically strong, a developer may be ill-advised to make a sizable investment, regardless of prevailing economic forces.

Once the indirect economic areas have been reviewed, and if no major constraints have been discovered, the next step is the analysis of the economic factors. It should be emphasized that real estate market analysis consists of neither a fixed routine of procedures nor a standardized end product. Market analysis is not a precise process that utilizes formulas to develop an unqualified and certain answer. Market analysis is limited by the accuracy of statistical data and derivations, the reliability of the estimates developed, the competency of the individuals whose judgments must be incorporated into the analytical process at every step, and the inherent uncertainties of projections of future economic events.

Direct Economic Factors

After a thorough review of the indirect economic constraints, a market study should focus on the determinants of demand and supply. However, there is inherent difficulty in differentiating the many economic factors influencing the real estate industry between supply and demand, and it is largely for purposes of analysis that we do so here. Although there are large areas of overlapping influence, there are certain basic forces which most clearly affect one side of the equation more than the other. On the demand side there are rather clearly established functional relations such as:

$D = f$ (population, income, employment, relative prices, taxes, interest rate, down payment requirements, and future expectations)

On the supply side there are also identifiable functional relations such as:

$S = f$ (expectations of demand, planned supply, competitive environment, availability, and cost of land, labor, and capital)

Numerous other factors could be included in either of the above functional relations. In most market studies, however, a much narrower definition of demand and supply relations is necessary because: (1) there is a general lack of comprehensive data for many factors considered to have some effect on the market, (2) the relative importance of certain factors on the market has not been clearly established, (3) the time and expense required to quantify many factors that may have only marginal significance cannot be justified by any measure of increased accuracy for the study's economic projections, (4) many of the factors are influenced by forces at the national and international level and therefore can be neither predicted nor effectively analyzed within the scope of a local market study, and (5) the time and financial constraints within which most market studies must be conducted severely limit the extent to which the various factors may be analyzed.

Given the above limitations, most market studies will analyze only those elements of supply and demand that have the most direct impact and that are relatively easy to quantify. On the demand side, population, income, and employment are considered to be the most significant factors and should be analyzed in depth.

Other factors, such as relative prices, taxes, interest rates, and down payment requirements, are taken as given, and little or no effort is made to predict their future direction. These *ceteris paribus* variables may be arbitrarily changed in a subsequent cash flow analysis just to see the effect of such a change on the project's profit position. But generally, no effort is taken to predict future national and international events which may cause these changes to come about. If actual changes do occur in these variables, they tend to affect all projects the same, neither enhancing nor detracting from any one project's competitive position.

In analyzing the supply side, the most important considerations are existing supply conditions and the competitive environment. The other general variables, such as the availability of land and financing, are typically not considered within the purview of a market analysis. These factors are extremely important but depend for the most part on the entrepreneurial ability of a developer. However, in some cases—for example, where a project may be in a remote recreational area—it may be necessary to assess the availability and cost of labor and building materials. In a normal urban market this is generally not necessary, since even in the short run the supplies of building materials and labor are readily available.

A typical market study then concentrates on economic factors generally considered to be the principal forces in the real estate market, such as:

Demand Side
1. Population
2. Total community income and distribution
3. Sources of employment

Supply Side
1. Existing and planned supply
2. Competitive environment

There are basically five essential steps to be undertaken in the analysis of these economic factors.

Demand

Population.   Step 1, in the residential analysis which we are using for an example, is to analyze the characteristics of the population in the study area. Historical growth trends must be developed and synthesized with current developments, and future projections must be made. The basic forces which affect changes in population characteristics are:

1. The natural birth rate of a population
2. The natural death rate of a population
3. Migration of population
4. Average family size

The natural birth rate of a population will be a partial determinant of the overall rate of growth of that population group. The birth rate minus the death rate will give the natural rate of growth. This natural rate of population growth is a key determinant of demand and is perhaps the easiest factor to quantify. Birth rates and death rates change only slowly over time. A historical trend analysis of a population's growth rate is a rather simple process to conduct. Projecting these historical trends into the foreseeable future would normally give a reasonably reliable estimate of a future population. However, there is another factor—the most difficult population factor to predict—that may dramatically offset population growth trends: migration. America is truly a nation on wheels. The mobility of our population is attested to by the high rate of turnover of residential units. The average American homeowner will move every 7 years and the apartment dweller every 12–18 months, and nearly 6 million dwelling units change hands each year.

Although the natural rate of growth of the population in the U.S. has declined rather steadily for the last decade (it now hovers around the zero population growth rate), many areas of the country have experienced explosive growth rates. Cities such as Atlanta, Denver, Phoenix, Tucson, Albuquerque, and Houston, to name a few, have grown much faster than the national growth rate. The phenomenal rates of growth in these cities are due primarily to in-migration, i.e., people leaving other parts of the country to resettle in these urban areas. One of the principal reasons for this continuing migration is changing employment opportunities. Other areas of the country have experienced net declines in population as a result of out-migration. Still other areas of the country have experienced net increases in population during the 1960s and 1970s, but this increase is less than would be expected from a natural rate of population growth.

There have been many sophisticated techniques developed to build population growth models, such as the cohort survival model. However, the accuracy of such models depends on the reliability of the input data. With migration being such a difficult variable to quantify, population projections made by well-informed people and practicing professionals within the market area are often more accurate and obtained at considerably less expense than those obtained by model building.

The basic formula for determining population growth is:

$$\text{Births} - \text{Deaths} +/- \text{Migration} = \text{Population Growth}$$

Once the annual rate of population growth figure has been developed and projected to a predetermined future date, the forecaster must then take into consideration the average number of persons per dwelling unit. This figure is, normally, roughly equivalent to the average number of persons per family. Changes in family formation have caused a rather marked increase in housing demand per capita since the early 1900s. The 1890 census indicated that there was an average of 4.9 persons per family; by 1970 this figure had declined to 3.2. This reduction in the average number of persons per family has had a significant impact on housing demand. Given today's present population of approximately 240 million, only 48.9 million dwelling units would be required if the average number of persons per family had remained constant. However, with this figure now at 3.2 or less, the number of units required is 75 million—a 53% increase.

Although the national average number of persons per household is now approximately 3.0, this figure varies widely from one locality to another and, in many cases, from one part of a city to another. One reason for these variances is age distribution. For example, many communities in the sunbelt have developed into retirement areas. The age distribution of these communities is heavily weighted in the 55–70 age bracket. Many of these households consist of one or two adults, with very few young couples with children. Consequently, it is not unusual to have an average household size figure of 1.8 or even less. Under these conditions the dwelling unit requirements for each 100 persons are much higher than in an area with a normal age distribution. Other reasons for a lower than average number of persons per household are the national trends toward smaller families with fewer children, the increase in single-person households, increasing economic independence of women, and the delaying of marriages. The parts of cities characterized by low income groups tend to have a higher than average number of persons per household. This generally results from doubling up and from a larger number of children per family unit. The average number of persons per household is a rather critical number to a market study, and the market analyst should take great care in determining the appropriate figure.

The overall objective of a population study for a residential market analysis is to determine the average annual population increase of the market area, to divide this figure by the appropriate average number of persons per household, and to estimate the annual housing need. For example, assume the average annual population increase between 1986 and 1990 is estimated to be 15,000 persons and the average household size is 3. Then we would have 15,000 ÷ 3 = 5,000. Therefore, 5,000 dwelling units would be required each year to 1990 to house the expanding population.

During the process of analyzing a community's overall population growth, the analyst should also determine how this population growth is spatially distributed over the community. Some areas of a community will expand more rapidly than others. If the population were increasing more rapidly in the area surrounding the subject site, then an increasing rate could be anticipated.

The principal data sources available to a market analyst conducting a population study are the following.

1. U.S. Census of Population and Housing, U.S. Department of Commerce, Bureau of the Census. The material contained in these documents is very useful and may well be essential in determining

historical population trends. The drawback with this source is that it is nearly always dated. The census is only conducted once every 10 years, and by the time it is tabulated and published, it is already 1 or 2 years out of date. Current sources of data are required to depict the present situation and to indicate impending trends.

2. State bureaus of employment generally keep monthly tabulations on total employment and unemployment at the state as well as local levels. Given a historically stable employment-to-population ratio in the market area, these figures would also give a clue to present and future population movements.

3. Utility and telephone companies are also excellent sources of population information. The number of utility and telephone connections provides a unique and up-to-date data base from which to estimate population growth.

4. School enrollments are also a convenient source of data which would give some indication of existing trends in migration patterns and household formations. This information can be obtained from local school boards.

5. Bank deposits, specifically demand deposits, are a good primary data source. If an area's population is growing, so will the local banks' demand deposits. This information is published by each local bank and by the Federal Reserve Bank servicing the market area. It is also a good idea for a research analyst to talk to several of the key bank officers in the market area to obtain their opinions not only on population trends but also on the overall feasibility of the project being studied.

6. Newspaper circulation rates will also give a good clue to the direction of population movements. Larger urban newspapers often will have their own research facilities which will continually monitor local business activity and population movements.

7. State automobile registration data are readily available to a researcher. There is a high correlation between the change in annual automobile registrations and a change in population. This information is compiled by state, county, and local governmental units.

8. State sales tax collections for a local area will also provide a good indication of the rate and direction of growth. Total sales tax receipts may be broken down to a per capita basis for some number of years in the past when the population figures were known, such as census years. By plotting past sales tax receipts and extrapolating into the future and dividing by an average per capita figure, a researcher would have another indicator of population trends.

9. The U.S. Postal Service in the local community may also be able to indicate present population trends. The local postal service may periodically take a postal survey conducted by its letter carriers. If this information is available, it should provide valuable insights into population growth patterns and family formation figures.

10. County and city building permits issued will also be an indicator of population growth and household formations. A researcher should not, however, put a great deal of weight on these figures since, as we have seen, the supply side of the real estate market is very inelastic in the short run. There may be a significant lag in building permits issued and actual population movements.

11. Regional Planning Commissions and local universities should also be consulted by a market analyst. Planning agencies and individual professors frequently will conduct original research that may be useful for the prediction of future population movements.

Community Income.   The second step is to determine how a community's income is distributed over its population. Since residential market studies are conducted primarily for private-sector developers, they must be concerned essentially with the nonsubsidized portion of the housing market. A market study conducted for the private sector must distinguish between *need* and *effective demand*. Effective demand is represented by those households that can afford to purchase new housing. In order to quantify this effective demand, a market researcher must analyze the community's income pattern.

Since income is not evenly distributed among households, the income distribution and its probable change over time must be determined. One reason the distribution pattern changes is that many families are experiencing rising incomes and are therefore moving out of low-income categories into higher-income categories. Most market analysts will measure the average rate of change between established income categories in past years, by using the 1960 or 1970 census with the 1970 or 1980 census, and assume this average rate of change to remain constant into the near-term future. The analyst may then make an estimate of annual effective demand for the projected future. A shorter and perhaps just as accurate method, when no dramatic income shifts are indicated and when projections are to be made for 10 years or less, would be to use the estimated income distribution pattern for the middle year of the projection for each year's estimate of effective demand. This may have the effect of overestimating near-term effective demand and underestimating the second half of the market study's projected time frame. But the overall projected absorption rate would be the same. In most local markets the rate of change in income distribution patterns would not be high enough to cause serious distortions in estimates of future effective demand using the "middle-year" approach. Other market forces weigh more heavily in the margin of error concerns of market analysts and developers.

Table 2–3 is an example of a middle-year income distribution pattern for the Milwaukee area; the period is from 1975 to 1985. Column 1 in Table 2–3 lists the various income categories. Column 2 lists the actual number of projected annual household formations falling into the various income categories. Column 3 indicates what percentage the corre-

Table 2–3. Annual Household Formations by Income Levels and Affordable Monthly Payments. Milwaukee SMSA[a] 1975–1985

Net Income Level	Annual Household Formations per Income Category	Percent of All Household Formations	Average Affordable Monthly Payment[b]
$ 0–2,000	195	.031	$31
2,000–2,999	176	.028	52
3,000–3,999	195	.031	73
4,000–4,999	208	.033	94
5,000–5,999	220	.035	115
6,000–6,999	245	.039	135
7,000–7,999	321	.051	156
8,000–8,999	441	.070	177
9,000–9,999	479	.076	198
10,000–10,999	440	.070	218
11,000–11,999	434	.069	240
12,000–12,999	434	.069	260
13,000–13,999	434	.069	280
14,000–14,999	434	.069	302
15,000–15,999	131	.021	323
16,000–16,999	131	.021	344
17,000–17,999	131	.021	365
18,000–18,999	131	.021	385
19,000+	1,120	.178	—
TOTAL	6,300	1.000	

[a] SMSA = Standard Metropolitan Statistical Area.
[b] Payments assume that 25% of a family's net income can be spent on housing. The middle of the income range is used in estimating the monthly payment.

sponding household formation in column 2 is of total annual household formations. The fifth and sixth years of the study were averaged for these figures. Column 4 gives an estimated average dollar amount that those families within each income category can afford to pay for monthly rent or mortgage payments.

An analyst may, by constructing a similar table, determine the approximate number of annual household formations that could compete in the unsubsidized housing market. Given today's prevailing costs of construction and financing, it would be very doubtful that any household earning a gross amount less than $11,500 annually could afford any type of new unsubsidized construction. Using our example in Table 2–3, this would mean that nearly 50% of the annual household formations cannot afford new housing. This leaves, of course, only 50% of the annual household formations representing effective demand.

Employment.   The third basic step in a residential market analysis is to review the community's overall employment picture. The smaller the community, the more important this aspect becomes. For example, in small communities it is not unusual to find one or two manufacturing firms employing a sizable percentage of the total labor force. If these firms were planning on relocating outside of the community, perhaps in a different state, the resultant unemployment and decline in community income and reduction of effective demand would certainly be significant. By contrast, large cities with diverse economic bases seldom have significant percentages of their total employment in any one firm, and their economies are not dramatically affected by the relocational decisions of a few firms every year. Therefore, the larger the community, the less meaningful are employment projections as indicators of population growth. Although there are a few large cities that have industrial agglomerations—such as Detroit and the auto industry—which may be more than noticeably affected by an industry shutdown or strike, these effects are generally short-run and are not necessarily contingent on normal market forces.

While reviewing a community's employment trends, an employment-to-population ratio should be developed. The employment-to-population ratio is generally stable over long periods of time in most communities, although it will vary between communities. In the above example, with a population of 200,000 and a labor force of 100,000, the community would have an employment-to-population ratio of 100,000/200,000 = .5. This figure is used primarily as a check on population and employment projections. Assuming a population projection of, say, 350,000 persons by 1990 and a historically stable employment-to-population ratio of .5, by 1990 the community would have to produce 175,000 total jobs. If, in reviewing the various employment sectors, the market analyst deems it unrealistic to project an increase of 75,000 jobs within this period of time, then it would be advisable to revise the population projections downward since the projected population cannot support itself given the available jobs. Generally, out-migration and a decline in family formations will occur when employment is scarce. Consequently, the analyst's prediction of a community's employment potential will impact the estimates of effective demand.

In the example, further assume the researcher discovered that several firms were relocating out of the market area at various times in the future. As a result, total employment projections were reduced by approximately 24%. The community would not be able to generate the 75,000 jobs required to support the projected population increase of 150,000. Instead the analyst estimated that only 57,000 additional jobs would be created by 1990 with total employment at that time of 78,500. Thus, with a population-to-employment ratio of .5 and projected total employment of 157,000, the community could only support a population of 314,000 by 1990 and not the originally projected 350,000.

In Figure 2–1, Projection A indicates the analyst's original population estimates. These projections were based on a study of existing population data only. Population projection A in Figure 2–1, given a population-to-employment ratio of .5, would require employment levels of Projection C in Figure 2–2. However, the analyst's employment projections indicated lower employment levels would prevail, resulting

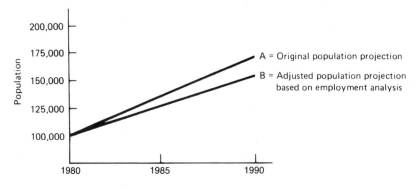

Figure 2–1. Population projections.

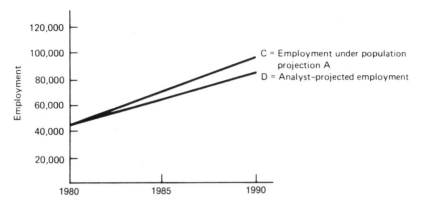

Figure 2–2. Employment projections.

in Projection D. Consequently, a downward adjustment in the population estimates from Projection A in Figure 2–1 to Projection B may be in order.

Table 2–4 indicates how these adjustments would affect estimates of housing requirements.

The above example was presented as if a hard and fast relationship existed between employment projections and population projections. This was done for explanatory purposes. The development of a broad but realistic constraint on population projections—which may be overly optimistic or distorted by a year or two of unsustainable growth—is the principal purpose of employment projections. In the longest of long runs, a direct relationship between employment and population may exist; however, during the normal planning horizon of

Table 2–4. Population Estimates and Housing Demand

Population Projection to 1990	Estimated Annual Population Increase, 1980–1990	Annual Housing Requirement, A.H.S. = 3[a]	Annual Effective Demand @ 50%
Original 350,000	15,000	5,000	2,500
Adjusted 314,000	11,400	3,800	1,900

[a] A.H.S. = Average Household Size.

the typical real estate development, a variety of factors may distort this relationship. In the face of increasing unemployment the population-to-employment ratio may also change, while transfer payments, savings, unemployment benefits, welfare benefits, and borrowing may sustain effective demand for long periods of time. New industries may also be attracted by a labor surplus area, thereby reestablishing a normal employment-to-population ratio. Employment-related adjustments to population projections cannot be made with mathematical precision, and care must be exercised by the analyst in doing so.

However, developers could face a serious problem of overbuilding, particularly in smaller communities, if they were to construct dwelling units using market projections based solely on estimates of future populations with little regard for future employment opportunities. The same may be said for a failure to analyze income distribution and the consequent overestimation of effective demand.

Just as population projections were adjusted downward in this example, so might they be adjusted upward due to an optimistic outlook for future employment and increases in effective demand.

While the first, second, and third steps deal primarily with determination of demand, the fourth step is concerned with the supply side of the equation.

Supply

Existing and Planned Supply.   In the process of analyzing the supply side, an equilibrium position between supply and demand may be determined. Table 2–5 exhibits the 15 items that are necessary to determine the equilibrium position of supply and demand.

Item 1 is taken from the adjusted population projections. The figure used is the total population projected to the final year of the time frame used in the analysis.

Item 2, estimated required housing, is the determination of the total number of dwelling units required to house the future population. To arrive at this figure, the adjusted population projection of 314,000 is divided by the average household size for the community; in the example, the average size is 3. The resultant figure of 104,666 is the number of housing units required to exactly house the expanding population. Since it is generally believed that a 5% vacancy rate is the normal condition of most residential markets, Item 3 adds a 5% vacancy figure to the total housing requirement figure. In the above example, the total estimated housing required by 1990 is 109,898 units, listed as Item 4.

Table 2–5. Supply and Demand Equilibrium[a]

Items		
1. Population projection, adjusted, to 1990		314,000
2. Estimated required housing, 314,000 ÷ 3 =		104,666
3. Plus 5% vacancy factor		5,233
4. Total estimated housing required by 1990		109,898
5. Minus units presently constructed	66,808	
6. Minus units permitted but not constructed	8,016	
TOTAL EXISTING HOUSING STOCK	74,824	74,824
7. Additional housing required by 1990		35,074
8. Required per year to 1990: 35,074 ÷ 10		3,508
9. Estimate of present population		200,000
10. Estimate of present housing requirement: 200,000 ÷ 3		66,666
11. Plus 5% vacancy factor		3,334
12. Estimate of total present housing requirement		70,000
13. Minus housing stock existing under construction (items 5 and 6)		74,824
14. Existing supply condition (oversupply)		4,824
15. Estimated time to deplete existing and planned stock: $\frac{4,824}{3,508} =$		approximately 1.4 years

[a] Conversions in are assumed to equal conversions out, and persons living in group quarters are not considered significant in numbers.

Items 1–4 show the total figure demand requirements, and Item 5 is an estimate of the number of dwelling units physically existing in the community at the present time. This information may be obtained by various methods. Community planning departments, as well as the property tax office, will generally have up-to-date statistics. This information will frequently have to be supplemented by on-site surveys of the newer developments.

Item 6 refers to those housing units planned for construction and for which building permits have been issued. However, the issuance of a building permit does not necessarily mean that the unit will be constructed. On-site surveys may be necessary to see if construction has actually started. If construction has started, for the most part it may be safely assumed that the units will be completed. In the absence of any visible construction, the permit holders should be contacted to determine whether they intend to move ahead with construction.

It may seem strange that anyone would apply for building permits and then not actually construct the buildings. However, this often happens. Even after the building permit is issued, there remain many obstacles prior to construction. A building moratorium may be anticipated, due, for instance, to overloaded water and sewage systems, and even with no firm commitments to build, developers will apply for building permits to beat the deadline. These events will distort the normal pattern of building permits issued and must be discounted accordingly.

The number and type of building permits issued will also indicate the prevailing conditions of various real estate submarkets. The trend and number of building permits issued for multifamily rentals, for instance, would indicate how well they are being accepted in the marketplace relative, for example, to single-family detached units. Table 2–6 depicts a hypothetical trend in construction types.

Table 2–6 indicates that, although single-family units are still the dominant form of housing, multifamily units (which are primarily rentals) are increasing as a relative percentage of new construction. Current conditions would indicate that approximately 65% of new household formations would prefer multifamily or rental units while the remainder of the market would be sales or single-family units.

Item 7 in Table 2–5 is the housing required beyond the presently existing supply to meet the community's total housing requirements to 1990. This figure is derived by subtracting Items 5 and 6 from Item 4.

Item 8 is the number of housing units required in every year of the study period to meet the total housing requirement projections made in Item 4. In the absence of any data to the contrary, it is generally assumed that the community will expand at an even rate. Item 8 is arrived at by dividing Item 7 (additional housing required) by the total number of years in the time frame of the study.

Table 2–6. Building Permits by Type of Structure

Year	Building Permits Issued	Single Family	Multi-family	Percent Multifamily
1980	2,000	1,500	500	25
1981	2,100	1,300	800	38
1982	2,200	1,200	1,000	45
1983	1,500	795	705	47
1984	1,150	494	656	57
1985	980	343	637	65
Total	9,930	5,632	4,298	43

In the example, the study period was 1980–1990, a 10-year span. This results in an annual housing requirement of 3,508 units per year during the period of time under study, assuming normal market conditions.

Items 1–8 are basic to the determination of future demand, while Items 9–15 assess the impact of existing supply on the projections of future demand.

Item 9 is an estimate of the community's present population. Item 10 is the estimate of the number of dwelling units required to house the existing population. Using the example, the estimated present population of 200,000 is divided by 3, the average number of persons per household, to give a present housing requirement of 66,666. To this is added a 5% vacancy factor (Item 11), characteristic of a normal market vacancy rate. Item 12 is the estimate of the total number of dwelling units needed in the community to house the existing population. From this figure is subtracted the estimate of existing housing stock, the sum of Items 5 and 6.

If the existing housing stock (Item 13) is greater than the present housing requirements (Item 12), then an oversupply condition exists. On the other hand, if present housing requirements exceed the existing housing stock, then an undersupply condition may exist. If the two figures are approximately equal, then a general equilibrium condition would be indicated.

Item 14 indicates an oversupply condition of 4,824 units. Annual requirements are estimated to be 3,508, so that it would take approximately 1.4 years (Item 15) with no new construction for the oversupply to be absorbed by the market. In this case a developer would be well advised to set aside any plans for new construction for at least a year. If a developer were to continue adding to the supply of housing, he or she would be in a very difficult competitive position with a lower than normal absorption rate and would quite possibly face financial collapse. This would certainly be the case if all developers continued to add to the housing stock during conditions of excess supply.

There is another factor that must be taken into consideration: distinguishing housing requirements or need from effective demand. For example, if it were determined in the income analysis that only 50% of the new annual household formations represented effective demand, then Item 8 would have to be adjusted accordingly. The model indicates that there is an annual housing requirement of 3,508 units. However, if effective demand were only 50% of this figure, then the unsubsidized market would only be 1,754 units. Consequently, the oversupply condition would be much worse, i.e., 4,824 ÷ 1,754, and it would take approximately 2.75 years to remove the excess supply from the market.

Competitive Environment.   The fifth step in a residential market analysis is to survey the competitive environment. The overall effective demand for housing is determined from Step 4, while Step 5 analyzes the specific submarket within which the subject property will be competing. Those projects which are, or will be, in direct competition with the subject project must be analyzed in order to determine how the proposed project might best be marketed and what competitive pressures it may come under. One approach to use in organizing and analyzing the data is to construct a matrix such as the type in Table 2–7.

Table 2–7 demonstrates in a somewhat simplified fashion the data necessary to make a study of competing projects. These data are normally collected by on-site inspections of the various projects and by interviews of project managers. The information for planned units may generally be found on file with a community's land planning department. Often the developers themselves should be contacted for information on newly planned developments.

Table 2–7 is a sample of the type of matrix an analyst might construct when surveying large multifamily rental projects. In a comprehensive housing market analysis, a similar table should be constructed for each submarket, such as single-family detached subdivision developments, condominiums, cooperatives, and mobile homes.

When a matrix has been completed, several questions concerning the competitive environment may be answered. By using the above example, an analyst would be able to tell how the competition has distributed the types of units between one-, two-, three-, and four-bedroom units. He may also conclude that the one-bedroom units seem to be the most marketable, while the four-bedroom units are not in much demand. Consequently, he may recommend more one-bedroom units and very few, if any, four-bedroom units. He will also be able to determine how large the units should be in order to remain competitive; in the above example the smallest one-bedroom unit is 775 square feet and the largest is 875 square feet. The largest, in Projects 1 and 2, even though they were more expensive, were all absorbed by the market; while the smaller and less expensive one-bedroom units in Project 3 have high vacancy rates.

The competitive price range will also become apparent. The number of units per acre is also an important competitive concern. The above

Table 2–7. Existing and Planned Supply

Name and Location of Competitive Projects	Number and Types of Units	Size of Units in Square Feet	Rent or Sales Price per Unit	Number of Acres	Density or Units per Acre	Time on the Market	Number of Units Sold or Rented to Date	Absorption Rate–Number of Units Sold or Rented per Yr.	Number of Units Remaining on Market	Type of Amenities Offered	Parking
Existing											
#1	20–1Bd	850	$225				20	10	0	Outdoor	Surface,
Willow Wick Apts.	50–2Bd	975	295				15	7–8	35	Pool,	1 space
2308 N. Maple	15–3Bd	1,050	350				15	7–8	0	Laundry	per unit,
	15–4Bd	1,150	400				0	0	15		No Chg.
Total	100			10	10	2 yrs.	50	25	50		
#2	30–1Bd	800	$255				30	10	0	Indoor	Underground,
River Bend Apts.	180–2Bd	925	340				60	20	120	Pool,	1 space
2000 Water St.	80–3Bd	1,050	395				30	10	50	Tennis,	per unit,
	15–4Bd	1,150	445				2	0–1	13	Laundry	$20 Mo.
Total	305			15.2	20	3 yrs.	122	41	183		
#3	75–1Bd	775	$195				55	11	20	Laundry	Surface,
Normandy Apts.	75–2Bd	875	225				35	7	40		1 space per
5800 Eagle Pt. Rd.				5	30	5 yrs.	90	18	60		unit, $10 Mo.
Total	150										
Total Existing	540	931.5 Avg.	$312 Avg.	21.6	20 Avg.	3.3 Avg.	262	85	293		
Planned											
#1	15–1Bd	875	$275			Planned				Indoor	Underground,
Bradford Arms	60–2Bd	950	350			Date to				Pool,	1 space
1700 Lake Drive	25–3Bd	1,075	425			Go on				Sauna,	per unit,
	10–4Bd	1,150	500			Market				Tennis,	$20 Mo.
Total	110			11	10				110	Laundry	
Total Planned	110	986 Avg.	$387 Avg.	11	10				110		

example indicates that Project 3, with the lowest price but very high density, i.e., units per acre, has the lowest annual absorption rate. An analyst may conclude then that the proposed project should have a density of no more than 20 and no less than 10 units per acre. The absorption rate for each project is determined by dividing the total number of units sold or rented by the number of years the project has been on the market.

The type of amenities, access, and parking are also important competitive concerns. The number of units remaining on the market at the time of the study and the inclusion of all planned developments that will be in direct competition with a proposed project will allow an analyst to determine competition at least into the foreseeable future. In determining what projects will be in direct competition with the proposed project, transportation time to the major employment and shopping facilities should also be considered.

Data Synthesis and Recommendations

The final step of a typical residential market study is to synthesize all the collected data and to make the resultant developmental recommendations. These recommendations generally use the analytical results of the overall study to comprehensively answer the six basic questions discussed in the beginning of this chapter.

The first question (What are the indirect economic constraints?) would be answered in the first section of a study dealing with the indirect economic factors. These indirect economic factors would normally establish certain constraints within which the project would have to be developed. Zoning and utility availability would most certainly establish type, density, and land planning configurations. Each of the indirect economic factors should be explained very clearly in the market report with obstacles clearly defined and alternatives explored.

What is the size of the future market, and what percentage of the overall market can be attracted to the subject site? This second question is perhaps the most crucial and most difficult to answer. The size of the future market is largely determined by the analysis and projections of population, income, and employment, and is well suited to quantification. The answer to the second part of the question (what percentage of the overall market can be attracted to the subject site?) depends upon the ability of the analyst to interpret both the quantitative and the qualitative aspects of a proposed project.

If management, marketing ability, design, amenities, price, and location were all equal, and if the population were expanding at an even rate everywhere in the market area, then the determination of the subject site's absorption rate would be relatively simple. An analyst would review the competitive environment matrix and find, for example, that there were four competing projects, each absorbing 25% of the market annually. Assuming these same projects would not be fully absorbed for another 2 years or so, then the proposed fifth project would reduce each of their absorption rates equally by 5%. Each of the five projects would then absorb only 20% of the market annually. However, in the real world few, if any, of the variables mentioned are similar, so the analyst is forced to deal with rough averages and make qualitative judgments based on the best available, but always insufficient, data. Indeed, if perfect knowledge existed, then real estate investments would be as safe as investments in U.S. government bonds!

The development of a thorough competitive environment matrix is essential in answering the second half of Question 2. The matrix should include not only existing developments that are not fully absorbed and future planned projects, but also past developments—especially those in the immediate area surrounding the subject site. By analyzing the absorption rates of past as well as present developments, an overall average annual absorption rate can be estimated. By using the matrix in Table 2–7, it may be seen that the total annual average absorption rate of the three existing projects listed is 85 units, with 36% being one-bedroom, 41% two-bedroom, 21% three-bedroom, and less than 2% four-bedroom units. If this sample were truly representative of a given market area, and if a similar absorption rate was indicated for older projects, then a new project would be competing for a percentage of an estimated annual demand in the area of 85 units. If population movements in the surrounding market area were expected to increase, then this demand estimate should be increased. The timing of developments is also important to the estimate of an absorption rate. When other competing projects are fully absorbed, then the absorption rate of newer projects should increase.

In general, an analyst should review the overall size of the market, the population trends in the immediate market area, the number of units sold or rented in similar and competing projects (past and present), the annual absorption per project by type of unit, the number of unsold or unrented units remaining on the market, and the time estimated for the absorption of the remaining units. The impact of future planned developments should also be assessed. From these quantitative data the analyst should develop an estimate of the percentage of the overall market that the subject site should attract. Where there are gaps in the data, the analyst's best judgment must prevail. Adjustments may be made to the absorption rate based on subjective judgment of the project design quality, managerial capabilities, marketing style, and overall track record.

A note of caution should be mentioned—subjective judgments often cause inflated absorption rates to be predicted in market studies and subsequently to be used in a project's cash flow analysis. Using overly optimistic absorption rates will produce a glowing cash flow projection, but if it does not reflect reality, then it may be costly for the developer and lender. Analysts should not feel they are doing their client a favor by inflating an absorption rate even if it means the project may get financial backing, for if the projected sales or rentals do not materialize, the project will in all likelihood fail. The failure will ultimately reflect on the individual or organization which produced the data upon which the developmental decisions were based.

The answer to Question 3 (What is the market-determined price range?) is determined by construction costs, the income level the project is designed to appeal to, and the pricing policies of competitive projects. In Table 2–7 the price ranges for the various competing units are:

One-bedroom – $195–275
Two-bedroom –   225–350
Three-bedroom – 350–425
Four-bedroom –   400–500

These price ranges and the absorption rate for each type of unit will serve as guidelines to the number of, and pricing policy for, the various units in the planned project. The price ultimately recommended by the researcher does not mean that the project can be built and rented or sold for that price and make a profit. Construction costs may have risen considerably since the surveyed projects were built, so that no new project could be built and priced competitively with the existing projects.

Besides competitive prices, the other limiting factor on price is effective demand. Using the household formation and monthly payment data from Table 2–3 to construct a housing demand curve (Figure 2–3), it becomes readily apparent that relatively small increases in monthly housing costs will cause large segments of the market to drop out of the effective demand category. For example, an increase in monthly housing costs from $300 to $325 (an 8% increase) will cause approximately 500 household formations to drop out of the effective demand category (a 21% decrease).

Question 4 (What type of dwelling unit is justified by market demand?) is answered by reviewing several factors in the market study. First, the zoning for a specific site might specify the type of dwelling units that can be built there. The question then becomes how many units, not what type. The second major limitation is again effective demand. Assume the first major division between types is single-family or rental units. Further assume that the cost to construct an average

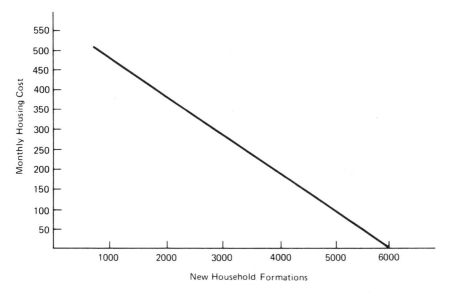

Figure 2–3. Annual effective demand curve.

single-family residence is $45,000 and that 95% financing is available. The mortgage payment alone would then be approximately $360 per month. In Figure 2–3 it may be seen that only about 20% of the market could afford an average, unsubsidized, single-family unit. Depending on the supply of existing unsold single-family units, a developer may not wish to speculate on such a small segment of the market and may choose to construct rental units. The question then becomes what type of rental unit, and this is determined again by estimated cost vs. effective demand and by a survey of the competitive environment.

Questions 5 and 6 (How large should the units be? and What amenities should be provided?) are largely answered by surveying the existing supply and determining what the planned project will require in this respect in order to effectively compete.

Once completed, the market analysis will serve as a planning tool and will provide much of the essential information necessary in the construction of a project's cash flow statement. Although a market analysis cannot eliminate all the risks from real estate investments, it can reduce them to a known and perhaps manageable level.

It should also be noted that many consulting firms and independent analysts are including consumer surveys as an element in the market analysis. There is a limit of what can be deduced from microeconomic and macroeconomic analysis, and this limiting factor has generated a keen interest in properly conducted consumer surveys. These surveys are especially relevant when dealing with the questions of type, size, and amenities.

SUMMARY

This chapter has explained the principal elements involved in a comprehensive real estate market analysis. The key questions that a market analysis should answer are indicated for residential, commercial, and industrial land use potential. In order to answer these questions in an appropriate manner, certain techniques of analyzing markets should be understood.

The described techniques of market analysis allow the investigator to analyze the supply and demand side of any real estate market, as well as to establish a development program, and to determine the highest and best use for a given site.

The supply side of the analysis is primarily concerned with the existing competitive environment and the planned supply. The demand side of the analysis is primarily concerned with population, income, and employment trends which, when properly analyzed, clearly distinguish between need or desire and effective demand.

The following chapter will explain the feasibility analysis, Phase 3 of the planning process, and, more specifically, the techniques and procedures that may be used to develop a cash flow model.

3

The Feasibility Analysis: How to Construct a Cash Flow Model

This chapter is concerned with the techniques involved in determining the financial feasibility of a real estate project. The information flow necessary for the construction of the feasibility analysis comes from the understanding and application of the concepts and methodology developed in the market study, sketch plan, and pro forma analysis as explained in Chapters 1 and 2. This chapter will first review basic investment objectives and related risks. Secondly, the chapter will discuss the traditional appraisal approach to determining the value of income-producing property. The distinction between fair market or appraised value and investment value to a particular investor will be made clear.

The principal components of the 1986 Tax Reform Act (TRA) which affect real estate will be reviewed and where appropriate compared with prior tax law. A discounted cash flow model will be developed which incorporates the relevant laws from the 1986 TRA.[1] The model will move from a static cash flow structure to a dynamic or time-related discounted cash flow. The model will demonstrate the interrelated nature of the financial variables involved in a real estate transaction, and the impact of individualized concerns such as federal tax and financing. The determination of project feasibility as it relates to real property requires a much broader knowledge of the physical and financial variables directly related to the investment than do most other forms of investment. An investment analysis, at the most general level, should consist of defining the investor's objectives, assessing the inherent risks, and analyzing the financial feasibility of the individual project.

INVESTMENT OBJECTIVES

A properly executed real estate investment analysis will first delineate the investor's specific objectives. Although the investment objectives of all investors are not the same, the basic objectives which should be considered by all investors are similar in nature. The same level of consideration should be given to the basic investment risks.

Current Cash Flow

The current cash flow resulting from the investment may be top priority for some real estate investors and not for others. For many investors, the return on their investment portfolio is their sole source of income; for others it may be only a percentage. For those investors whose standard of living depends upon the return on their investment, current cash flow may be of principal concern to them. However, other investors may have current income from other sources and may place more emphasis on appreciation and future income. Still others may be solely concerned with the tax ramifications of the investment.

Future Cash Return

Investors who are not currently dependent on the cash flow from their investment may prefer future income to current returns. In real estate this usually takes the form of property appreciation with profits being taken at the time of sale. This is a common investor posture in today's real estate markets. Investors in this market must have disposable income from other sources. The estimates of future market conditions and sales prices also become important considerations.

Liquidity

Liquidity is generally considered to mean the rapidity with which the property purchased can be turned into cash. Real estate is among the most illiquid types of investment. For example, 100 shares of XYZ Corporation may be disposed of at prevailing market prices within a matter of minutes, whereas it may take months or even years to sell certain types of real property. In the real estate market a single-family housing unit is perhaps the most liquid type of property, with an average "offer"-to-"close" period of approximately 90 days.

Inflationary Hedge

Many investors are acutely aware of the decline in the purchasing power of the dollar resulting from inflationary forces. Investments which serve as a hedge against inflation are those that maintain their relative purchasing power as the general price index increases. For example, an investment of $1,000 in long-term certificates of deposit paying a 6% rate of return will be worth $1,060 at the end of 1 year. However, if we assume an increase in the general price index of 10% during the same time, the actual purchasing power of the $1,000 at the end of the year is $960—a decline of 4%. However, if that same $1,000 were invested in income property such as an apartment house or in personalty such as diamonds, the price of the commodity might increase at the same or nearly the same rate as the general price index. Thus, the value of the investment relative to other goods remains the same.

Ordinary Income Tax

To many, the impact of an investment on the amount of tax liability to which an investor will be subject is a vital consideration. If an investment results in an increase in taxable income for an investor, he or she will tend to view it differently than if it resulted in a tax loss or tax shelter, i.e., reducing the amount of income subject to ordinary income tax. Real estate investments remain quite popular among persons in high tax brackets because depreciation and other allowable deductions often result in a tax shelter, thereby protecting a certain percentage of their income from other sources from taxation. Indeed, many real estate developments are undertaken for the primary purpose of creating a tax shelter. However, it should be noted that it is entirely possible for a project to create a tax shelter and at the same time to generate a positive cash flow. This will be explained more fully in the section on cash flow analysis.

Capital Gains Treatment

Many investors, prior to the 1986 Tax Reform Act, sought to have their income or profits classified as capital gains and thus qualify for a more favorable tax treatment. Real estate lent itself well to this objective. Under normal market conditions an investor would hold an ownership interest in real property for the 6-month required period. During this time the investor would hope to see the property appreciate in value.

Current cash flow might or might not be an important consideration. At the time of sale the profit would be taxed as capital gains and not as ordinary income. However, as we will see, the 1986 Tax Reform Act has eliminated this consideration.

INVESTMENT RISK

Along with the establishment of investment objectives, an investor should carefully assess the risks involved. The risks are basically the other side of the "objectives" coin. The risks which should be analyzed may be classified under the following headings: (1) market changes, (2) inflation, (3) interest rate movements, (4) liquidity, (5) legal risks, (6) changes in political climate, and (7) natural hazards. These risks overlap but are sufficiently different so that each should be considered separately. All investments may, to some extent, be influenced by all of the above risks; however, some types of investment are more susceptible to a certain type of risk than others.

Market Changes

Changes in the supply and demand conditions that create the competitive environment for any investment pose a risk to most investments. Changed conditions of a neighborhood, changed traffic patterns because of the opening of a new street, and the development of new competition will all affect the profitability of an investment in the local real estate market. Other forms of investment may also be dramatically affected by changing market conditions. The commodities market, stocks, and options market are the best examples of investments which may be dramatically affected—even in the short run—by fluctuations in the supply or demand side of that particular market.

Inflation

The forces of inflation are certainly destroyers of wealth, and the higher the rate of inflation, the more wealth that is lost. A high rate of inflation is more destructive to some types of investments than to others. Savings accounts are among those investments which are hurt the most by inflationary forces, while a real estate investment is generally considered to be a good hedge against inflation.

During times of rapid inflation, when the purchasing power of the dollar declines sharply, there may be a "flight from dollars." Under these conditions, an investment in just about any physical good is considered to be a hedge against inflation. The impact of inflation should be seriously considered when making any investment.

Interest Rate Movements

The fluctuation in interest rates will impact some types of investments more than others. Those affected most are direct monetary instruments such as fixed-interest mortgages, negotiable paper, and bonds of all sorts. Real estate will also be affected by fluctuations in interest rates. Long-term securities will normally be affected more than short-term assets. The effect on existing real estate is due primarily to the influence of interest rates on the capitalization rates used in determining appraised value. For example, an increase in interest rates will have a tendency to drive up capitalization rates. Thus, in the formula $NOI/R = Value$ (where NOI is net operating income and R is the capitalization rate), it may be seen that an increase in R will decrease the appraised value. This will eventually affect general sales prices in the market.

Liquidity

The sudden unexpected need for cash is always a risk factor confronted by most investors. Savings accounts, stocks, and bonds can generally be converted to cash with little effort. Investments in real property or personalty are generally more difficult to dispose of on short notice. Real estate also has the disadvantage of immobility. For example, stocks, bonds, cars, refrigerators, and other valuable property may be sold anywhere or, in the case of personalty, moved to more favorable market areas. Real estate, however, is physically fixed within the local market and in an individual liquidity crisis may have to be sold at a distressed sale price.

Legal Risks

An investment in real estate entails legal risks unlike other types of investments. There are certain legal risks which directly relate to the title to property. There may be prior claims of ownership as yet uncovered or unexpressed. Other legal risks associated with real property are mortgages, notes, liens, easements, taxes, building codes, environmental restrictions, tenant actions, and liability claims. Various types of insurance are available as a safeguard against claims arising from these risk areas, but the insurance is itself another legal risk area. As a general rule, the larger the investment, the larger the legal risk exposure is to the investor and, consequently, the more legal assistance required in analyzing the investment.

Changes in Political Climate

For any given type of investment an investor is well advised to review any pending legislation at all levels of government which may affect the investment. Any changes in tax legislation may be particularly important. Political climate also includes intangibles such as the public's attitude toward business.

Natural Hazards

This area of risk is peculiar to most types of real estate investment. However, "Acts of God," i.e., earthquakes, floods, hurricanes, and hail, are especially difficult to predict. They are nevertheless a real risk associated with real property investment. The value of the potential damage from these hazards may be calculated and insured against, and the investor in real estate should be well aware of the natural disaster(s) most likely to occur in the geographical area of the investment.

INVESTMENT VALUE

At the very heart of assessing the financial feasibility of a real estate investment is the determination of the value of the real property to the individual investor. This is referred to as the investment value of the property. The investment value may differ from investor to investor, and may differ also from the appraised market value.

Unlike other forms of investment, the prevailing sales prices of a class of real property are never unambiguous and certain at any given point in time. In the stock market, investors know the minimum amount they will have to pay for, say, 100 shares of Xerox Corporation's stock. Buyers and sellers may be instantly apprised of the supply and demand conditions surrounding a particular stock. The same may be said for most bonds, options, and commodities. However, in the real estate market each property, even within a class of property, is unique and therefore requires special analysis to determine its value. The term *value* is a nebulous one in real estate, since the estimate of value may differ among investors and analysts alike.

In the final analysis, the sales price paid would normally be indicative of the property's value. However, it is often misleading to use past sales prices to arrive at an estimate of value for a similar property. Sales prices are often distorted by the variety of ownership interest involved, the multitude of mortgages and notes that may be exchanged in the transaction, the location, and physical differences in the properties. The very nature of the interaction between buyers and sellers will also have an impact on sales prices. Due to the fragmented nature of real estate markets, i.e., no focal point for buying and selling, there is often a lack of knowledge on the part of buyers as to who is selling what and on the part of sellers as to who is a potential buyer. In a tight market, a buyer may have to be very persuasive to get any owner to sell.

There are certain classes of property, in those cities that are experiencing rapid growth, that do not get listed with brokers because the demand is competitive. In an attempt to avoid paying large commissions, buyers contact on a regular basis all the known owners of that class of property. For example, the investor demand for large apartment complexes is so strong in Atlanta, Georgia, that a corporation was formed for the sole purpose of analyzing and publishing data on the apartment market. Land Data Corporation has accumulated information on every apartment complex in Atlanta, including recent sales information and the owner's or agent's name, telephone number, and address. These properties are listed by geographical areas and in alphabetical order by owner. Readily accessible information of this sort will expedite the meeting of minds between buyers and sellers. The situation mentioned above, however, is unique to the Atlanta market. Information in other markets is still scarce.

Figure 3–1 is a simplified model of the buy/sell process in most markets. In a competitive market the situation is normally one of informed sellers and informed buyers, so that a seller would be aware of the appraised value of his property but would also be aware that there might be investors to whom the property would be worth more; i.e., their estimate of investment value would be higher than the appraised market value. The seller would also be aware that there would be other investors who would value the property at less than the appraised market value. A seller who is trying to maximize his return would set his asking price at point C in Figure 3–1, hoping that the competitive

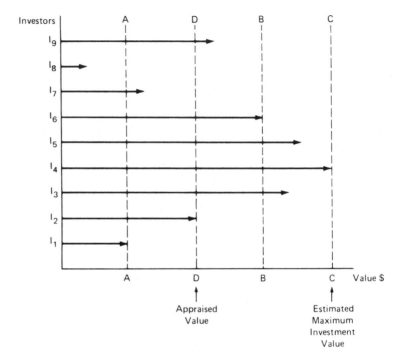

Figure 3–1. Range of investment values.

environment and the characteristics of his property would attract that investor who would place the highest possible investment value on his property. In Figure 3–1, that would be investor 4. However, the seller realizes there may be other properties for sale that are at least as equally attractive to investor 4 as his property, and he also realizes that not all investors are in the market at the same time. Therefore, in order to assure himself of a sale, he may be willing to negotiate a lower price between point D (the appraised value and his minimum acceptable price) and point C (the maximum he could expect). This range of negotiation then puts the property within the investment capabilities of several more potential buyers. In Figure 3–1 the price range between D and C includes investors 2, 3, 4, 5, 6, and 9. How quickly the property sells and who will be the final purchaser depend on many factors— such as how many of the potential investors are in the market during the duration of the offering, how well the property is marketed, and which of the investors makes an acceptable offer first. It may be that investor 6 makes an immediate offer at his maximum investment value, point B. The seller, not knowing who the other potential investors are, their time frames, or property interest, may accept investor 6's offer, believing it to be the best and most timely offer he might receive. If, on the following day, investor 4 made an offer equal to his maximum investment value, the seller could not legally accept, assuming the first offer was a properly executed and accepted contract to purchase.

So then, what is the value of the property, and how representative is the sales price of prevailing market conditions? Should the sales price be used as an indicator of value for similar properties? It sold for more than the appraised market value but less than it could have.

The questions could be argued, but perhaps the most appropriate stance to take would be that in a normally competitive market there is a range of investment values within which sales prices of similar class properties will fall. The exact sales price will fall somewhere between the minimum amount acceptable to the seller and the maximum invest- ment value to the investor, with the appraised market value being only one input to the decision process and its primary influence being on the determination of the amount of the mortgage.

Point A in Figure 3–1 might represent the asking price of an unin- formed seller, a forced sale, a quick sale, or a deteriorated property, since it falls considerably below the range of prevailing investment values for a similar class of properties. Since there are few if any "steals" in a normally functioning real estate market, the property would be suspect and the asking price would not be representative of prevailing values.

In order to clearly understand why the appraised market value may differ from investment value and why investment values will differ among investors, we must review the procedures and assumptions involved in the determination of fair market value.

APPRAISED MARKET VALUE

The traditional approaches used in determining value are generally referred to as the sales approach, the cost approach, and the income approach. The approach that is the most influential when estimating the value of income-producing property is the income approach. In- deed, many practitioners in the field believe it is the only relevant approach to use with income property. Therefore, in our review of the traditional approaches to value, the focus will be on the income approach. It should also be emphasized that much of the criticism we shall note may be remedied by being more concerned with the income approach as it is normally practiced.

At the basis of the income approach is the formula:

$$\text{Value} = \frac{\text{Net Operating Income}}{\text{Capitalization Rate}}$$

The formula seems simple enough, and indeed it is. The problems, however, are the assumptions underlying the development of both the numerator and denominator of the formula; they may not reflect reality. The assumptions necessary to arrive at a value figure using this approach relate directly to either the computation of the NOI or the capitalization rate.

Net Operating Income Assumptions: Tax Shelter, Appreciation, and Equity Buildup

By using only the NOI as the amount to be capitalized, the traditional approach ignores other sources of income and stores of value. The other sources are tax shelter, appreciation, and equity buildup, and are important considerations to informed investors. Tax shelter results from tax laws which allow interest and depreciation to be deducted from income before determining tax liability. These deductions will often result in a property operating at a loss for tax purposes. The loss may be used to reduce the investor's tax liability on income from other sources, although the 1986 TRA has greatly reduced this benefit.

Most income properties in today's market produce very little cash flow after debt service. Therefore, the investors in these properties expect to take their profit at the time of sale. The gains at the time of sale have traditionally resulted from appreciation in the property's value. This appreciation has occurred for three reasons: (1) rental increases, (2) increasing demand, and (3) inflationary forces. Without appreciation in a property's value, investment in real estate would undoubtedly decline. The traditional approach does not consider potential appreciation.

Since the vast majority of real property in this country is mortgaged, equity buildup is an important source of value and is often used as leverage for additional investments. Equity buildup results from the reduction in the mortgage principal as successive mortgage payments are made. Even though the reduction in the principal amount of the mortgage increases the investor's equity in the property, it is not considered in the traditional income approach.

Level Annuity

The traditional income approach normally assumes that the projected NOI is level for the entire economic life of the property. This does not take into account fluctuating vacancy rates or changes in rental rates. For example, an investor could reasonably predict annual increases in rents of 5, 10, or 15% (these increases are commonly included in leases). The traditional income approach could not accommodate this except by taking the average of the increases over the life of the project or by assuming that increases in rents will not be offset by increases in costs, thereby having no net effect on NOI. Many income properties now have their leases pegged to consumer price indices; this tends to increase the NOI over time. Also, there is a movement toward indexing costs such as property tax, utilities, insurance, etc., so that increases in operating costs will be passed along to the consumer while the NOI, also being pegged to a Consumer Price Index (CPI), will not lose its purchasing power. However, the traditional approach may still assume a level NOI, which causes a reduced estimate of market value.

Financing

The traditional income approach assumes that the real estate transaction is an "all-cash deal" and ignores the ramifications of financing on the value of the property. It is estimated that more than 90% of all real estate transactions in the United States are financed to some extent by using a variety of financing techniques. Large differences between investment value and appraised market value are caused because the traditional approach does not consider financing and its impact on tax shelter and equity buildup.

Economic Life

The traditional approach includes the unrealistic assumption that the investor will hold the property for the duration of its economic life, when in fact most investors will sell or trade their project within a 7- to 10-year time span. The capitalization of an income stream projected for 20, 30, 40, or more years in the future simply does not reflect the investment holding periods of today's investors. The reason that most investors will sell long before the end of the economic life of the project is because they want to recoup their capital and profits resulting from appreciation or because their tax shelter has been reduced significantly due to decreasing interest and depreciation allowances.

Capitalization Rate Assumptions.   Although the capitalization of income is a legitimate and commonly accepted method of determining present value, in some cases the traditional approach to determining the capitalization rate will add to the differences between appraised market value and investment value.

In many cases the rate developed in the traditional approach will bear little resemblance to the actual required rate of return of the investor. The capitalization rate employed in the income approach is generally determined by using the average of rates which were derived by using the sale prices of properties that are comparable to the subject property. That is, the capitalization rate may be derived by dividing the NOI (net operating income) by the sales price of comparable properties. Although comparable, these properties may be dissimilar in many ways to the subject property. These differences may require further adjustments to the capitalization rate. A second method often used is based on the prevailing mortgage rates in the local market for properties similar to the subject property. However, mortgage rates are, in general, determined by capital market forces and a concern with the overall rate of return on a lending institution's mortgage portfolio. An investor, on the other hand, is looking at the return on equity in a specific property, which may include tax shelter, appreciation, and equity buildup.

No matter how the traditional approach determines the capitalization rate, it may differ significantly from that required by an individual investor.

Because the assumptions underlying the traditional income approach to value do not relate to the reality of today's real estate investment practices, the approach cannot be used as a dynamic tool for investment analysis. This situation has been widely recognized; one of the earliest attempts to develop a method that would accurately reflect investor concerns in the determination of fair market value was pioneered by L. W. Ellwood.[2]

Mortgage Equity Capitalization.   The Ellwood mortgage equity approach, first introduced in 1959, represented a significant departure from the traditional appraisal approaches to value. The Ellwood technique attempts to take into account the idea that most real estate is financed and that most investors sell long before the end of the economic life of the property. The approach also takes into consideration any appreciation or depreciation which may be projected. However, this technique also has many shortcomings as an indication of investment value. The approach basically is the adjustment of a market-determined equity yield rate to arrive at an overall rate of capitalization. The equity yield rate is adjusted for decreases in the mortgage principal balance (equity buildup) and anticipated appreciation or depreciation, and these adjustments are put within the time frame of a typical investor's holding period.

A review of the basic formula will help to clarify these adjustments.

$$R = Y - MC + \text{dep} \times 1/S_n$$

or

$$R = Y - MC - \text{app} \times 1/S_n$$

where

R = adjusted overall capitalization rate
Y = market-determined equity yield rate
MC = basic adjustment to the equity yield rate to account for equity buildup. The reader should bear in mind that a reduction in capitalization rate will increase the resultant estimate of value.
M = ratio of mortgage to value
C = (mortgage coefficient) $Y + P \times 1/S_n - f$
P = percentage of mortgage paid off
$1/S_n$ = sinking fund factor for the equity yield rate for the holding period of the investment
f = mortgage constant
dep = anticipated depreciation
app = anticipated appreciation

The interested reader should attempt to apply this approach using the data provided in the sample cash flow problem that follows.

A brief analysis of the factors making up the formula will point out some of the dangers inherent in using the formula as an indicator of investment value. The determination of an appropriate Y is in practice very difficult, and it is the single most important factor. The data required for Y must come from the market, either from other investors who are willing to divulge personal financial data or from the analysis of the results of similar investment liquidations. The factor Y also influences the determination of C, and of course $1/S_n$ depends directly on Y and will change as Y changes. The depreciation and appreciation factors are highly subjective inputs, and small changes in either direction could cause significant differences in the final estimate of value. The overall shortcoming of using the formula is that it concentrates on adjusting one uncertain capitalization rate (Y) with uncertain factors (C and appreciation or depreciation) to arrive at an equally uncertain overall capitalization rate (R). This R is then divided into an NOI which is subject to the following limitations:

1. Current income levels, expenses, and residual cash flow are considered to remain constant throughout the period of ownership. This is in direct contrast to the norm of increasing rents and spiraling costs in today's markets.
2. The effect of tax consideration on income is not considered. It was not long ago that the effect of tax on a real estate investment was not considered to be a sufficient economic motive for investing, and that if tax shelter was the only benefit of ownership, the property was not worth owning. In 1974 L. W. Ellwood wrote, ". . . the combination of conditions has to be very rare to make tax shelter the paramount benefit of ownership."[3] By 1976 the rarity had become commonplace, and by 1978 the price of income properties had been bid so high it was a rarity to find a property that provided any benefits besides tax shelter.

Although the Ellwood Mortgage Equity Approach is a departure from the more traditional approaches to value, it still suffers from many of the same constraints as the traditional approaches and is not an effective tool for investment decision making.

The most effective tool for real estate investment decisions and for the determination of investment value is the discounted cash flow model. Even though many technical corrections remain to be made to the 1986 TRA, the basic changes made to the prior tax law should bring market value, as determined by the traditional appraisal approach, much closer to today's investment value.

REAL ESTATE AND THE 1986 TAX REFORM ACT

Before investors can structure and analyze a meaningful investment model, they must have a fundamental grasp of the various tax laws affecting the project's cash flow. The purpose of this section is to survey the principal federal tax laws relating to real estate and to indicate their potential impact on cash flow and the real estate investment decision. Tax laws are extremely complex and do change from time to time. Their actual application will vary from one project for a particular investor to another project and investor. Any attempt to cover in detail all tax laws relevant to real estate investment would, by far, exceed the scope of this section. Competent professional tax counseling should be sought before making any sizable investment in real estate. However, there are several areas of tax law that clearly affect real estate far more than other types of investments. These areas are dealt with below.

The 1986 Tax Reform Act is the most drastic overhaul of federal taxes in the last 40 years. It is so encompassing that in the future it will not be called a tax "reform" but rather the Internal Revenue Code of 1986. Most of the law changes take effect after 1986.[4]

Tax Rate Changes

The first item that needs to be mentioned in any review of the 1986 TRA is the dramatic change in tax rates. The immediate effect of lower tax rates is that the value of tax shelters will be reduced. Before the 1986 TRA, there were 15 different tax rates ranging from 11% to a top rate of 50%. The new law creates essentially two rates, 15% and 28%, although there is a phase-in period during which time a taxpayer could end up paying a rate as high as 38.5%.

Tax Rate Schedules

Single Taxpayers

New Bill: 1987

If Taxable Income Is More Than	But Not More Than	The Tax Rate Is	Of Amount Over
$ 0	$ 1,800	$ 0 + 11%	$ 0
1,800	16,800	198 + 15%	1,800
16,800	27,000	2,448 + 28%	16,800
27,000	54,000	5,304 + 35%	27,000
54,000	—	14,754 + 38.5%	54,000

(*Continued*)

New Bill: 1988

If Taxable Income Is More Than	But Not More Than	The Tax Rate Is	Of Amount Over
$ 0	$17,850	$ 0 + 15%	$ 0
$17,850	—	$2,678 + 28%	$17,850

A taxable income of more than $43,150 is subject to a 5% additional tax liability (surcharge) intended to eliminate the benefits of having the first $17,850 taxed at the 15% rate. The surcharge 15% tax bracket is followed by the elimination of the personal exemption; this could put a taxpayer in the 33+% tax bracket. When the phaseout is completed, the taxpayer will pay a flat tax of 28 percent on all taxable income.

Married Filing Joint

New Bill: 1987

If Taxable Income Is More Than	But Not More Than	The Tax Rate Is	Of Amount Over
$ 0	$ 3,000	$ 0 + 11%	$ 0
3,000	28,000	330 + 15%	3,000
28,000	45,000	4,080 + 28%	28,000
45,000	90,000	8,840 + 35%	45,000
90,000	—	24,590 + 38.5%	90,000

New Bill: 1988

If Taxable Income Is More Than	But Not More Than	The Tax Rate Is	Of Amount Over
$ 0	$29,750	$ 0 + 15%	$ 0
$29,750	—	$4,463 + 28%	$29,750

For married taxpayers filing jointly a taxable income of more than $71,900 is subject to the 5% additional tax liability.

Phaseout of 15% Bracket.   The additional surcharge to phase out the benefit of a tax bracket less than 28% is 5% of the taxable income within specified taxable income ranges:

Surcharge Schedule

Filing Status	Specified Ranges[a]	
If the Taxpayer Is:	Increase Tax by 5% of Taxable Income	
	From	To
Single	$43,150	$89,560
Head of household	$61,650	$123,790
Married, joint	$71,900	$149,250

[a] A 33% marginal tax rate applies in the phaseout range.

Corporate Tax Rates[a]

	1986	1987
$ 0–$25,000	15%	15%
$25,000–$50,000	18%	15%
$50,000–$75,000	30%	25%
$75,000–$100,000	40%	34%
Over $100,000	46%	34%
Phaseout	N/A	[b]

[a] The 1988 rate schedule is effective July 1, 1987.
[b] The graduated rates would be phased out for corporations with taxable incomes over $140,000, and so the corporations with taxable incomes of $360,000 or more would pay, in effect, a flat tax at the 34% rate.

Homeownership

Although the 1986 TRA eliminated many of the benefits of real estate investing, it did leave many of the advantages of homeownership intact.

Mortgage Interest.   Mortgage interest, with qualifications, is still tax-deductible. Mortgage interest expense on two homes may be taken as a deduction on the taxpayer's income tax return. However, the interest on the two homes, referred to as "qualified residence," is deductible only to the extent that the amount of the mortgage loan does not exceed the original purchase price plus improvements. The debt must be secured by a security interest perfected under local law on both residences.

The one exception to this general rule is when the interest expense is incurred for the payment of educational or medical expenses. If the interest expense is incurred for education or medical expenses, then the home mortgage interest on debt in excess of the purchase price plus improvements, but not more than the fair market value of the residence, is deductible. The interest paid on a mortgage loan in excess of the fair market value is not deductible as "qualified residence" interest, even if used for educational or medical expenses. This law was made retroactive and took effect on August 17, 1986.

A principal residence is not specifically defined by the IRS. It depends upon all the facts and circumstances in each case, including the good faith of the taxpayer. Examples listed are single-family dwellings, condominiums, cooperatives, houseboats, trailers, and even yachts. The above definition and example also apply to second homes. The taxpayer designates the two homes, not the IRS, and the taxpayer may change these designations each year under current law.

A husband and wife, even if filing separate returns, may only deduct the interest on two qualified residences. They may each deduct the interest on one qualified residence.

Rental/Vacation Home.   If property is used partly for rental purposes and partly for vacation purposes, then interest is allocated to the rental use in the ratio of the number of days the property is rented at fair market retail value to the number of days the property is used by the owner.

The interest expense on a second or third vacation home is nondeductible and is considered consumer interest. All consumer interest is no longer deductible under the 1986 TRA.

Property Tax Deduction.   The two-residences limit does not apply to property tax. State and local property taxes, both real and personal, continue to be deductible without limitations. State and local income taxes also remain as deductible items.

Rollover Provision.   This provision was retained. The tax on the total gain from the sale of a principal residence is postponed provided that the seller buys a replacement dwelling costing the same or more than the old residence. The replacement purchase must be completed 24 months before or after the sale of the original residence. If the homeowner buys a property which costs less than the original residence, then taxes need be paid only on the difference between the adjusted sales price of the old residence and the cost of the replacement residence.

The $125,000 Exclusion of Gain.   This provision is retained in the 1986 TRA. It is a one-time election to taxpayers, age 55 and over, for the permanent exclusion of up to $125,000 of the gain realized from the sale of the principal residence. The homeowner must have occupied the dwelling unit for 3 of the last 5 years immediately preceding the sale in order to qualify.

Residential Energy Credit.   The residential energy credit was allowed to expire as of January 1, 1986. Prior law allowed a 15% credit on the first $2,000 of qualifying expenditures for a personal residence on energy-saving equipment such as insulation, storm doors, and other related energy-saving devices.

Investment Property

Depreciation.   Depreciation is a major and, in many cases, a decisive factor in investment decisions. In today's investment climate, the tax shelter provided by the depreciation deductions may be the most important benefit provided by a project. Depreciation and the resulting tax shelter may be the sole motivation of many investors. To understand the tax benefits of depreciation, the distinction between tax depreciation and economic or actual depreciation must be understood.

Actual Depreciation vs. Tax Depreciation.   Actual depreciation may be referred to as the loss in value of an asset for any reason. The primary reasons for an actual loss in value are physical deterioration, functional obsolescence, and economic obsolescence resulting from changing market conditions such as a declining neighborhood or a new expressway that reroutes traffic away from a commercial site.

In contrast, tax depreciation is a statutory accounting concept that permits the investor to recover the actual cost or other basis of an asset over the useful life of that asset. It is a cost-recovery concept written into law and has little or no relationship to the actual depreciation of a real property asset. The concept is based on the idea that an investor ought to be able to recover the original capital investment from a project over its useful life and that the recovered capital should not be taxed as income. Viewed another way, some of the building's value is "consumed" in the process of earning income for the investor.

However, not all real property is subject to tax depreciation allowances. There are certain criteria to which a property must conform before depreciation for tax purposes may be taken:

1. The property must have a finite useful life span.
2. The useful life span must be determinable.
3. The property must be used in the taxpayers' trade, such as a piece of capital equipment, or used in the production of income.
4. Depreciable property may not be an item of inventory.

Accordingly, land is normally not a depreciable component of real property because land is not considered to have a limited useful life but rather is considered to exist in perpetuity. Normally, only attachments or improvements to land may be depreciated. There are certain types of mineral- or ore-producing land which may be depreciable, but these are special limited cases—each with a unique set of circumstances and applicable laws—and will not be dealt with here.

A taxpayer's residence is also excluded from tax depreciation since it is not considered income-producing. It may also be the case that a dealer or broker of real property may not be allowed a depreciation deduction on certain income property since it may considered by the IRS to be part of the broker's inventory of properties for sale and not in itself used for the production of income. Thus a developer normally may not depreciate units that are for sale in a subdivision.

Tax depreciation is allowed annually and must be taken within the tax or fiscal year in which it occurs. The depreciation allowance may not be accumulated, i.e., carried forward or back, and so failure to claim depreciation for any given year will result in the loss of that depreciable amount. Tax law also requires that the depreciable base of the property (i.e., the total amount of depreciation allowed over the useful life of the property) be reduced annually by the prescribed amount whether or not depreciation was actually taken.

Allocation of Depreciation.   Since land is normally a nondepreciable asset, on improved properties an allocation of total purchase price must be made between land and buildings. The buildings or improvements are the only depreciable components of improved property and therefore must be assigned a value separately from the land. If a traditional appraisal approach is not used to assign a percentage of total purchase price to the improvements (which commonly occurs), certain other procedures are generally accepted by the IRS. A prior year's local property tax receipt that assigns independent values may be used. Even though the dollar amount of a prior year's property tax receipt may not be representative of the actual purchase price, the percentage of total value assigned to the improvements may be used. Another popular method is for the purchase contract to explicitly state the percentage of the purchase price assigned to the land and the percentage assigned to the improvements. Any reasonable allocation made by informed parties would normally be accepted by the tax authorities. An investor should bear in mind that the higher the percentage of total value assigned to the depreciable components of improved property, the higher the annual depreciation allowance will be and, hence, the lower the tax obligation will be.

The New Accelerated Cost Recovery System.   The pre-1987 depreciation system was subject to radical changes under the 1986 TRA. All tangible depreciable property purchased and placed in service on or after January 1, 1987, is expensed using a straight-line or accelerated depreciation method over predetermined recovery periods. This law results in real property being depreciated over substantially longer periods of time than under prior law; these periods may range from 27.5 to 33 years. Investors may continue to use the pre-1987 depreciation methods (i.e., the 15/18/19-year accelerated method for real property purchased between January 1, 1981, and December 31, 1986) even after the effective date of the 1986 TRA of January 1, 1987.

The tax reform act created eight new classes of accelerated cost recovery systems (ACRSs). These classes are based on the "midpoint lives" of the properties as determined by the IRS's asset depreciation range (ADR) system. The term *midpoint lives* means the average useful life of an asset. These averages are based on the IRS's research of broad classes of similar properties. By using this method the IRS hopes to keep conflicts over individual useful lives at a minimum. One, however, has to question the wisdom of this approach when thinking, for example, of a 40-year-old commercial building purchased on December 30, 1987, being put into a 33-year depreciation schedule. The likelihood of a 30- or 40-year-old building having an economic life of 33 more years is very low, given rapidly changing land use patterns.

All property is put into eight new ACRS classes, replacing the four previous classes (3-year, 5-year, 10-year, and 15/18/19-year). The eight new classes are titled for the number of years over which the property is to be depreciated. Table 3–1 lists the new classes and examples of the types of property which may fall into each class.

Tables 3–2 to 3–5 are the prescribed accelerated statutory ACRS rates (in percentages) which are applicable to the eight new ACRS classes. Table 3–2 is the 200% declining balance schedule for personal

Table 3–1. Post-1986 ACRS Classifications

3-Year Class	*5-Year Class*
ADR midpoint of 4 years or less.	ADR midpoint of more than 4 years to less than 10 years.
EXAMPLE: Over-the-road trailers, 2-year-old race horses.	EXAMPLE: Automobiles, pickups, computers, typewriters, adding machines, copiers, cattle, most construction equipment.
7-Year Class	*10-Year Class*
ADR midpoint of 10 years or more and less than 16 years, and all other property with no ADR midpoint or class.	ADR midpoint of 16 years or more and less than 20 years.
EXAMPLE: Office furniture and fixtures, desks, chairs, single-use agricultural and horticultural buildings, and most farm equipment.	EXAMPLE: Machinery used to convert grain into flour, etc., mobile homes.
15-Year Class	*20-Year Class*
ADR midpoint of 20 years or more and less than 25 years.	ADR midpoint of 25 years or more, other than real property in 27.5-year or 31.5-year class.
EXAMPLE: Depreciable land improvement, e.g., roads, fences, landscaping.	EXAMPLE: Farm buildings, sewer pipe.
27.5-Year Class *Residential Rental Real Property*	*31.5-Year Class*
Buildings from which 80% or more of gross rental income comes from "dwelling units."	All other real property that is not residential rental property.
EXAMPLE: Duplexes, apartments, condos and co-ops.	EXAMPLE: Office buildings, shopping centers, hotels, motels.

Table 3–2. Personal Property Tables

If the Recovery Year Is	The Depreciation Percentage For Each Class Is:					
	3-Yr. Class	5-Yr. Class	7-Yr. Class	10-Yr. Class	15-Yr. Class	20-Yr. Class
1	.33	.200	.143	.100	.050	.038
2	.45	.320	.245	.180	.095	.072
3	.15	.192	.175	.144	.086	.067
4	.07	.115	.250	.115	.077	.062
5		.115	.089	.092	.069	.057
6		.058	.089	.074	.062	.053
7			.089	.066	.059	.049
8			.045	.066	.059	.045
9				.065	.059	.045
10				.065	.059	.045
11				.030	.059	.045
12					.059	.045
13					.059	.045
14					.059	.045
15					.059	.045
16					.030	.045
17						.045
18						.045
19						.045
20						.045
21						.017
	100%	100%	100%	100%	100%	100%

property in the 3-, 5-, 7-, and 10-year classes. The schedules switch to straight-line at a time that maximizes the depreciation allowance. For property in the 15- and 20-year classes, the 150% declining balance is used. Table 3–3 is the straight-line schedules for property in the 3-, 5-, 7-, 10-, 15-, and 20-year classes. The schedules switch to straight-line at a time that maximizes the depreciation allowance.

Tables 3–4 and 3–5 are the depreciation schedules for commercial and residential rental property. For residential rental property the depreciation period is 27.5 years. For nonresidential real property the depreciation period is 31.5 years.

Both the half-year and half-month conventions are built into the 5-, 7-, 10-, 15-, and 20-year classes, while the half-month convention is built into the 27.5- and 31.5-year classes.

Table 3–3. Straight-Line Depreciation For Personal Property

If the Recovery Year Is	The Depreciation Percentage For Each Class Is:					
	3-Yr. Class	5-Yr. Class	7-Yr. Class	10-Yr. Class	15-Yr. Class	20-Yr. Class
1	.167	.100	.071	.050	.033	.025
2	.333	.200	.143	.100	.067	.050
3	.333	.200	.143	.100	.067	.050
4	.167	.200	.143	.100	.067	.050
5		.200	.143	.100	.067	.050
6		.100	.143	.100	.067	.050
7			.143	.100	.067	.050
8			.071	.100	.067	.050
9				.100	.067	.050
10				.100	.067	.050
11				.050	.067	.050
12					.067	.050
13					.067	.050
14					.067	.050
15					.067	.050
16					.029	.050
17						.050
18						.050
19						.050
20						.050
21						.025
	100%	100%	100%	100%	100%	100%

The half-year convention treats all applicable property as if placed in service, or sold, or disposed of on the midpoint of the taxable year. For example, for all calendar-year taxpayers, all property purchased will be assumed purchased on July 1 no matter when during the year the property was actually purchased. The same is true for the year of disposition.

The half-month convention applies only to residential rental property and nonresidential real property. Under this convention, property is assumed to be bought and sold on the 15th of the month.

Alternative Depreciation System (ADS). This optional depreciation system is required for some types of property and electable by all taxpayers. The option is a straight-line method which uses longer de-

Table 3–4. 31.5-Year Nonresidential (Commercial) Real Property Tables

If the Recovery Year Is:	Jan.	Feb.	Mar.	Apr.	May	Jun.	Jul.	Aug.	Sep.	Oct.	Nov.	Dec.
				The Applicable Percentage Is: (Use the Column For the Month That the Property Was Placed in Service)								
1	.030	.028	.025	.022	.020	.017	.015	.012	.009	.007	.004	.001
2	.032	.032	.032	.032	.032	.032	.032	.032	.032	.032	.032	.032
3	.032	.032	.032	.032	.032	.032	.032	.032	.032	.032	.032	.032
4	.032	.032	.032	.032	.032	.032	.032	.032	.032	.032	.032	.032
5	.032	.032	.032	.032	.032	.032	.032	.032	.032	.032	.032	.032
6	.032	.032	.032	.032	.032	.032	.032	.032	.032	.032	.032	.032
7	.032	.032	.032	.032	.032	.032	.032	.032	.032	.032	.032	.032
8	.032	.032	.032	.032	.032	.032	.032	.032	.032	.032	.032	.032
9	.032	.032	.032	.032	.032	.032	.032	.032	.032	.032	.032	.032
10	.032	.032	.032	.032	.032	.032	.032	.032	.032	.032	.032	.032
11	.032	.032	.032	.032	.032	.032	.032	.032	.032	.032	.032	.032
12	.032	.032	.032	.032	.032	.032	.032	.032	.032	.032	.032	.032
13	.032	.032	.032	.032	.032	.032	.032	.032	.032	.032	.032	.032
14	.032	.032	.032	.032	.032	.032	.032	.032	.032	.032	.032	.032
15	.032	.032	.032	.032	.032	.032	.032	.032	.032	.032	.032	.032
16	.032	.032	.032	.032	.032	.032	.032	.032	.032	.032	.032	.032
17	.032	.032	.032	.032	.032	.032	.032	.032	.032	.032	.032	.032
18	.032	.032	.032	.032	.032	.032	.032	.032	.032	.032	.032	.032
19	.032	.032	.032	.032	.032	.032	.032	.032	.032	.032	.032	.032
20	.032	.032	.032	.032	.032	.032	.032	.032	.032	.032	.032	.032
21	.032	.032	.032	.032	.032	.032	.032	.032	.032	.032	.032	.032
22	.032	.032	.032	.032	.032	.032	.032	.032	.032	.032	.032	.032
23	.032	.032	.032	.032	.032	.032	.032	.032	.032	.032	.032	.032
24	.032	.032	.032	.032	.032	.032	.032	.032	.032	.032	.032	.032
25	.032	.032	.032	.032	.032	.032	.032	.032	.032	.032	.032	.032
26	.032	.032	.032	.032	.032	.032	.032	.032	.032	.032	.032	.032
27	.032	.032	.032	.032	.032	.032	.032	.032	.032	.032	.032	.032
28	.032	.032	.032	.032	.032	.032	.032	.032	.032	.032	.032	.032
29	.032	.032	.032	.032	.032	.032	.032	.032	.032	.032	.032	.032
30	.032	.032	.032	.032	.032	.032	.032	.032	.032	.032	.032	.032
31	.032	.032	.032	.032	.032	.032	.032	.032	.032	.032	.032	.032
32	.010	.012	.015	.018	.020	.023	.025	.028	.031	.032	.032	.032
33	0	0	0	0	0	0	0	0	0	.001	.004	.007
	100%	100%	100%	100%	100%	100%	100%	100%	100%	100%	100%	100%

preciation periods and the half-month and half-year convention. Table 3–6 indicates this ADS.

The following property must use the ADS method:

1. Any property at taxpayer's election.
2. Most property leased to tax-exempt entities.
3. Property financed partially or totally by tax-exempt bonds.
4. Property imported from a trade-restricted country as determined by the President.
5. Predominantly foreign-used property.

Leasehold improvements must be depreciated over the life of the property under the new ACRS, not over the life of the lease. Additions

Table 3–5. 27.5-Year Residential Rental Real Property Tables

If the Recovery Year Is:	The Applicable Percentage Is: (Use the Column For the Month That the Property Was Placed in Service)											
	Jan.	Feb.	Mar.	Apr.	May	Jun.	Jul.	Aug.	Sep.	Oct.	Nov.	Dec.
1	.035	.032	.029	.026	.023	.020	.017	.014	.011	.008	.005	.002
2	.036	.036	.036	.036	.036	.036	.036	.036	.036	.036	.036	.036
3	.036	.036	.036	.036	.036	.036	.036	.036	.036	.036	.036	.036
4	.036	.036	.036	.036	.036	.036	.036	.036	.036	.036	.036	.036
5	.036	.036	.036	.036	.036	.036	.036	.036	.036	.036	.036	.036
6	.036	.036	.036	.036	.036	.036	.036	.036	.036	.036	.036	.036
7	.036	.036	.036	.036	.036	.036	.036	.036	.036	.036	.036	.036
8	.036	.036	.036	.036	.036	.036	.036	.036	.036	.036	.036	.036
9	.036	.036	.036	.036	.036	.036	.036	.036	.036	.036	.036	.036
10	.036	.036	.036	.036	.036	.036	.036	.036	.036	.036	.036	.036
11	.036	.036	.036	.036	.036	.036	.036	.036	.036	.036	.036	.036
12	.036	.036	.036	.036	.036	.036	.036	.036	.036	.036	.036	.036
13	.036	.036	.036	.036	.036	.036	.036	.036	.036	.036	.036	.036
14	.036	.036	.036	.036	.036	.036	.036	.036	.036	.036	.036	.036
15	.036	.036	.036	.036	.036	.036	.036	.036	.036	.036	.036	.036
16	.036	.036	.036	.036	.036	.036	.036	.036	.036	.036	.036	.036
17	.036	.036	.036	.036	.036	.036	.036	.036	.036	.036	.036	.036
18	.036	.036	.036	.036	.036	.036	.036	.036	.036	.036	.036	.036
19	.036	.036	.036	.036	.036	.036	.036	.036	.036	.036	.036	.036
20	.036	.036	.036	.036	.036	.036	.036	.036	.036	.036	.036	.036
21	.036	.036	.036	.036	.036	.036	.036	.036	.036	.036	.036	.036
22	.036	.036	.036	.036	.036	.036	.036	.036	.036	.036	.036	.036
23	.036	.036	.036	.036	.036	.036	.036	.036	.036	.036	.036	.036
24	.036	.036	.036	.036	.036	.036	.036	.036	.036	.036	.036	.036
25	.036	.036	.036	.036	.036	.036	.036	.036	.036	.036	.036	.036
26	.036	.036	.036	.036	.036	.036	.036	.036	.036	.036	.036	.036
27	.036	.036	.036	.036	.036	.036	.036	.036	.036	.036	.036	.036
28	.029	.032	.035	.036	.036	.036	.036	.036	.036	.036	.036	.036
29	0	0	0	.002	.005	.008	.011	.014	.017	.020	.023	.026
	100%	100%	100%	100%	100%	100%	100%	100%	100%	100%	100%	100%

or improvements to property are to be computed in the same manner as the deduction for the underlying property would be.

Interest and Property Tax. The interest and property tax deductions for residential rental and commercial property were basically unchanged by the 1986 TRA. A taxpayer may deduct all interest accrued

Table 3–6. Alternative Depreciation System

Type of Property	Straight-Line Recovery Period
1. Residential rental property	40 years
2. Nonresidential real property	40 years
3. Personal property with no class life	12 years
4. Property not mentioned in 1, 2, or 3 above	The class life

within the taxable year on related indebtedness, subject to such limitation rules that may apply, i.e., investment interest limitation rule, construction period interest rule, and the new passive loss rules.

Investment Tax Credit (ITC).   Under prior law, 10% of a taxpayer's investment in qualified tangible personal property (6% for property in 3-year class) could be used as a credit against a taxpayer's income tax liability. This ITC has been repealed retroactive to December 31, 1985. Although this credit was never available for buildings and other real property, it was a significant consideration when those properties contained personal property such as stoves, refrigerators, furniture, etc. A 10% ITC could be taken on the value attributable to those items that were considered personal property.

Investment Interest Deductibility Limitations.   All interest that is incurred in connection with a trade or business is deductible. However, the deduction by noncorporate taxpayers of interest on investment indebtedness is limited. For the tax year 1986, just prior to the 1986 TRA, the deductibility of investment interest is limited to $10,000 per year, plus the taxpayer's net investment income. Table 3–7 demonstrates the calculation of deductible investment interest for 1986.

Table 3–7. Investment Interest Calculation—1986

Investment	*Income*
Income Source	
Interest from CD	$3,000
Stock dividends	1,500
Interest from limited partnership	2,000
Royalties	1,000
Total investment income	$7,500
Minus Investment Expenses	
Brokers' fees paid	$ 200
Investment counseling	1,000
Property maintenance expense	500
Legal fees	2,000
Total investment expenses	$3,700
Net investment interest allowed	$ 3,800
Plus additional allowance	10,000
Total deductible investment interest for 1986	13,800

Beginning in 1987, the $10,000 excess is being phased out over a 5-year period, 1987–1991. The phaseout is scheduled as follows:

Year	Allowed Amount	Percentage not Deductible
1986	$10,000	N/A
1987	6,500	35%
1988	4,000	60%
1989	2,000	80%
1990	1,000	90%
1991	0	100%

Interest and income from activities subject to the passive loss rules are not treated as investment interest and investment income. The passive loss rules are explained in a later section.

Capital Gains Treatment.   Effective January 1, 1987, net capital gains deductions have been eliminated. Under pre-1987 rules, taxpayers were taxed on only 40 percent of the net long-term capital gains. They did not pay taxes on 60 percent of the gains made on the sale of a capital asset held for more than 6 months. Table 3–8 demonstrates the effect on the net proceeds from the sale of a property generating capital gains.

Even though the maximum tax bracket has been reduced from 50% to 28%, the overall effect has been an increase in the tax on capital gains of 40% or more. Most taxpayers were not in the 50% tax brack-

Table 3–8. Capital Gains Treatment

	Sale on 12/31/86	Sale on 1/1/87
Sale price	$100,000	$100,000
Less basis	−60,000	−60,000
Total gain	$ 40,000	$ 40,000
Less 60% (1986)	−24,000	− 0
Taxable gain	$ 16,000	$ 40,000
Maximum tax rate	× 50%	× 28%
Tax	$ 8,000	$ 11,200
Net proceeds	$ 32,000	$ 28,800

ets, so that the increase in taxes paid would be even more severe. Using the example in Table 3–8, note the difference in taxes paid by a taxpayer who was previously in the 30% tax bracket. For such taxpayers the new rates will increase the tax bite.

Taxable gain	$16,000	$40,000
Tax rate	× 30%	× 28%
Tax	$ 4,800	$11,200

The difference represents an effective increase of 133% in taxes paid on capital gains. All gains are treated as ordinary income under the 1986 TRA.

Installment Sales.   Installment sales contracts made before the 1986 TRA are also affected by the new tax laws relating to capital gains treatment. Table 3–9 demonstrates this impact. Many taxpayers who may have had their retirement years planned around their net proceeds from installment contracts have been adversely affected by the 1986 TRA. The lower their prior tax rate, the worse the relative effect may be.

At-Risk Rules.   Under the 1986 TRA the at-risk rules now apply to real estate. The at-risk rules of current law reflect the fact that, as an economic matter, an investor cannot lose more than the amount that he or she has directly invested plus any additional amount for which the

Table 3–9. Installment Contract

Sold $100,000   80% Gross Profit $10,000 Payment $8,000 Capital Gains

	1985	1986	1987	1988
Payment	$10,000	$10,000	$10,000	$10,000
Long-term capital gains	8,000	8,000	8,000	8,000
−60%	−4,800	−4,800	−0	−0
Taxable gain	3,200	3,200	8,000	8,000
Tax rate—maximum	× 50%	× 50%	× 28%	× 33%
Tax due	$ 1,600	$ 1,600	$ 2,240	$ 2,640
Net	$ 8,400	$ 8,400	$ 7,760	$ 7,360

investor is liable. The purpose of the at-risk rules is generally to restrict the use of limited-risk transactions by individual taxpayers who shelter from taxes their income from other sources.

For example, assume the following:

- Susan purchases a building in January 1987 for $100,000.
- The land is leased.
- Susan puts $5,000 down and gives the seller a $95,000 nonrecourse mortgage note for the remainder.
- Gross income is $10,000.
- Operating expenses or vacancy loss is $3,000.
- Debt service is, say, $9,500 (interest only).
- Depreciation in the first year amounts to $3,636.
- Susan's total loss for the year is

$$
\begin{array}{lr}
\text{Gross Income} & 10,000 \\
\text{Expenses} & -16,136 \\
\hline
\text{Total loss} & (6,136)
\end{array}
$$

Since Susan has only paid $5,000 in cash (or "cash-like") of the $100,000 total investment, she can only deduct $5,000 of the total loss of $6,136. The balance of the loss may be carried forward until used in a following year or until the time of sale, where the losses carried forward may be used to increase the basis in the property. The total accumulated losses that Susan may use in any year is limited to her accumulated equity in the property.

Had Susan financed the property with a conventional loan and recourse note, then the at-risk rules would not have limited the deductible losses.

Recourse notes are considered personal obligations and therefore, for at-risk purposes, may be added to the basis of the properties. In case of default in nonrecourse financing, the holder of the financing instrument can only look to the property for financial protection and cannot get a deficiency judgment in case of foreclosure. In many states, trust deeds and real estate contracts are considered nonrecourse financing and are the principal instrument for owner financing. Thus owner financing will be greatly affected under the 1986 TRA.

However, certain exceptions for nonrecourse financing are available under the TRA of 1986. Nonrecourse loans from qualified lenders are exempt as long as the purchase price does not exceed $150,000. Qualified lenders are banks, S&Ls, and other institutions which are regularly engaged in lending money for mortgage purposes. Certain financing by related parties is also exempt.

Passive Loss Rules.   Before the Tax Reform Act of 1986, no limitations were placed on the ability of a taxpayer to use deductions, losses, or credits from one business or investment to offset the profits of another business or investment. This allowed taxpayers to offset, or "shelter," the income from one source with deductions and credits from another.

> **EXAMPLE:** Dr. Goldman is a professor with a 1986 income of $40,000. She is married with no children and has itemized deductions of $8,000. She purchased a historic apartment house for $5,000, plus a mortgage, and "rehabilitated" it. At the end of the year she received a rental income statement from her accountant which reported a $15,000 rental loss and a $5,600 investment tax credit. The following tax worksheet indicates that her total tax due in 1986 was $1,000. Without the tax shelter, it would have been $4,650.

Schedule E (Form 1040).   Rental Income or Loss Schedule

Rental income	$37,500
Rental expenses & vacancy	−18,500
NOI	19,000
Mortgage interest	−19,000
Before-tax cash flow	0
Minus depreciation expense	−$15,000
Income or loss from rental property	(15,000)
Rehab. investment tax credit	500

Tax Calculations

	Tax Shelter	No Tax Shelter
Gross income:	$40,000	$40,000
Less deductions from gross income	(15,000)	None
Adjusted gross income	$25,000	$40,000
Less: Itemized deductions	− 8,000	− 8,000
Less: Personal exemptions	− 2,160	− 2,160
Taxable income:	$14,840	$29,840
Tax due before credits:	1,500	5,150
Less: Investment tax credits	− 500	− 500
Net tax due	$ 1,000	$ 4,650

However, Congress believed that tax laws before 1987 created an income tax system that promoted abusive tax shelters. The Congressional solution to limiting abusive tax shelters without eliminating tax preferences to certain businesses and activities was to give limited benefits and incentives to taxpayers who are active in or materially participate in the businesses to which the preferences are directed. In addition, Congress created a barrier against the use of losses from business activities in which the taxpayers do not materially participate to offset positive income sources such as salary and portfolio income.

Beginning in 1987, taxpayers must materially participate or otherwise be actively involved in the activities to which the tax preferences relate in order to pass through losses to shelter other income. This barrier is called the *passive loss limitation rule*.

The basic rule is that "Deductions (and Credits) from passive trade or business activity, to the extent they exceed income from all such passive activities, generally may not be deducted against other income, such as services rendered, salary, or portfolio income."

Disallowed losses and credits are carried forward and treated as deductions from passive activities in future taxable years. If the disallowed losses are not fully utilized when the taxpayer disposes of his or her entire interest in the activity, in a taxable transaction, the remaining losses are deductible in full, even against active income.

Active income is income that is generated from activities in which the taxpayer materially participates. Passive income is income that is generated by an activity in which the taxpayer does not materially participate. All businesses except rental activities, in which the taxpayer materially participates in the activity, are excluded from the passive loss rule. Material participation means that the taxpayer must be "regularly, continuously and substantially" involved. These terms remain to be clearly defined.

Rental activity involving apartment houses, office rentals, commercial space rentals, etc., have been generally defined as passive activities *whether or not the taxpayer "materially participates."* All rental activities are subject to the passive loss rule unless significant services are performed along with the rental activity. Examples of excluded rental activities are hotels, motels, and time rentals such as auto and VCR movie rentals. A limited partnership is, by definition under the 1986 TRA, a passive activity.

There is, however, a relief provision for middle-income taxpayers who may own rental property. In the case of rental real estate in which the taxpayer "actively" participates, there is a special provision that allows the deduction of up to $25,000 in passive losses against active income from another source. "Active" participation is a less stringent requirement than is "material" participation. To be "actively" involved a taxpayer must own at least 10% interest in the property and participate in the day-to-day management decisions of the property. An "active" participant may, however, have a property manager. The taxpayer must be an individual and not a corporation. However, this relief provision phases out as the taxpayer's adjusted gross income, determined without regard for passive activity losses, increases from $100,000 to $150,000. There is a $1 decrease in relief for every $2 of adjusted gross income over $100,000.

Portfolio Income.   The term *portfolio income* takes on a new meaning under the 1986 TRA and must be defined. Portfolio income is not treated as income from a passive activity, and passive losses and credits, in general, may not be used to offset it. Portfolio income will now normally include such items as:

- Interest income on debt obligations
- Dividend income
- Royalty income from the licensing of property
- Gains or losses from the sale of assets producing the above interest, dividend, or royalty income such as stocks and bonds
- Gains or losses from the sale of investment property such as unimproved raw land and vacation homes (but not the sale of depreciable trade or business property)
- Interest earned on working capital

The following section of this chapter will give the reader an in-depth review of the methodology used in structuring a discounted cash flow program. The inputs to this program should be carefully considered and related to the relevant tax law cited in the above section. The passive loss rule should be given special consideration as it affects the ability of the sample investor to pass through his or her tax losses to shelter other income from taxes.

STRUCTURING THE CASH FLOW MODEL

It has long been understood by sophisticated investors that a dynamic cash flow model that incorporates discounted rates of return is essential to the determination of a reasonably accurate estimate of their investment value. If the variables in a cash flow could be readily changed to reflect alternative assumptions, then it could be an invaluable investment tool. In the early 1960s very few real estate investors were using dynamic cash flow models as investment tools. The relationship between variables was complicated, and the physical development of a model was prohibitively time-consuming. However, by the early 1970s these models were used extensively by planning groups and large developers. The widespread use of computers was primarily responsible for the increasing reliance on cash flow models. Computers allowed the rapid development of models with no limits on the number of variables and changes in variables that could be tested.

Static Investment Value Model

Before exploring a complete cash flow model it would be helpful to demonstrate the essential factors involved in the model and their relationship to one another in a static presentation. In this sample analysis we will use the following assumptions:

1. There are 80 rental units, renting at $220 per month per unit.
2. Cost of building is $1,000,000.
3. Land value is $200,000.
4. Total project cost is $1,200,000.
5. Loan-to-value ratio is .75.
6. Depreciable life is 27.5 years (rates from precomputed table).
7. Mortgage is for 26 years at 9% with a debt service constant of .100715. Mortgage is conventional financing from an S&L.
8. Annual debt service is $90,643.
9. Investor is in the 28% tax bracket.
10. Date of purchase is January 15, 1987.
11. Investor's adjusted gross income is expected to be $90,000 annually without consideration of passive (rental) activities. Investor is actively involved in the management of the property.
12. Gross rent is expected to increase by .025 per year compounding.
13. Operating expenses are expected to increase by .025 per year compounding.
14. Property is expected to sell at the end of the fifth year. Price will be the capitalized value of the NOI projected for the sixth year. Cap rate will be

$$.0922 = \frac{\text{Current NOI}}{\text{Current Sale Price}}$$

Table 3–10 serves as an introductory cash flow model and is presented in a fashion similar to an annual operating statement. The principal cash flow items have been listed in two columns; the first is referred to as the "Cash Account," and the second is the "Tax Account." The cash account details the actual amount of cash available to the investor, and the tax account demonstrates the investor's tax liability. The purpose for these two accounts is to clearly demonstrate the impact that tax laws have on investment decisions. Both accounts are exactly the same up to the determination of NOI. It would be at this point that the traditional income approach to value would stop. The NOI figure of $110,640 would be capitalized by using some market-determined capitalization rate. However, investment analysis requires that several other factors be taken into consideration. An investor is primarily interested in how much actual cash is available after all ex-

Table 3–10. Static Cash Flow—Year 1

Items	Cash Account	Tax Account	
Gross revenue	$211,200	$211,200	
Minus vacancy & collection loss (5%)	−10,560	−10,560	
Effective gross	$200,640	$200,640	
Minus operating expenses	−90,000	−90,000	
Net operating income	$110,640	$110,640	
Minus debt service	−90,643	−81,000	(Interest only)
Before-tax cash flow	$ 19,997	$ 29,640	
Plus tax savings	1,500	−35,000	(Depreciation)
After-tax cash flow	$ 21,497	($5,360)	(Tax shelter)
		× .28	(Tax rate)
		$ 1,500	(Tax savings)
Future cash benefits:			
Equity buildup	$ 9,643		
Appreciation	$30,000		
Total ownership benefits:			
First year	$61,140		

Return on equity, cash only: $\dfrac{21,497}{300,000} = .0716$

Return on equity, total benefits: $\dfrac{61,140}{300,000} = .2038$

penses are paid and what this cash amounts to in terms of a rate of return on the equity investment; therefore, debt service must be considered.

In the cash account in Table 3–10, total debt service is subtracted from the NOI and leaves $19,997 as the before-tax cash flow. If there were no tax benefits to consider, this figure would represent the actual flow of money into the investor's pocket. However, looking at the tax account, other factors must be considered before arriving at the actual rate of return. The standard mortgage payment is composed of two parts: (1) the principal payment and (2) the interest payment. In the above example the debt service payment is approximately $90,643, of which $81,000 is interest and the remainder is payment of principal.

Total amount of mortgage (.75 × $1,200,000)	$900,000
Debt constant .100715	× .100715
Level of annual debt payment	$ 90,643
Interest at 9% (.09 × 900,000)	−81,000
Principal reduction	$ 9,643

Interest payments, along with operating expenses and depreciation, are tax-deductible items. The interest component is therefore subtracted from the NOI figure in the tax account. Depreciation must be considered next. Straight-line depreciation is $35,000 per year. The first year's depreciation may be calculated as follows:

Depreciable base (improvement only)	$1,000,000
Straight depreciation rate (taken from Table 3–5)	× .035
Depreciation taken first year	$ 35,000

The first year's depreciation is then subtracted from the remaining tax balance of $29,640. The resulting figure of −$5,360 is the investor's tax liability. This, however, is a negative figure, and therefore for tax purposes the project is being operated at a loss; no tax is owed. Thus, the $19,997 before-tax cash flow indicated in the cash account is tax-free income.

In addition to the tax-free income from the project, the tax loss will produce an additional benefit referred to as tax savings. Existing tax law allows this tax loss to be used to offset the investor's tax liability on income from other sources, subject to the qualifications previously discussed. Assuming the investor is in the 28% tax bracket, the tax savings would have a value of $5,360 × .28 = $1,500. Thus, the $5,360 tax loss results in a $1,500 tax savings; i.e., the investor will reduce the taxes paid on other income by $1,500. This is a real cash benefit and should be added to the $19,997 before-tax cash flow. The after-tax total cash benefits are $21,497.

Two additional considerations round out the computations of the first year's total benefits to the investor. The principal component of the debt service, $9,643, is an increase in the owner's equity in the property. As the mortgage principal is reduced, the investor's or owner's equity interest increases. In addition to the equity buildup, expected appreciation or depreciation should be considered. In the above example an appreciation in the property of 2.5% is expected on the initial project cost. The total first year's benefits from the project may be broken down into present and future cash benefits.

Present cash benefits:	
Before-tax cash flow	$19,997
Tax savings	1,500
Total present cash benefits	$21,497
Future cash benefits:	
Equity buildup	$ 9,643
Appreciation	$30,000
Total future benefits	$39,643
Total of first year's benefit	$61,140

The future cash benefits will not be actually recognized until the property is sold or refinanced.

The returns on equity shown above are for the first year only. Many of the factors in the cash flow statement will change over time so that the total benefits to equity will also change. For this reason the direct capitalization method cannot be used to determine the present value of these future benefits. The direct capitalization approach assumes a level or stabilized income stream, which is not the case in a typical real estate investment.

The changing factors and their impact on investor benefits are demonstrated in Figures 3–2 through 3–8. The slopes and intersects of these figures are not calculated; they are used here for illustrative purposes only. Figure 3–2 shows the two components of debt service: principal and interest. The interest component declines over time as the principal increases. Since interest is a tax-deductible item, it ap-

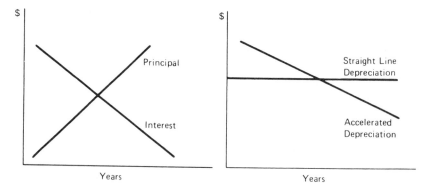

Figure 3–2. Components of debt service.

Figure 3–3. Depreciation schedule.

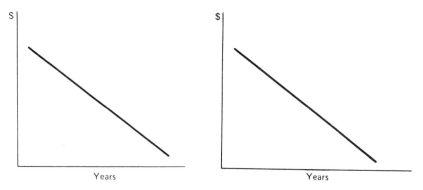

Figure 3–4. Tax shelter.

Figure 3–5. Annual cash benefits.

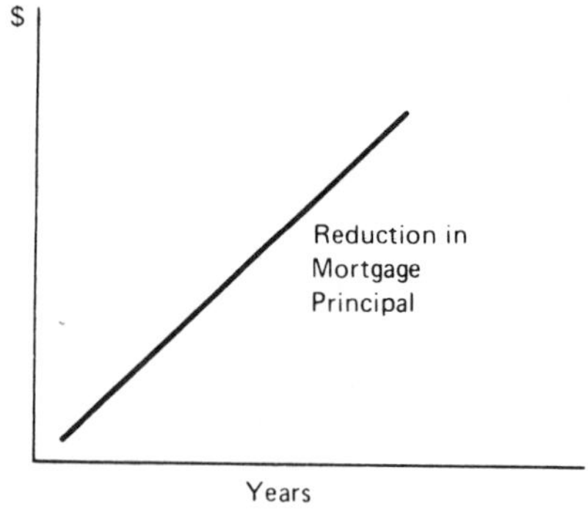

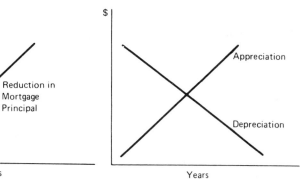

Figure 3–6. Equity buildup.

Figure 3–7. Appreciation and depreciation schedules.

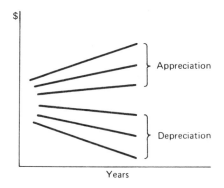

Figure 3–8. Range of future cash benefits.

pears in the tax account in Table 3–10. The declining interest function would cause the taxable income to become less negative, i.e., move in a positive direction, thereby reducing the tax shelter over time. Figure 3–3 exhibits the functions of a straight-line depreciation schedule and an accelerated schedule. A declining depreciation schedule would also cause the tax shelter to become less negative. The tax shelter exhibited in Figure 3–4 is a declining function resulting from the declining interest and increasing before-tax cash flow.

The taxable income figure will eventually move above zero and turn into a positive figure. At that time the tax shelter disappears, and a tax liability is incurred. The taxes due must be paid out of the project's cash flow.

The annual cash benefits demonstrated in Figure 3–5 may decline over time as the tax shelter declines and taxes must eventually be paid. This assumes that the income and expense stream remain constant. It may be possible to raise rents each year in order to offset the decline in annual cash benefits, but the possibility of doing this would depend on the competitive environment.

Future cash benefits which would occur at the time of sale would depend on equity buildup and expected appreciation or depreciation. Equity buildup would be a mathematically predictable amount, assuming mortgage payments are made as agreed. The biggest influence on future cash benefits would be the degree of appreciation or depreciation in the property. Figure 3–8 demonstrates the range of future cash benefits which might be expected based on the anticipated appreciation or depreciation in the value of the property. The future cash benefits anticipated at time of sale must be adjusted to net figures since there will be additional tax liabilities on the proceeds from the sale.

After reviewing the sample analysis, it should be clear that the simple capitalization of a level NOI stream would not normally be indicative of an individual's investment value of the project. All benefits of ownership should be considered. However, since many of the benefits change over time, a simple discounting process is not suitable in determining their present values.

The following is presented as a synopsis of ownership benefits and what is necessary to determine the present value of each.

Cash Flow before Tax. If this is projected to be constant over the ownership period, then a simple capitalization procedure using an appropriate discount rate would indicate the present value. However, if the property is financed and there is a variable interest function, the before-tax cash flow will change. It will also change as a result of increases or decreases in projected rent and/or operating expense.

Tax Shelter. A tax shelter, created by declining interest and depreciation schedules, will itself be a declining function. The determination of the present value of these future benefits will require the separate discounting of each projected year's figure.

Equity Buildup. The dollar value of the equity buildup must be calculated on an annual basis. The following formula may be used.

$$P = \frac{Sp - 1}{Sm - 1}$$

where P = the percentage of the mortgage paid off
Sp = the amount to which $1 will grow with interest compounded at the effective mortgage interest rate during the term of the projection
Sm = the amount to which $1 will grow with interest compounded at the effective mortgage interest rate for the term required for full amortization

Since equity buildup may only be realized at time of sale or upon refinancing, it may, but need not, be discounted annually. The equity benefits will be a component of the net proceeds at time of sale. The entire net projected proceeds would be discounted from that future point in time in which the sale of the property is expected.

Appreciation. Like the equity buildup, any appreciation in the property would be realized at the time of sale and would be an additional component of the net proceeds of the sale. The net proceeds need be discounted only once: at the projected time of sale.

The sum of these present values of the ownership benefit would be the present value of the equity investment. The present value of the equity investment plus the present mortgage amount would then equal the total investment value of the project.

It should be clear from the above discussion that investment value is a dynamic concept that does not lend itself to the usage of the traditional static tools of value determination. The determination of investment value requires that all ownership benefits be analyzed. The proper analysis of all ownership benefits in turn requires the development of a dynamic cash flow model. The model, in addition to establishing the investment value, may serve as an investment tool. The model allows for variable changes and the "testing" of various inputs to see what conditions would maximize return on equity and alternatively what conditions would make the project unfeasible.[5]

In the recent past there were two limiting factors to the widespread use of cash flow models. First was the level of knowledge required to properly analyze and interpret the output from such a model. Second was the access to computer facilities, which is essential to the rapid development of the initial output and to the testing of alternative inputs.

The latter problem, access to computer facilities, is rapidly being overcome. Computer equipment and programs are readily available in most areas. As computer technology and miniaturization continue to advance, access will cease to be a rational argument against the use of the more sophisticated investment model.

The level of education required to deal with cash flow models is the more serious limiting factor. This is being overcome—albeit slowly—by continuing education programs in the professions and the gradual acceptance that the traditional tools of value determination are becoming less relevant in light of today's tax laws and investor motivations.

Dynamic Cash Flow Model

A simplified dynamic cash flow model that may be used for feasibility analysis is presented next. The model is presented to further explain the nature and determination of investment value and to underscore the relationship between the market-determined and investor-required inputs to the outputs used in the final determination of investment value.

Any discounted cash flow analysis may be broken down into several distinct parts. The following cash flow model is divided into four basic sections. Section I (shown in Table 3–12A) itemizes the necessary data input requirements for the general model. In Section I there are 10 (A–J) relevant inputs, i.e., information that is developed outside of the model. The inputs provide the basic data that the cash flow model uses to compute those items that are essential to the determination of investment value. The method or methods by which these inputs are developed is directly related to the validity of the cash flow results. A comprehensive market analysis, as discussed in Chapter 2, would be the most appropriate method for developing the input data. The basic assumptions underlying the input data will determine whether the cash flow is a conservative or optimistic estimate of future events. Conservative figures are viewed more favorably by lending institutions and other financial analysts.

The remainder of Table 3–12B is separated into 3 basic sections. The table is an example of a computerized discounted cash flow model. Although the meaning of some of the items in the cash flow is more apparent than others, to help achieve a complete understanding of the model each item will be reviewed and the relationship of each to the rest of the model will be explained. The model presented is only one of many that are in use. Even though formats may differ, the basic input data are generally similar and the relationships among the variables are the same.

All items in Table 3–12B are referenced by their item numbers as indicated. Section II, Items 1–14, relates to the annual cash benefits available from the investment. Section III, Items 15–25, relates to the investment liquidation and analyzes on an annual basis the financial impact on the investor of selling the property. Section IV, Items 26–29, contains the items that are the most relevant indicators of investment performance, i.e., present value of all returns to equity, net present value, internal rate of return, and the investment value. Each of these will be explained in turn. The input items will be reviewed first so that their importance to the rest of the program may be put in a proper perspective. Following the review of the input items, the program's output items will be reviewed and their impact on investment value assessed.

Section I: Main Input Items and Assumptions.   The input items and assumptions used in the cash flow analysis are essentially the same as those used for the development of the static cash flow analysis in Table 3–10. Input items are data, essential to the cash flow, which are developed outside of the model itself.

Item A, Estimated Acquisition Price.   This input is generally developed by using the asking price of an existing property or the total cost of a new project. The analysis could be "turned on its head" to reveal the extent, if any, to which the asking price of an existing property would have to be adjusted to meet the investment requirements of the purchaser. In this analysis the estimated price for an existing 80-unit apartment building and land is $1,200,000.

Item B, Estimated Land Value.   The value of the land and improvements must be differentiated. This input is essential to the computation of book value, depreciation, capital gains, and tax considerations. Land value is a nondepreciable component of total value and therefore must be determined separately from the building. The estimated value of the land in this sample is $200,000. The land area is 3 acres, averaging a cost of $1.53 per square foot. Land value may be determined by comparing the prices paid for unimproved land at comparable sites. The value may also be estimated by determining the cost to reproduce the building new, subtracting depreciation, and then subtracting the estimated value of the building from the total estimate of project cost. The remainder would represent the land value.

Item C, Estimated Building Value.   The estimated depreciated value of the building in this model is $1,000,000. This figure represents an average cost per unit of $12,500, which compares favorably with sales of similar properties in the market area, exclusive of land. The building is 52,000 square feet. Construction costs new are estimated to be $30 per square foot. Therefore, the cost to construct the building new would be $1,560,000. The building is several years old, and depreciation is estimated to be 36% of the cost to construct the building new.

Item D, Depreciable Life of Improvements.   The depreciable life of the building is predetermined under the TRA of 1986. The depreciable life of residential real estate is 27.5 years, with the exact percentages of allowable depreciation taken from precalculated tables. The percentage of depreciation given for the sample property, which was put in service on January 15, 1987, is 3.5% the first year and 3.6% per year thereafter (see Table 3–5). The depreciable base is the $1,000,000 attributable to the building.

Item E, Mortgage—Financial Structure.   The mortgage interest rate is usually determined by assessing the prevailing rates in the local market or by using the exact rate quoted by the lending institution most likely to advance the mortgage money. The mortgage in the model is for 26 years at 9% with a debt service constant of .100715. The mortgage in the model is for 75% of the cost of the property, $1,200,000 × .75 = $900,000. The annual debt service payment is $90,643. Annual figures are used for compounding and discounting purposes. The mortgage is conventional financing from a savings and loan. The type of financing is an important consideration with respect to the at-risk rules discussed earlier.

Item F, Project Revenues.   The projected revenues and expenses of a project must be reviewed very carefully for accuracy. It is sometimes unwise to assume the future will be exactly like the past. A reconstructed operating statement should be developed by the potential investor so that all of the revenue and expense numbers accurately reflect the estimates of the investor, not the seller, and should be based on market-determined comparables. Table 3–11 is a reconstructed operating statement for the sample problem.

From Table 3–11 it may seem that the gross potential revenue of the project is estimated to be $211,200 the first year. There are 80 rental units at an average rent of $220 per month. Rents are expected to increase at an annual compound rate of 2.5%. The vacancy rate, based on historical evidence and a review of comparable projects, is estimated to be on the order of 5%. Even in those cases where a project may have 100% occupancy, some vacancy factor should be included to be on the conservative side.

Item G, Holding Periods.   A necessary task in cash flow analysis is to make an estimate of when the property will be sold and to determine the present value of the net gain from sale. In the model employed the calculations are made on an annual basis; i.e., what are the financial results if the project is sold at the end of the first year of ownership, the second year, the third year, and so forth. The sale price is determined by capitalizing the projected net operating income for the following year. The sale price for the end of year 1 is:

$$\frac{\text{NOI Year 2}}{\text{Cap Rate}} = \text{Sale Price} \qquad \frac{\$113,406}{.0922} = \$1,230,000$$

Table 3–11. 80-Unit Rental Apartment Reconstructed Income and Expense Statement—Year 1

Estimated income:		
40 one-bedroom units @ $210 per month		$100,800
40 two-bedroom units @ $230 per month		110,400
Gross possible income		$211,200
Less vacancy and rent loss @ 5%		−10,560
Effective gross income		$200,640
Operating expenses:		
Real estate taxes	$19,800	
Insurance	4,330	
Wages	18,000	
Gas	13,600	
Water	3,700	
Electricity	3,070	
Advertising	2,890	
Repairs and maintenance	5,720	
Supplies	1,350	
Management @ 5%	7,142	
Transportation	5,898	
Miscellaneous	4,500	
Total operating expenses	$90,000	
Net operating income (NOI)		$110,640
Less: Debt service		−90,643
Before-tax cash flow		$ 19,997

The cap rate used is the same cap rate that was generated using the current sales price and current NOI:

$$\frac{\text{NOI, Earned}}{\text{Sale Price}} = \frac{\$110,640}{\$1,200,000} = .0922$$

The assumption is that a future purchaser would be willing to accept a similar rate of return on his or her investment as that of the current investor. This also assumes relatively constant interest rates and inflation. The appreciation is estimated conservatively. The effect of changes in these variables can be tested easily in a computerized version of the model.

Item H, Operating Expenses.   The estimated operating expenses must be reviewed for accuracy and compared with known figures from comparable properties. Often this information is difficult to obtain for the average investor. It may be necessary to consult with an appraiser or other analyst who has experience in the property area in question. Operating expenses should be calculated as a percentage of effective gross, and this overall percentage should be compared as well as the relative percentage of each item of operating expense. Operating expenses for similar classes of property will vary from one part of the country to another. Snow removal would be one item that would be an example of differences in operating cost from region to region. However, within a given market area the operating costs for similar classes of property should all be close to an average figure. Significant deviations from the average should be reviewed closely and the reasons why determined. The operating expenses of the model are expected to increase by 2.5% per year compounding.

Item I, Required Return.   Information relative to the investor must be developed as inputs to the cash flow model. The investor in the sample model requires a 10% rate of return on investment. This required rate of return is the interest rate that is used to discount all cash flows.

Item J, Investor Tax Situation.   The investor in the model is in the 28% tax bracket and is expected to have an adjusted gross income (AGI) of $90,000 or less in the ensuing years. This AGI does not include passive (rental) activities. The investor is expected to be actively involved in the management of the property and will own 100% of the equity interest in the property. These management, income, and ownership conditions will allow the investor to pass through the tax losses of the property to partially shelter income from other sources.

Section II: Cash Flow Items.   Items 1–14, in Section II of Table 3–12, are fundamental to any cash flow analysis. Each input item will be discussed separately. Table 3–12 is functionally the same method used in Table 3–10; however, the tax account and cash account have been collapsed into one annual column.

Item 1, Estimated Gross Income (Input).   This figure is the basis upon which the other dollar inflow figures are formed. An overly optimistic gross income figure will distort all income figures and the resultant estimate of investment value. This figure should be closely scrutinized so that it truly reflects realistic conditions. This gross income figure should be one result of a market study. The income may be changed from year to year to reflect increases in rents or changing market conditions. It need not be a level annuity as in the income or mortgage equity approaches. In the above model, the gross income figure is increased annually at 2.5% compounding.

Item 2, Vacancy and Rent Loss.   This figure should be based on prevailing occupancy rates in the local market area and the historical occupancy rate of the property involved. A prior market study would also provide this figure. This figure may also be changed annually, or remain a constant percentage as in the above model.

Item 3, Effective Gross Income.   This item is the first output of the program. It is computed by subtracting the vacancy rate from the gross income.

Item 4, Total Operating Expenses.   Operating expenses may be estimated to be a constant percentage of effective gross income. These figures should also come from a market analysis that has made a comparison of the operating expenses of similar properties.

Item 5, Net Operating Income (NOI).   The net operating income is calculated by subtracting operating expenses from the effective gross

Table 3–12A. Model Inputs

Section I

Basic Facts and Assumptions

A. Acquisition price—$1,200,000
B. Land value—$200,000
C. Building value—$1,000,000
D. Depreciable life—27.5 years; see TRA Guidelines
E. Mortgage—$900,000 at 9%, for 26 years
F. Project revenues—200,640, increasing 2.5% annually
G. Holding period—1–5 years
H. Operating expenses—$90,000, increasing 2.5% annually
 I. Required return—10%
J. Tax situation—28% marginal tax rate, active, 100% equity interest

Table 3–12B. 80-Unit Apartment Building
5-Year Income & Expense Statement
Discounted Cash Flow

Section II

#	*Cash Flow Items*	*Year 1*	*Year 2*	*Year 3*	*Year 4*	*Year 5*
1.	Estimated gross income	$211,200	$216,480	$221,892	$227,439	$233,125
2.	Minus: Vacancy & rent loss @ 5%	−10,560	−10,824	−11,095	−11,372	−11,656
3.	Effective gross income	$200,640	$205,656	$210,797	$216,067	$221,469
4.	Minus: Operating expenses	−90,000	−92,250	−94,556	−96,919	−99,341
5.	Net operating inc. (NOI)	$110,640	$113,406	$116,241	$119,147	$122,128
6.	Minus: Debt service	−90,643	−90,643	−90,643	−90,643	−90,643
7.	Before-tax cash flow	19,997	22,763	25,598	28,504	31,485
8.	Plus: Principal	9,643	10,511	11,457	12,489	13,613
9.	Minus: Depreciation	−35,000	−36,000	−36,000	−36,000	−36,000
10.	Taxable gain or loss	−5,360	−2,726	1,055	4,992	9,097
11.	Before-tax cash flow	$ 19,997	$ 22,763	$ 25,598	$ 28,504	$ 31,485
12.	± Tax savings/tax due	1,500	763	−295	−1,398	−2,547
13.	After-tax cash flow	$ 21,497	$ 23,526	$ 25,303	$ 27,106	$ 28,938
14.	Discounted value of ATCF @ .10	19,543	19,443	19,010	18,513	17,968

Section III

Investment Liquidation

Tax Due on Sale:

15. Sale price (net) estimated	$1,230,000	$1,260,748	$1,292,266	$1,324,598	$1,357,705
Minus: Adjusted basis (book value)					
16. Land cost	200,000	200,000	200,000	200,000	200,000
17. Improvements (cost – depreciation)	965,000	929,000	893,000	857,000	821,000
18. Gain on disposal	65,000	131,748	199,266	267,598	336,705
19. Times: Tax rate	× .28	× .28	× .28	× .28	× .28
20. Tax due on sale	$ 18,200	$ 36,889	$ 55,794	$ 74,927	$ 94,277
21. Sale price (net) estimated	$1,230,000	$1,260,748	$1,292,266	$1,324,598	$1,357,705
22. Minus: Tax due on sale	−18,200	−36,889	−55,794	−74,927	−94,277
23. Minus: Mortgage balance	−890,356	−879,844	−868,386	−855,897	−842,284
24. After-tax equity reversion	$ 321,444	$ 344,015	$ 368,086	$ 393,774	$ 421,144
25. Discounted value of equity reversion	292,222	284,310	276,549	268,953	261,497

Section IV

Measures of Investment Performance

26. Present value of all returns to equity	$ 311,765	$ 323,296	$ 334,545	$ 345,462	$ 355,974
27. Net present value	11,765	23,296	34,545	45,462	55,974
28. Internal rate of return	14.32%	14.33%	14.34%	14.34%	14.33%
29. Investment value	$1,211,765	$1,233,296	$1,234,545	$1,245,462	$1,255,974

income. The NOI is the first indicator of the economic performance of a project. The NOI is used to calculate an overall cap rate: NOI ÷ Sale Price = Overall Capitalization Rate.

Item 6, Debt Service.   The debt service does not change from year to year on a typical fixed-rate, fixed-amortization-period mortgage. The debt service payment is typically calculated internally by most computerized cash flow programs once the mortgage life and interest rate are given. The debt service payment is calculated by multiplying the debt service constant (amortization rate) times the amount borrowed. The above model uses a 9% interest rate and a 26-year amortization period, which results in a debt service constant of .100715. This may be calculated or taken from a 9% discount table, column 6 at the 26th year; it is the combination of the discount rate (9%) and the sinking fund factor in column 3 (.010715). The debt service constant of .100715 times $900,000 equals a debt service payment of $90,643. The debt service amount is subtracted from the NOI, which results in the before-tax cash flow.

Most computerized cash flow programs will also calculate an entire amortization schedule that details the specifics of the loan and repayments. Table 3–13 is an example of such an amortization schedule. The calculations made in Table 3–13 are based on annual payments and compounding assumptions. The five outputs of the annual amortization schedule, i.e., remaining principal balance, principal paid this year, interest paid this year, total principal paid to date, and total interest paid to date, are necessary inputs to further calculations in Sections II and III.

Item 7, Before-Tax Cash Flow.   The before-tax cash flow is the actual cash generated by the project that flows to the owners. Debt service has been subtracted from the NOI, and so the resultant figure is attributable to the investor's equity contribution to the project. However, this figure is a before-tax amount.

Item 8, Principal Reduction.   In addition to the actual before-tax cash flow, the investor will increase the equity interest by reducing the amount of money owed on the mortgage. Every debt service payment made consists of interest on the debt plus some amount of principal repayment. The principal component of the debt service payment reduces the amount owed on the mortgage, thereby increasing the investor's equity ownership in the property. This reduction in principal is an

Table 3–13. Annual Amortization Schedule

Purchase price	1,200,000.00		Annual rate		9.00
Down payment	300,000.00		Term in years		26.00
Amount financed	900,000.00		Loan constant		10.07153556
Balloon payment	0.00		Annual payment		90,643.82

End of Year	Principal Balance	Principal Paid This Year	Interest Paid This Year	Principal, Total Paid to Date	Interest, Total Paid to Date
1	890,356.18	9,643.82	81,000.00	9,643.82	81,000.00
2	879,844.42	10,511.76	80,132.06	20,155.58	161,132.06
3	868,386.59	11,457.82	79,186.00	31,613.41	240,318.05
4	855,897.57	12,489.03	78,154.79	44,102.43	318,472.85
5	842,284.53	13,613.04	77,030.78	57,715.47	395,503.63
6	827,446.32	14,838.21	75,805.61	72,553.68	471,309.24
7	811,272.66	16,173.65	74,470.17	88,727.34	545,779.40
8	793,643.38	17,629,28	73,014.54	106,356,62	618,793.94
9	774,427.47	19,215.92	71,427.90	125,572.53	690,221.85
10	753,482.12	20,945.35	69,698.47	146,517.88	759,920.32
11	730,651.69	22,830.43	67,813.39	169,348.31	827,733.71
12	705,766.52	24,885.17	67,758.65	194,233.48	893,492.36
13	678,641.69	27,124.83	63,518.99	221,358.31	957,011.35
14	649,075.62	29,566.07	61,077.75	250,924.38	1,018,089.10
15	616,848.61	32,227.01	58,416.81	283,151.39	1,076,505.91
16	581,721.16	35,127.45	55,516.37	318,278.84	1,132,022.28
17	543,432.25	38,288.92	52,354.90	356,567.75	1,184,377.19
18	501,697.33	41,734.92	48,908.90	398,302.67	1,233,286.09
19	456,206.27	45,491.06	45,152.76	443,793.73	1,278,438.85
20	406,621.01	49,585.26	41,058.56	493,378.99	1,319,497.41
21	352,573.09	54,047.93	36,595.89	547,426.91	1,356,093.31
22	293,660.84	58,912.24	31,731.58	606,339.16	1,387,824.88
23	229,446.50	64,214.34	26,429.48	670,553.50	1,414,254.36
24	159,452.87	69,993.63	20,650.19	740,547.13	1,434,904.54
25	83,159.80	76,293.06	14,350.76	816,840.20	1,449,255.30
26	0.37	83,159.44	7,484.38	899,999.63	1,456,739.68
27	0.00	0.00	0.00	0.00	0.00
28	0.00	0.00	0.00	0.00	0.00
29	0.00	0.00	0.00	0.00	0.00
30	0.00	0.00	0.00	0.00	0.00
31	0.00	0.00	0.00	0.00	0.00
32	0.00	0.00	0.00	0.00	0.00
33	0.00	0.00	0.00	0.00	0.00

important consideration in valuing any real estate investment that utilizes amortizing debt service payments.

Item 9, Depreciation. Depreciation is a noncash expense item which is basically a method of capital recovery allowed under current tax law. Allowable depreciation techniques and amounts have fluctuated dramatically with each tax revision. The current model uses the 1986 TRA depreciation schedules. The precalculated rates for residential rental property are given in Table 3–5.

Depreciation is subtracted from the before-tax cash flow, since depreciation, along with interest and operating expenses, is a tax-deductible item. The resultant figure is the investor's taxable gain or loss. In the above model the investor shows a loss for tax purposes in Year 1 and Year 2. This means that the before-tax cash flow is tax-free income because for tax purposes the property shows a loss. Table 3–14 demonstrates a capital cost recovery depreciation schedule. In the above model the depreciable base is the value of the building, $1,000,000. The allowed percentage of depreciation, from Table 3–14, is 3.5% the first year and 3.6% thereafter. The amount of depreciation from this schedule is used as the input for Item 9. The remaining book value is the difference between the original depreciable base of $1,000,000 and the accumulated amount of depreciation taken. The remaining book value is a necessary input to Section III, Investment Liquidation.

Table 3–14. Capital Cost Recovery Depreciation Schedule

Year	Depreciable Base		Percentage from Tables		Depreciation Amount	Remaining Book Value
1	1,000,000	×	.035	=	$35,000	$965,000
2	1,000,000	×	.036	=	36,000	929,000
3	1,000,000	×	.036	=	36,000	893,000
4	1,000,000	×	.036	=	36,000	857,000
5	1,000,000	×	.036	=	36,000	821,000
6	1,000,000	×	.036	=	36,000	785,000

Item 10, Taxable Gain or Loss. This tax loss may be used by the investor to offset taxes on income from another source, such as salary from a job. However, in Years 3–5 this tax shelter disappears and the property generates taxable income.

Item 11, Before-Tax Cash Flow.   This item is a repeat of Item 7, and is generated to demonstrate its relationship with tax savings, Item 12. Together they make up the after-tax cash flow or the cash-on-cash return to equity.

Item 12, ± Tax Savings/Tax Due.   This item is either the approximate tax savings generated by the project or the tax due to be paid for each year. In the above model, Item 10 indicates that in the first 2 years the property is showing a loss for tax purposes. This tax shelter is converted to the actual tax savings to the investor by multiplying the tax loss by the investor's tax bracket. In Year 1 the tax shelter is (5,360) × .28 = $1,500; the $1,500 represents actual tax savings. Table 3–10 presents a slightly different view of the same problem. This approach to the determination of tax savings is not the exact method found on IRS tax forms, but it will generate approximately the same results without the necessity of reviewing and working with tax forms.

In Years 3–5 the model property is generating taxable income (Item 10), and therefore the investor must pay taxes on those amounts for those years. For example, in Year 3, the taxable gain (Item 10) is $1,055 × .28 = $295, which is the amount of tax owed in Item 12.

Item 13, After-Tax Cash Flow.   The after-tax cash flow is the combination of the before-tax cash flow and the addition of tax savings or the subtraction of tax due. The resultant amount represents the actual cash return for the year to the investor and his or her equity investment.

Item 14, Discounted Value of the After-Tax Cash Flow.   This item, generated by most computerized cash flow programs, converts the after-tax cash flows to their present values. Dollars that are received in the future are worth less today. Therefore, in order to determine what the investor would be justified in paying today for the dollars that are expected to be generated by the property in the future, we must convert those future dollar amounts to their present values. The rate at which we discount those future dollars is the discount rate which equates to the investor's required rate of return. In the above model, the investor requires a 10% rate of return. This is the return that is necessary to induce the investor to purchase the property rather than, say, put money in United States Treasury bills. Item 14 gives the present values of each of the future years' cash flow. The future values are discounted at 10%. Table 3–15 demonstrates the calculations re-

Table 3–15. 80-Unit Apartment Building
Measures of Investment Performance (ATCF)

End of Year	After-Tax Cash Flow	Present Value Factor at 10%	Discounted Cash Flow
1	$21,497	.909091	$19,543
2	23,526	.826446	19,443
3	25,303	.751315	19,010
4	27,106	.683013	18,513
5	28,938	.620921	17,968

quired to determine the present values of the future cash flows. The present value factors may be taken from any 10% discount table.

Section II has determined the investor's actual after-tax rate of return of the annual cash flows from the project. Section III deals with the question: If the project is sold at the end of any given year, what will the effect be on the investor's position?

Section III Investment Liquidation.   Investment liquidation is an area of utmost concern to investors. The potential gain made upon the sale of a property is an important part of the overall return on an investor's equity. Therefore the calculation of this potential should be handled in a realistically conservative manner; i.e., the assumptions should not be exaggerated.

The model calculates the impact of an assumed sale of the property as if it occurred at the end of each year. This allows the investor to ask the question: What if I sold at the end of Year 3, or 4, or 5, and so forth?

Item 15, Net Sale Price.   The sale price is calculated by assuming that a future investor would require the same rate of return on his or her investment as the model investor. Therefore the net sale price (exclusive of transaction costs) is calculated at the end of each year by capitalizing the next year's NOI by the same overall cap rate that was generated in the original sale of the model property. The sale price at the end of Year 5 would be

$$\frac{\text{NOI}}{R} = \text{Sale Price}$$

$$\frac{\$125,180}{.0922} = \$1,357,705$$

Adjusted Basis (Book Value).   From the net sale price the investor must subtract his or her remaining basis in the property. The basis is the original cost minus any amount taken as depreciation. This is done so that the investor's original capital investment in the property will not be taxed.

Item 16, Land Cost.   The first item to be subtracted from the net sale price is land cost. Since land cannot be depreciated for tax purposes, the entire amount of the original cost of the land is subtracted from the net proceeds from sale.

Item 17, Improvements.   The second item to be subtracted is the remaining basis in the improvements, i.e., buildings. The amount of depreciation already taken is first subtracted from the original investment in the building to arrive at the remaining basis. The depreciation is subtracted because that amount has been used to reduce the tax liability of the investor in prior years.

Item 18, Gain on Disposal.   The final gain after sale of the property is the difference between the net sale price and the adjusted basis. Since the 1986 TRA no longer allows special tax treatment for capital gains, the total gain on disposal is taxed.

Item 19, Tax Rate.   The investor's tax rate is multiplied by the gain on disposal to determine the amount of tax due.

Item 20, Tax Due.   This item is simply the result of the above calculation and is the dollar amount of the tax that would be due if the property were to be sold at the assumed sale price at the end of that period of ownership.

Item 21, Net Sale Price.   This item is an informational repeat of Item 15. It is used here to calculate the actual returns to the investor after taxes and the remaining mortgage balance are paid off.

Item 22, Tax Due on Sale.   This figure is the amount of tax due on the sale. It is subtracted from the sale price.

Item 23, Mortgage Balance. In addition to taxes, the investor must pay off any remaining balance on the mortgage at the time of the sale. The remaining mortgage balance is calculated in the amortization schedule presented in Table 3–13.

Item 24, After-Tax Equity Reversion. This figure represents the difference between the net sale price minus taxes and mortgage balance due. This is the amount that actually goes to the investor after the sale of the property.

Item 25, Discounted Value of Equity Reversion. Just as the model discounted to present values the annual cash flows from the project (Item 14), the model should also discount to their present values the anticipated proceeds from the sale of the property that the investor would hope to get. The after-tax equity reversion should be discounted using the same discount rate as that used for the annual cash flows. Table 3–16 demonstrates the method used to calculate the present value of the equity reversion for any given year of sale.

The equity reversion, i.e., the proceeds from the sale that actually go to the investor, and the annual cash flows from the project represent the total financial benefits to the investor for his or her investment in the property. These two items then, taken together, determine the total rate of return on the investor's equity position.

Section IV: Measures of Investment Performance. A fourth section of most cash flow models will calculate and present the more commonly accepted measurement of the economic performance of the project.

Table 3–16. Measures of Investment Performance (Equity Reversion)

Assumed Sale at End of Year	Equity Reversion	Present Value Factor @ 10%	Discounted Equity Reversion
1	$321,444	.909091	$292,222
2	344,015	.826446	284,310
3	368,086	.751315	276,549
4	393,774	.683013	268,953
5	421,144	.620921	261,497

Item 26, Present Value of All Returns to Equity.   This item is the sum of Item 14, the discounted value of the after-tax cash flows, and Item 25, the discounted value of the equity reversion. This sum represents the actual present value of the equity investment, assuming that all of the assumptions and projections materialize. This sum is the highest amount that the investor could actually invest in the project and still earn the required rate of return. In the above model the required rate of return is 10%.

Table 3–17 exhibits the relationship of these variables. The second column is the accumulated present value of the after-tax cash flows for all the years of ownership. The third column is the present value of the net proceeds from sale (equity reversion) for any given year that actually go to the investor (after tax and mortgage deductions). This last amount is not accumulated from year to year, but rather represents the proceeds from the sale of the property, assuming the sale took place at the end of the indicated year. The final column is the sum of these present values.

Item 27, Net Present Value.   The net present value (NPV) of a project is a key determinant in the investment decision-making process. The NPV is simply the difference between the present value of all returns to equity and the original or anticipated equity investment. There are basically three possible outcomes: (1) the difference is zero, (2) the difference is positive, or (3) the difference is negative. If the difference between the two values is zero, then the investor is earning exactly his or her required rate of return, i.e., the discount rate that was used to convert future cash flows to present values. If the difference is a posi-

Table 3–17. Measures of Investment Performance (Present Value of All Equity Returns)

Assumed Sale at End of Year	Accumulated Present Value of After-Tax Cash Flow	Present Value of Equity Reversion for Given Year	Present Value of All Returns to Equity
1	$19,543	$292,222	$311,765
2	38,986	284,310	323,296
3	57,966	276,549	334,545
4	76,509	268,953	345,462
5	94,477	261,497	355,974

tive number, then the investor is earning a rate of return in excess of his or her required rate of return. The exact rate of return requires additional calculations and is referred to as the internal rate of return. If the difference is a negative number, then the investor is not earning the required rate of return.

The following examples will serve to illustrate the development of the net present value figure.

1. Zero Difference

Present value of all returns to equity	$355,000
Minus actual or expected equity investment	−355,000
Difference	0

The present value of all returns to equity is exactly equal to the actual or anticipated equity investment; therefore the investor is earning exactly the required rate of return. The investment then could be said to be a good one; i.e., it is providing the investor with the rate of return necessary to make the actual investment.

2. Positive Difference

Present value of all returns to equity	$355,000
Minus actual or expected equity investment	−300,000
Difference	$ 55,000

In the above example the difference (net present value) is a positive $55,000; therefore the investor is earning a rate of return in excess of the required rate of return. However, the exact rate of return is not known. Even though the exact rate of return is not known, the positive NPV indicates that the investment is a good one in that the rate of return is above the minimum required to actually make the investment.

3. Negative Difference

Present value of all returns to equity	$355,000
Minus actual or expected equity investment	−360,000
Difference	(5,000)

In the above example the difference (NPV) is a negative ($5,000). This indicates that the present value of the future cash flows is less than the actual equity investment, and therefore this actual rate of return to the investor is less than that which is required. In this case the investment is not a good one, since the investor will not receive the necessary rate of return. One solution would be to negotiate a lower price for the property, thereby requiring a lesser amount for the equity requirement.

Table 3–18 demonstrates the method for calculating the NPV for the sample cash flow. The table indicates that for each year in which a sale is assumed, there is a positive NPV. Therefore the investor in the cash flow example would be earning a rate of return in excess of the 10% minimum requirement for any year that he or she may decide to sell the property. Table 3–18 also indicates the actual or internal rate of return (IRR).

Item 28, Internal Rate of Return.   The internal rate of return is the discount rate that converts the future cash flows to a present value that is exactly equal to the actual or expected equity investment. For example, assume a sale at the end of Year 5. It may be seen in Table 3–19 that at a 10% discount rate the NPV is a positive $55,974, at a 15% discount rate the NPV is a negative ($7,616), and at a discount rate of 14% the NPV is a positive $3,845. The calculations in Table 3–19 indicate then that the discount rate that would generate a zero NPV is somewhere between 14% and 15%. The actual rate is 14.33% and is the internal rate of return. That is the actual rate of return the investor may expect from the project.[6]

Table 3–18. Measures of Investment Performance (NPV/IRR)

Year	Present Value of All Returns to Equity		Required Equity		Net Present Value	Internal Rate of Return
1	311,765	–	300,000	=	$11,765	14.32%
2	323,296	–	300,000	=	23,296	14.33%
3	334,545	–	300,000	=	34,545	14.34%
4	345,462	–	300,000	=	45,462	14.34%
5	355,974	–	300,000	=	55,974	14.33%

Table 3–19. Measurements of Investment Performance Internal Rate of Return

End of Year	After-Tax Cash Flow	× Present Value Factor at 10% =	Discounted Cash Flow (DCF)	
1	$ 21,497	.909091	$ 19,543	
2	23,526	.826446	19,443	
3	25,303	.751315	19,010	
4	27,106	.683013	18,513	
5	28,938	.620921	17,968	
Sale Proceeds	$421,144	.620921	$355,974	Total DCF
			−300,000	Equity
			$ 55,974	NPV

End of Year	After-Tax Cash Flow	× Present Value Factor at 15% =	Discounted Cash Flow	
1	$ 21,497	.869565	$ 18,693	
2	23,526	.756144	17,789	
3	25,303	.657516	16,637	
4	27,106	.571753	15,498	
5	28,938	.497177	14,387	
Sale Proceeds	$421,144	.497177	209,383	
			$292,384	Total DCF
			−300,000	Equity
			(7,616)	NPV

End of Year	After-Tax Cash Flow	× Present Value Factor at 14% =	Discounted Cash Flow	
1	$ 21,497	.877193	$ 18,857	
2	23,526	.769468	18,102	
3	25,303	.674972	17,079	
4	27,106	.592080	16,049	
5	28,938	.519369	15,029	
Sale Proceeds	$421,144	.519369	218,729	Total DCF
			$303,845	Total DCF
			−300,000	Equity
			$ 3,845	NPV

The actual calculation of the IRR by a trial-and-error method is time-consuming and cumbersome. A computerized cash flow program designed to generate this indicator of performance can save a great deal of time and aggravation. This is especially true when one wants to change one or more of the input assumptions and generate the entire cash flow program a second, third, fourth, or more times.

Item 29, Investment Value. This last item in the sample cash flow is the indicator of the total investment value of the project. This amount is the sum of the present value of all mortgages (current mortgage amount) and the present value of all returns to equity. If the investment value is equal to the cost of the project, then all parties are receiving their required rates of return. If the investment value is greater than the actual cost of the project, then the overall rate of return on the investment is in excess of the minimum requirement necessary to make the investment.

In summary, the sample cash flow indicates that the project would be a profitable investment. The project would generate a positive NPV and an IRR of 14.3%. The actual investment value is in excess of the actual total investment requirements of $1,200,000. A student of real estate investment analysis should review all of the interrelationships of the variables in the sample cash flow analysis and then construct a separate one based on a different set of input assumptions.

The above model is presented here as a sample of the type of model that is required to determine the investment value of a property. A variety of formats may be used, and the amount of informational data printed may be expanded or contracted. The most important elements are the calculations of the present value of all the cash flow benefits and the benefits from investment liquidation.

Although the inputs to a cash flow model may be varied to test the possible results of a variety of investment and market conditions, those who advocate the use of the model for valuation purposes argue that the inputs could be based on "average" or "typical" investor requirements. These average requirements could be determined by surveying the general market and using general market averages. The key averages to be determined would be: (1) required rates of return on equity, (2) tax brackets, (3) investment holding periods, (4) mortgage interest rates, (5) loan-to-value ratios, (6) operating ratios for various classes of properties, and (7) appreciation rates.

In addition, they argue that because the financing of real property is in most cases based on the personal aspects of borrower creditworthiness, the property valuation methods should—to some extent—be personalized.

Investment Indices

Most investors and lending institutions, whether or not a cash flow model is employed, will calculate several useful indices as rough indicators of a project's performance.

Operating Ratio. The operating ratio is the relationship of operating expenses to gross income. For example, in the above cash flow model the operating ratio for the first year is:

$$\frac{\text{Operating Expenses}}{\text{Gross Income}} = \frac{\$90,000}{\$211,200} = .42$$

The lower the operating ratio, the more efficient the property. Operating ratios will vary between classes of properties and from one part of the country to another. Operating ratios are typically developed for similar classes of properties so that their efficiencies may be compared. They may also serve as a partial indicator of the capabilities of the property management. Operating ratios for various classes of properties tend to range from 25% to 50% of gross revenues.

Break-Even Cash Throw-off Ratio. This ratio indicates the relationship between operating expenses, total mortgage payment, and gross income. The break-even point would be indicated by a ratio equal to 1. In the above cash flow model the break-even cash throw-off ratio would be:

$$\frac{\text{Operating Expenses} + \text{Mortgage Payment}}{\text{Gross Income}} = \frac{\$180,643}{\$211,200} = .85$$

This ratio would indicate to the investor the relative margin of safety between total expenditures and the potential gross income of the project.

Payback-Period Ratio. This ratio indicates the time it will take for the project to totally pay back the investor's equity investment from the cash flow only. It may be calculated as follows:

$$\text{Payback Period} = \frac{\text{Equity}}{\text{Annual Cash Flow after Tax}} = \frac{\$300,000}{\$21,497} = 13.9 \text{ years}$$

However, this method of calculating the payback period may only be used when the annual cash flow after tax is constant over the projected years. In most models the cumulative cash flow will be calculated so that the payback period may be seen at a glance.

Debt Service Coverage Ratio.   This ratio indicates the margin of safety between the mortgage payment and the actual NOI. The ratio is calculated as follows:

$$\text{Debt Service Coverage} = \frac{\text{Net Operating Income}}{\text{Mortgage Payment}} = \frac{\$110,640}{\$90,643} = 1.22$$

Lending institutions are particularly concerned with this ratio. The higher the ratio, the more secure the lender's investment. If the lender is not satisfied with the ratio, he or she may reduce the loan-to-value ratio and thereby require a higher equity investment on the part of the investor.

These ratios are quite simple to derive once the data are known, and no special technology is required. However, many computerized cash flow models incorporate in their programming the computation for these ratios so that investors and lenders can see at a glance the various relationships that exist. These ratios will of course change as the input data are varied.

Even though discounted cash flow models are not widely used in determining the market value of income property, they can and do serve as invaluable investment analysis tools. They may be used in sensitivity analysis whereby various inputs are used to test their impact on profitability. The computerized models allow a range of inputs to be tested, from those estimated to be the least likely conditions to those estimated to be the most optimistic. The probabilities of each set of input data within this range may be derived so that investors may assess the degree of financial risk involved.

SUMMARY

This chapter brings together the concepts and methodologies presented in Chapters 1 and 2 and focuses them on the real estate investment decision process. Before the actual development of an investment model, investors should first define their investment objectives and weigh these objectives against estimates of risk.

Basic investment objectives are reviewed. These are as follows:

1. Current cash flow
2. Future cash return
3. Liquidity
4. Inflationary hedge
5. Ordinary income tax
6. Capital gains tax treatment

Investment risks should be evaluated relative to:

1. Market changes
2. Inflation
3. Interest rate movements
4. Liquidity
5. Legal risks
6. Changes in political climate
7. Natural hazards

Once the decision to make a real estate investment has been made, an understanding of the differences between appraised value and investment value is essential. The chapter presents a discussion of a bargaining model to highlight these differences and then critically explores the traditional approach to determining the value of income-producing property.

The traditional income approach to value is not a suitable method for determining investment value. Therefore, an analytical investment model is introduced which moves from a static first-year cash flow analysis to a dynamic model that tracks all the investment variables and their changes over time. All the investment benefits are discounted to arrive at an investment value figure.

Dynamic cash flow models may incorporate the financial characteristics of individual investors. The variables in these models may be changed to test for various possible results; for this reason they may also serve as tools for investment analysis. The development and use of dynamic cash flow models has been limited due to the necessity of computer facilities and the high level of expertise needed to analyze the results. These problems are being overcome by the rapid expansion and miniaturization of computer facilities and continuing educational programs in the real-estate-related professional organizations.

Although a dynamic cash flow model combined with sound judgment and knowledge of the local market is perhaps the best investment analysis tool, many investors and lending institutions employ several indices of a project's performance. These indices are referred to as:

1. The operating ratio
2. The break-even cash throw-off ratio
3. The payback-period ratio
4. The debt service coverage ratio

These indices, however, should never be substituted for thorough market and financial feasibility analysis. Chapter 4 describes how to analyze market and feasibility reports.

4

How to Analyze Market and Feasibility Reports, or What Every Lender Should Know

The preceding chapters demonstrated the nature and complexities of real estate market and feasibility studies. These studies should be required for any type of significant real estate development and, if properly conducted, will provide an essential and invaluable tool for use in the investment decision process. However, it has become painfully apparent that there are serious weaknesses in the state of the art. Many professionals in the real estate industry today believe that a large part of the collapse of the real estate market in 1973 and the oversupply of office and commercial space in most major markets in the mid-1980s could have been avoided if market and feasibility studies had been done correctly and if the consumers of these studies had known how to interpret them properly. As a result, there exists today a general skepticism about such studies. This skepticism could, however, prove to be beneficial. The field of real estate analysis is relatively young and in a stage of transition from a fragmented area of study fraught with careless practices to a well-defined discipline with a literature and methodology all its own. The present skepticism should prove to be a positive force bringing about some necessary changes hastening this transition.

In order for the producers and consumers of market and feasibility studies to avoid the practices and problems that became apparent in the mid-1970s and 1980s, they must have a clear understanding of just what the uncovered weaknesses were.

The weaknesses in the planning process and, more specifically, in the conduct of market and feasibility studies, fall into three general classifications: forces external to the planning process, shortcomings within the analysis, and lack of post-planning follow-through.

FORCES EXTERNAL TO THE PLANNING PROCESS

Forces external to the planning process are those pressures and practices that relate to the parties involved in the actual conduct of the studies. In nearly all cases the developer is responsible for the commissioning of the studies and typically will seek the expertise of an AE&P firm.[1] It is within the individual AE&P firm that the first weakness in the planning process appears.

Relationship between Analyst and Developer

One of the major external factors is the relationship that often evolves between the analyst and the developer. The analyst too often becomes an advocate for the developer and, hence, the project. Objectivity is lost when the analyst begins to feel personally involved with the success or failure of the project under study. Developers are by nature optimistic risk-takers. Their optimism will many times influence the individual or individuals conducting the market and feasibility studies. The employer-employee connection between the developer and analyst may in many cases be strong enough to influence the data and conclusions reached in the studies. An inexperienced analyst may tend to use, without question, market data provided by the developer. This happens frequently when actual market data are difficult to obtain and the analyst lacks sufficient experience to be certain of his or her own sources and objective judgment.

Developer-influenced studies are invariably biased, but this bias may be difficult to detect. Lending institutions can play a key role in correcting this weakness, for it is only natural that as long as developers are the ones commissioning the studies, the results will be subject to their influence. Lending institutions should begin to play a key role in the commissioning and overseeing of such studies.

Objectives of the Developer

A second external force involves the objectives of the developer. Often the developer will not have a clear set of objectives and will seek the advice of the consultants in formulating them. Too often these objectives are not clearly defined at the outset of the planning process, and consequently there is no precise focus to the following studies. When this happens, the resultant studies may be incomplete and inconsistent, and will be misleading to the developer and lender alike. In many instances the consultant will not fully explain the planning process itself and will fail to point out the distinction between market studies and feasibility studies. Consequently, feasibility studies are undertaken where market studies are warranted, and narrowly focused market studies are conducted when highest and best use investigations should be initiated.

Essential to a market study is a complete meeting of the minds between the developer and the consultant about the type of project envisioned by the developer vs. market realities, and about the developer's financial and political strength. Essential to a feasibility study is an understanding of the developer's profit objectives and willingness to take risks. Is the developer seeking cash flow, tax shelter, capital security, capital gains, or perhaps an estate for his or her heirs? These objectives should be clearly defined at the outset so that the studies will result in focused and meaningful recommendations.

Drive for Profits

A third major external force is the drive for profits. Any consulting firm is in business to make a profit, but in some instances this necessity will cause a distorted or biased development plan to emerge. Those consulting firms that offer a complete line of development services, i.e., market, economic feasibility, architectural, and engineering studies, will normally want a project to be developed. The market, economic feasibility, and land planning departments will typically be only small profit centers for these firms, while the architecture and engineering contracts will by far produce the largest dollar amount of billings.

If a project is not developed, then the AE&P firm will lose the potential earnings it could have made from the architectural and engineering fees. For example, the entire planning process for a $10 million project might result in $25,000–$100,000 in planning fees and perhaps $1 million–$1.5 million in architectural, land planning, and engineering fees. The relative differences in dollar amounts of billings are quite significant. For this reason, pressure may be exerted on the individual or team conducting the initial market and feasibility analysis to produce positive figures or at least play down any negative aspects in an effort to get the project financed and ultimately constructed. This is not to suggest that this is a common practice, for it is not. However, these internal pressures are real, and the persons working in the real estate industry, especially developers, investors, and loan officers, should be aware of them.

This concern has resulted in the formation of firms that conduct only market and feasibility studies, thereby avoiding conflicting internal interests. Although this independent approach often causes some problems of coordination and interpretation in the cash flow modeling and developmental programming stages, they may be overcome by a determined project director.

A note of caution should be mentioned here: many AE&P firms have become aware of the criticism of internal conflicts of interest and have separated their market and feasibility departments from the parent company. In all outward appearances the new market and feasibility firm is independent, but in fact it may be a wholly owned subsidiary of the original parent company and subject to many of the same pressures.

Disintegration of the Team Approach

A fourth external factor is referred to as the disintegration of the team approach. The team approach is essential to comprehensive planning. A team will generally consist of market analysts, financial analysts, land planners, architects, various engineers, computer programmers, and the developer. Disintegration of the team approach is generally the result of one or a combination of the following:

1. Personality conflicts
2. Differing professional opinions
3. Indifference
4. Work overloads resulting in scattered efforts and poor-quality reports
5. Budget constraints (the team approach is expensive)
6. One or more weak departments
7. Poor project timing
8. Too heavy a reliance on client input and pressures
9. Misunderstandings of client's objectives
10. Inability to incorporate client as a team member
11. Unrealistic promises in the original proposal, thereby causing time lags and budget breakdowns
12. Incompetent project director

The developer may be, but for the most part generally is not, aware that "his" team is not operating as a team at all. When the developer is present for discussions or presentations of findings, he is confronted with a group of individuals, each representing a different area of expertise, calling themselves his development team. However, it often happens that once the developer is gone, the team breaks apart, and each individual follows his own set of priorities and inclinations, each out of synchronization with all the others. This results in poor-quality reports at a high cost. An experienced and knowledgeable project director can resolve all of these problems, and for that reason it is essential for developers and lenders to assess the abilities and workload of the individual who will be directing the planning process in the specific project in question.

Fragmented Development Planning

Another external factor that is a common error on the part of AE&P firms is fragmented development planning, i.e., allowing client projects to enter the planning process at inappropriate points. The most common example is accepting a land planning and design project without a market study or preliminary economic feasibility analysis. Many clients have spent thousands of dollars on land use plans that later turn out to be economically impossible to develop. This seems, on the face of it, to be such an apparent mistake that it should seldom happen. However, in terms of wasted effort, dollars, and environmental degradation, it is more significant and common than is generally realized. When this happens, it generally involves inexperienced developers.

A case in point occurred recently in Florida when the vice president in charge of land use planning for a large AE&P firm, in an effort to increase his department's billings, signed a contract with two inexperienced developers to design the land use plans for a piece of property they owned at the interchange of a major interstate highway. The site was analyzed, and the land use planners developed a unique plan for interchange development. The plan included four motels, two service stations, a theater, a restaurant, curio shops, a campground, and play areas. After spending $20,000 on the land use plans, the developers then asked the uncomfortable question: Could any money be made on the development? It was only then that the project came to the attention of the economic analysts. A hurried market study indicated no effective demand on that site for motels, service stations, or campgrounds. A complete disaster was averted by a redesign for strip commercial land sales to various fast-food operations. An expensive lesson—in dollars, prestige, and credibility—for all concerned.[2]

Incompetent Personnel

One final consideration of the external forces weakening the planning process is that of inadequate, inexperienced, and incompetent personnel. In many instances, consulting firms will find themselves understaffed for the number of projects for which they have contracted. During boom periods in the real estate industry, it is not unusual to find a market analyst juggling several projects at one time. This is not necessarily harmful, but when the projects are diverse in nature, it may be impossible for the analyst to give each project the time needed for its proper completion.

Market and feasibility analysis is hard work and requires a great deal of experience to be completed properly. The job involves field work, on-site analysis, interviews, data collection and analysis, report writing, and numerous presentations to project directors, clients, and public bodies. But as is so often the case, the more experienced people are advanced up the corporate ladder where their expertise no longer is directed toward a specific project. The all-important work of market and feasibility analysis is left to the less experienced, who are often recent graduates with no prior real estate experience. Inexperience tends to produce errors in judgment in such critical areas as projected absorption rates, price ranges, type and design recommendations, and assessment of existing competition. Inexperienced analysts are also more subject to developer influence than their experienced counterparts.

The economic analysis of real estate markets is still a young and evolving field. The methodologies used are to a large extent borrowed from other disciplines, and to employ them properly requires knowledge that is as broad as it is deep. For these reasons there are many individuals working in the industry who not only may lack experience but are also generally incompetent. Many staff members, analysts, and administrators, in large as well as small consulting firms and lending institutions, lack the educational background that is essential to the successful fulfillment of their job requirements.

The consumers of market and feasibility studies, such as developers and lending institutions, should no longer assume that any consulting firm has at any given time adequate, experienced, competent personnel with which to carry out the planning process. Provisions should be made so that an ongoing review may be made of the personnel involved in the project planning process.

The above material pointed out the weaknesses external to the actual studies. The second general area of weakness in the development planning process is internal to the studies and is discussed below.

SHORTCOMINGS WITHIN THE ANALYSIS

There are 11 identifiable points of weakness in the planning process that could be considered to be internal to the studies. Many of these areas overlap but are sufficiently different to warrant individual attention and investigation.

Inadequate Analysis of Indirect Economic Forces

The first of these weaknesses is the general failure to analyze adequately the indirect economic forces that may exist in the market area in question. Chapter 2 demonstrated the basic techniques to be employed in market and feasibility studies. It was pointed out that a comprehensive market study would include three general areas of analysis: indirect economic forces, direct economic forces, and conclusions and recommendations. However, too often the indirect economic forces are ignored or only superficially reviewed. The indirect areas that are most often not covered properly are the environmental, social, and political concerns of the community, and more specifically, those interests that will be directly affected by the project. It is not an easy matter to properly assess the concerns of citizens and their elected representatives. There is no precise formula for carrying out this analysis, but no matter what the method used, it must result in a thorough sounding-out of all concerned parties. Some generally accepted methods for undertaking this type of analysis are surveys and extensive interviews with citizen groups and elected and appointed officials.

For every successful real estate project that is undertaken, developers, planners, and investors can usually point to an unsuccessful one. There is an increasing number of unsuccessful developments resulting from the failure to search out and consult with the special-interest groups that could possibly align themselves against the project under study. Many of these projects would never have been started, and millions of dollars would not have been lost, if the studies had been properly conducted.

A developer or investor commissioning a market analysis should be certain that all of the surrounding communities' attitudes toward the project will be uncovered. Furthermore, the developer should be familiar with the method used to study these attitudes. The developer, lender, and consultant should review the results of such an analysis.

"Best Case" Figures

A second internal shortcoming is the widespread practice of using overly optimistic, or the "best case," figures when making future cash flow projections. The "best case" absorption rate, along with the highest estimated unit or sales price, will typically be used in the projection. The high gross revenue projection results in an inflated estimate of value that may influence the lending decision. Many projects become over-leveraged due to inflated estimates of value, and the actual NOI may not be sufficient to cover the mortgage debt. Also, cost estimates for both production and operating expenses may be underestimated.

An alternative to the "best case" projections may be to give a range of possibilities with support given for the most likely case. The range of projections could include the best case, the worst possible case, and the middle or most likely case. The various scenarios would be a more useful decision-making tool and not as misleading as projections based solely on the best possible circumstances.

Misrepresentation of Data

A third significant concern is the misrepresentation or misuse of certain key pieces of data. In a few cases this may be done deliberately to enhance the project's potential, or, as is more often the case, the data may not be sufficiently substantiated by market facts. Some types of key data that may be distorted include: population projections, new household formations, household size, effective demand, price range, and the absorption rate or the percentage of the market that the project is expected to capture.

As an example of this type of distortion, assume a market analyst has developed the following information by analyzing prevailing market conditions.

Annual population increase	3,000
Average # of persons per household	3
Total housing units needed (3,000 ÷ 3 = 1,000)	1,000
Effective demand as percentage of total housing needed	.75
Total size of private-sector market (1000 × .75)	750
Percent of market to be captured (.10 × 750 = 75 units)	75

Price range of units	$50,000
Gross revenue projected for first year ($50,000 × 75)	$3,750,000

On the basis of the above information the project's gross revenue projection is $3,750,000. But now suppose that one piece of information is slightly altered. Take for example the average number of persons per household; this number will vary from community to community and even within communities, and is also difficult to check. If this number is reduced from 3 to 2.8, a slight change that would normally not be questioned, the resultant gross revenue projection is now $4,100,000, an increase of $350,000, or 9.3%. This may make the difference in a cash flow projection between a project appearing feasible or nonfeasible.

Every consumer of market and feasibility studies should be thoroughly aware of the items of information that, if slightly exaggerated, could transform a nonfeasible project to one that would appear to be potentially profitable.

Underestimation of Infrastructure Cost

A fourth problem frequently encountered in market and feasibility analysis is an underestimate of the total infrastructure cost of the proposed development. The cost of utility systems, roads, lighting, and other amenities has increased at an unprecedented rate in the last several years. The failure to anticipate and project these increases may lead to an initial glowing cash flow projection but will almost assuredly lead to financial disaster when the actual costs of 10–20% higher are encountered. It is true that some costs cannot be predicted with accuracy due to uncertain economic conditions; in 1972 who could have predicted the future cost of petroleum products? However, there is another reason that many costs are underestimated.

In a typical market and feasibility study, the analyst will request the consulting engineers to develop the cost estimates for the various components of the project infrastructure. If the resultant cost/revenue position is not favorable, the engineers will come under pressure and revise their estimates in a downward direction. Often this may be accomplished by substituting less expensive materials, reducing overhead and profit figures to barely acceptable levels, reducing the scope of the project or amenities provided, and eliminating the percentage usually included for unforeseen contingencies. The resultant cost figures have no margin for error or unforeseen price increases or construction delays. Cost figures arrived at in this manner will invariably fall short of the actual costs.

An increase in actual cost of 10% over projected costs can easily put a real estate project into bankruptcy. Infrastructure cost estimates should be reviewed closely by all those who share a financial interest in the project. The cost estimates should be varied to see the effect on the projected cash flow.

Inadequate Techniques of Analysis

A fifth major weakness internal to the planning process is that of utilizing inadequate techniques of analysis. The use of inadequate techniques of analysis may be partially or wholly the result of other weaknesses mentioned, such as inadequate personnel. Inadequate techniques of analysis usually result when the procedures used to collect and analyze data are not in-depth methods and consequently result in distorted projections and inappropriate recommendations. An example of this type of analysis would be a case where population growth patterns are given only a superficial review and aggregated historical growth rates are used to project future growth rates. There may be no analysis of the age distribution of the population or no effort to relate employment patterns and effective demand to population projections.

Other areas that may receive too little analysis relate to the cash flow study. Individual items of operating cost may only be assumptions with no market data to substantiate them. Level income streams may be projected when a discontinuous pattern would more closely reflect market conditions. Overly simplified income statements may be developed using current dollars when a more rigorous cash flow statement utilizing discounted values would be necessary to determine the real rate of return.

To avoid using inadequate techniques of analysis, it is imperative that the consumers of these reports be thoroughly familiar with accepted and appropriate methods for conducting market and feasibility studies and begin insisting that high-quality research be the norm. Any report that does not measure up to appropriate standards of quality research should be rejected.

Too Much Statistical Analysis

A sixth weakness that could be said to be the other side of the inadequate techniques of analysis is too much statistical analysis. Examples of this weakness are where highly sophisticated predictive models are used when their use is not warranted. Often, models are used to cover the fact that little or no practical data have been gathered and analyzed. Generalized models are seldom appropriate for use in a specific case. The practice of conducting market and feasibility studies is closer to an art than a science. They are by nature quantitative, but often the available data, to be meaningful, must be interpreted through the eyes of an experienced and educated analyst rather than subjected to rigorous statistical analysis or utilized in models that may be based on inappropriate and little-understood assumptions.

Lack of Relevant Data

A seventh internal weakness that plagues far too many reports is the general lack of relevant data. Market data are hard to come by. Most real estate transactions are not conducted in public, and the facts and figures relating to specific real estate developments are normally proprietary in nature. Where information is available, its true meaning is often hidden or distorted due to the individualized nature of every real estate transaction. In many cases the general lack of data cannot be overcome even by the most diligent research efforts. In these cases the situation should be made clear and the increased investment risk should be spelled out. However, the limited and uncertain data often are utilized in making market projections, and highly quantitative cash flow predictions are made with an implied accuracy that cannot be justified.

Lack of Consumer Surveys

An eighth internal weakness in most real estate market analysis is the lack of consumer surveys. Usually, studies will employ macroeconomic and microeconomic tools of analysis. These tools for the most part are necessary and appropriate and provide essential information. However, in most market studies it is necessary to address the question of consumer preferences. These preferences may relate to questions concerning specific types of dwelling units desired, size requirements, locational preferences, amenities desired, and ownership patterns. The present methods of economic analysis are only poorly suited to this important area of study.

The determination of consumer preferences with respect to the development of real estate resources is an area of study that is still in its infancy. There are a few firms that are active in the area of surveying consumer preferences and attitudes with respect to real estate, but this type of analysis is sorely lacking in the typical market study being produced today. Firms involved in producing market and feasibility studies should expand their abilities to include the surveying of consumer preferences.

Lack of Sensitivity Analysis

A ninth shortcoming inherent in most feasibility studies is a lack of sensitivity analysis. The profitability picture is not tested adequately to determine the impact of potential changes in the cash flow variables, thus reducing the feasibility study's overall effectiveness as an investment decision tool. The failure to construct a dynamic cash flow model that is capable of testing a variety of economic or financial variables is difficult to justify in light of today's easy access to computer programs and equipment.

Overvaluation of Land

A tenth internal weakness is the overvaluation of land caused by overly optimistic sales and revenue projections. This is usually due to an unrealistic estimate of an absorption rate and future appreciation in land prices. These high projections lead to an overestimation of the current value of land. If the present value estimate of the land is used as the basis for securing a highly leveraged loan, then an unsupportable burden of debt is incurred and project failure is ensured.

No Assessment of Management

One final internal weakness is a failure to properly assess the managing ability of the developer involved. In larger projects, the quality of management can mean the difference between success and failure. If any evaluation of management is done at all, the assessment is typically overly generous in defining the competencies of the developer's project management. Many market and feasibility studies will base overly optimistic absorption rates on the "superior quality" of the developer's project management with no justification for doing so. The past track record of individual investors is no indication of the strength of any individual project's management. The competitive nature of today's real estate markets demands that lenders require an analysis of any project's management team.

LACK OF POST-PLANNING FOLLOW-THROUGH

The third general area of weakness in the planning process consists of two parts. First is the failure on the part of the consultants to explain fully to the client all of the elements involved in the studies, their relationships, how they influenced the final recommendations, and what the possible consequences would be if some or all of the recommendations were not followed. Secondly, there is a general tendency not to monitor the progress of the project and the continued suitability of the studies, i.e., not to adapt the studies to changing conditions so that they continue to serve as effective decision tools.

Incomplete Client Presentations

The consultant may be called upon to make presentations of his or her reports to many different audiences. The following are a few of the most common types of presentations required:

1. Consultant presentation to the client and the client's associates
2. Consultant presentation to a lending institution
3. Consultant presentation to a group of private investors
4. Consultant presentation to a public forum
5. Consultant presentation to a planning and zoning commission
6. Consultant presentation to an environmental group

The focus of the presentation made to each of these groups is different, since these groups have different levels of interest in the project. Effective presentations can generally be made if the consultant has done a good job on the planning process and is well prepared for the presentation with a clear understanding of the interests of the audience. However, the most important presentation, and the one that is often mishandled, is the one to the client and the client's associates.

A point that consulting firms often overlook is that many clients need to be educated about the planning process, the elements involved, and the importance of each. The concepts behind the finalized development plan are often not properly presented to the client. For those working with a project on a daily basis, many of the elements within the market study, feasibility analysis, and development plan become so familiar that the analysts begin to think they are obvious to everyone. The same feeling can and does occur in the collective mentality of a development planning team. Consequently, during presentation to the client many important facets are glossed over or simply ignored. The client may never become aware of their importance or may feel that they are unimportant, allowing deviations from the development program, resulting in something less than optimum use of the land, and quite possibly endangering the financial stability of the project.

To avoid this problem when making a client presentation, no assumptions should be made on the part of the consultant about the client's knowledge of any point relating to the market study, the feasibility analysis, or the development program. All points should be covered thoroughly, no matter how tedious it may seem at the moment. Developers and lenders should insist on this type of presentation to test the quality of the reports and to ensure the adequate preparation for further presentations.

No Monitoring of Plans and Project

Too many consultants, developers, and lenders view the completion of the development plan as the end of the planning process and fail to integrate the market study, feasibility analysis, and development plan with the physical development itself. The documents produced in the planning process should be viewed and used as decision-making tools and as guidelines for the physical development of the project. The normal practice followed by developers and lenders is to forgo the continuing use of a consultant and to set the market and feasibility study aside once financing has been arranged. This is a mistake; the larger the project, the larger the mistake. Since large-scale developments require commitments for from 1 to 25 years and since economic, social, and political patterns change, developers and lenders should frequently review what they have accomplished, what unanticipated changes have occurred, and what impact these changes have had on the project. Changes in national and local real estate markets should be monitored and the market and feasibility analysis updated so they do not lose their effectiveness as decision-making tools. By following a continuing monitoring process, costly mistakes could be avoided— particularly when economic conditions change and various real estate markets may be approaching an oversupply condition.

SUMMARY OF POSSIBLE WEAK AREAS IN THE PLANNING PROCESS

I. Forces External to the Planning Process

A. Relationship between analyst and developer
B. No clearly defined developer objectives
C. Consulting company's drive for profit
D. Disintegration of the team approach
E. Poorly sequenced development planning
F. Incompetent personnel

II. Shortcomings within the Analysis

A. Inadequate analysis of indirect economic forces
B. Overuse of "best case" figures
C. Misrepresentation of data
D. Underestimation of infrastructure cost
E. Inadequate techniques
F. Too much statistical analysis
G. Lack of relevant data
H. Lack of consumer surveys
I. Lack of sensitivity analysis
J. Overvaluation of land
K. No assessment of management

III. Lack of Post-Planning Follow-Through

A. Incomplete client presentations
B. No monitoring of plans and project

There is no one simple solution to the deficiencies indicated above. The long-run solution is widespread education in the real estate industry about the purpose, nature, and use of market studies, feasibility analysis, and development plans. The producers of these studies must become more aware of the serious deleterious ramifications, to developers, investors, and the real estate industry in general, of producing reports that do not represent the reality of market conditions. Past practices have not held the producers of these deficient studies accountable; this may not be true in the future.

The principal consumers of these studies must insist on rigorous research practices and educate themselves on the proper methods of analysis and interpretation with an eye toward the potential shortcomings inherent in these reports. Where the in-house ability to properly analyze market and feasibility reports is lacking, qualified objective outside assistance should be sought. Also, many of the problems could be overcome if the lenders commissioned the studies in addition to, or instead of, the developer.

Section II expands on the social and economic forces at the national, local, and neighborhood levels which inevitably impact the way we use our land resources. The chapters in Section II will explore how to analyze these forces and interpret the analyses within the practical aspects of real estate markets.

SECTION II

Neighborhood, Regional, and National Influences on Land Development

The success of a real estate venture depends upon the project's environment. Market and feasibility studies necessarily included assumptions about the project's environment. Sometimes these assumptions are explicit, and sometimes they are not.

Section II examines the real estate environment from three perspectives: (1) the immediate neighborhood, (2) the city and regions, and (3) the nation.

5

Neighborhood Influences and Site Analysis

Almost every phase of real estate activity is concerned with the pattern of land use. A good location is important whether you are purchasing real estate for investment, business, or personal use. It is as important to understand the general forces that result in the emergence of land use patterns as it is to describe those patterns. Only if we understand how and why the current patterns of land use have developed can we begin to explore how patterns will change in the future.

The purpose of this section is to provide the conceptual tools necessary to understand the dynamics that underlie urban form. Cities, whether large or small, are composed of relatively distinct land use areas. Not only are broad classes of activities separated from each other, but various gradations within each category are discernible. Thus the high-priced homes in an exclusive subdivision are segregated from modest housing. Most individuals recognize fine gradations in the land use patterns of their community. They are aware of not only which is the "right" side of the tracks, but how Meadow Lane compares with Wood Lane. However, two facts might be overlooked by the casual observer. First, cities have similar patterns of land use, although the patterns are not identical because of the unique historical and geographical circumstances. Nevertheless, the similarity is striking and suggests that forces common to all cities influence land use patterns. Second, homogeneous land use districts are dynamic. Sometimes the shifts are rapid, but often they are so slow that they escape notice. For example, it may take 20 years for a residential neighborhood to change from primarily owner-occupied to renter-occupied. Regardless of the speed of change, these shifts have a major impact upon property values.

LAND USE PRINCIPLES

To study land use patterns, it is necessary to simplify numerous factors into a few principles. Complicated human settlement patterns cannot be totally explained by a few generalizations. Yet, attempts to understand general patterns of urban form must abstract from unique or particularistic details. This section focuses upon three important determinants of land use: (1) highest and best use, (2) accessibility, and (3) site value principles. Major models of urban development are introduced later in the chapter.

Highest and Best Use

Land will be employed in the use that the owners believe will give them the most satisfaction subject to the prevailing legal restrictions. In the context of this chapter "use" includes leaving property idle as well as developing it. Both pecuniary and nonpecuniary motives determine the land use distribution within a city. Leaving land in its natural state simply for the enjoyment of viewing its beauty may be the highest and best use for some individuals; the "income" they receive is psychic. Others may leave land undeveloped for speculative purposes. Often, land is partially developed while being held for speculation. Parking lots or agricultural uses provide modest revenues without committing land to long-term development. These temporary uses are referred to as "tax payers" because they provide enough revenue to cover a few of the fixed costs.

Land analysts have conveniently assumed that land will be used in the function that provides the greatest monetary returns to the owner within legal limitations of zoning and other regulations because the psychic income derived from a particular use is too difficult to predict. The most profitable legal use of land is called the *highest and best use*. The model that we will develop to explain land use patterns assumes land will be employed in the use most profitable to the owner. Non-monetary motives are ignored. Several points warrant discussion because of the importance of the concept of highest and best use.

First, the profitability of a particular land use comes about because consumers want the site used for that purpose and are willing and able to pay for the location. They are willing to pay enough for the goods and services offered at the location to outbid competing land uses. If a restaurant is profitable, it is at least partly due to the benefit individuals receive from the restaurant's location.

Second, the highest and best use is not necessarily the most socially desirable use. Land uses entail considerable positive and negative spillovers. Construction of a supermarket in the middle of a rare downtown open space may be the most profitable use, but some might argue that it is not "best" in a normative or ethical sense. Perhaps an outdoor concert hall would be a better use from the perspective of the entire society. Therefore, while private profitability and most socially desirable uses are not synonymous, there is a great deal of overlap between the concepts.

Third, the most profitable use of land is seldom the most intensive or most highly developed use. A high-rise apartment is usually more valuable—that is, it would sell for a higher price or generate a larger cash flow—than a single-family house, but this does not mean that it will be more profitable to construct high-rises rather than single-family houses on vacant land. Low-density housing is built in areas because: (1) the cost of construction for a high-rise is also greater than that of single-family construction and (2) rents per unit may have to fall in order to ensure adequate occupancy. If rents don't fall, higher vacancies may cause net revenues to decline. The second factor is apt to be particularly true for apartment units in areas with low population densities. The real question in the highest and best use determination is: What use will provide the greatest return to land after construction and operating costs have been subtracted?

Table 5-1 illustrates the relationship between intensity of development, cost, and the return to land. The economy of vertical construction is illustrated by the lower per story cost of the second level. However, construction costs per story start to rise after the second level because it becomes increasingly expensive to construct additional

Table 5-1. The Return to Land

Number of Stories	Construction Costs (Cost of Capital)	Present Value Net Operating Income	Present Value of Returns to Land
1	100,000	200,000	100,000
2	175,000	400,000	225,000
3	300,000	575,000	275,000
4	525,000	750,000	225,000
5	775,000	900,000	125,000
6	1,125,000	1,100,000	−25,000

units. At the same time, the present value of the rents increases—at a decreasing rate—reflecting the fact that per unit rents might fall due to increased vacancies or the need to lower rents to avoid increased vacancies. The combined result of these forces causes the present value of returns to land to fall after the third story. The present value of the returns to the land are maximized at three stories; a building of three stories is the highest and best use.

The example just discussed showed the highest and best use principle by examining different heights of a residential building. In all cases, the overall use of the land was residential. However, the same principle applies to the choice between types of uses. For example, to determine whether a bakery or a three-story apartment would be the highest and best use, a similar calculation could be utilized.

Market mechanisms reinforce the tendency of an owner to employ land in its highest and best use. For example, suppose an individual owns a parcel of land for which the most profitable use requires construction of a three-story residential building. However, the owner of the property intends to build a one-story apartment building. Perhaps the owner doesn't know a multistory structure is the highest and best use, or perhaps the owner lacks the financial or other technical skills necessary to complete the three-story unit successfully. The land would probably still be developed according to its highest and best use. Another developer might notice the vacant parcel (developers actively seek out such properties), and after analysis determine that a three-story building would be optimal. The developer could offer to buy the land for a maximum of $275,000. Since the value of the land is only $100,000 as a single-story building, there is ample bargaining space in which the two individuals may reach a mutually satisfactory deal. Perhaps the original owner will sell the land and use the proceeds to purchase a property elsewhere on which a one-story building would be the highest and best use. If the owner knows the initial market value of the property, he or she would find it more profitable to sell the land than to develop it as a one-story building.

Much of the discussion about highest and best use has been about use of land prior to development. An existing structure can often be converted from one function to another. The highest and best use principle also applies to changing existing structures. However, the concept requires slight modification. An analyst must estimate what uses will provide the greatest return after *additional* capital costs (including remodeling or demolition costs) have been subtracted from the total value of the property and the improvements. This approach implicitly assumes that existing construction costs ("sunk" costs) must be paid even if the building is demolished. Table 5–2 shows how the owner of a gas station should analyze the modification of the property either to add a convenience grocery or to convert the gas station into a body shop. The addition of a convenience grocery would cost more than the increase in the present value of the NOI. Consequently, the present value of the gas station/grocery does not warrant the extra spending. The conversion to a body shop is feasible because the present value of the post-conversion NOI is greater than the construction costs.

How to Conduct a Highest and Best Use Study. Determining the highest and best use of a site or an existing property is an important part of many appraisals and market studies. Frequently the highest and best use aspect is given light treatment. For instance, the analyst may simply assume that the existing or prevailing use is the highest and best. However, vacant and valuable land may be subject to an intensive highest and best use study. In such cases the highest and best use study can be an important part of the market and feasibility study.

Highest and best use studies can be performed for land as though vacant (the land is assumed to be vacant whether or not it is) or as improved. In the latter case the existing improvements are assumed to be given and the concern is for changes. In either case, the study attempts to narrow the range of choices prior to a detailed financial analysis. The process can be divided into five steps.

1. Develop Land Use Hypothesis. Theoretically a highest and best land use is the most valued of all possible legal uses. Of course, not all

Table 5–2. Highest and Best Use of Developed Property

Land Use	Extra Construction Costs	Increase Present Value of NOI	Present Value of Return to Land and Original Building
Gas station	$ 0	$ 0	$75,000
Gas station/grocery	25,000	20,000	70,000
Body shop	10,000	15,000	80,000

conceivable uses can be considered—that would be too costly. Thus, a limited set of possibilities must be considered initially. These can be either broad categories such as industrial land or very specific such as a box factory. The various value principles, particularly the principle of conformity, can be useful at this stage.

2. Assess Physical Possibility.   Some uses are physically impossible, whereas others face physical impediments that are so great as to be uneconomical. The physical suitability of a parcel to a particular use may depend upon shape, frontage, topography, and subsoil conditions. Because sites compete with one another for particular uses, if costs of a site preparation are significantly higher than costs for nearby similar sites, the use potential will be diminished.

Some sites can only reach their highest and best use as part of an assemblage of other properties. This is often the case with small parcels in the central business district. In this case the analyst will have to make a judgment of the possibility of assemblage and proceed accordingly.

A study of the highest and best use of an improved property should also consider the physical limitations imposed by the improvements. If the property is in good repair, the current use could be the highest and best use. The current physical characteristics will clearly affect potential conversion costs.

3. Assess Legally Permissible Uses.   Zoning is the most frequently discussed legal impediment to a particular land use. However, other legal restrictions that can limit land use are building codes, historic district controls, and environmental regulations. Private restrictions, including setback requirements, material specifications, and so forth, should also be considered. Long-term leases are also a legal restriction.

Legal restrictions can be changed. A report could suggest a nonlegal use as the highest and best use; in this case, the analyst should provide a realistic assessment of the cost and likelihood of success in changing the legal impediments.

4. Determine Preliminary Financial Feasibility.   After winnowing out uses that have major physical and legal impediments, alternative uses should be examined for financial feasibility. Is the property likely to generate an income sufficient to affect construction and operating expenses? All uses that generate a positive return are considered financially feasible.

5. *Determine Maximal Use.* The process thus far has been one of eliminating possible uses. The remaining two or three uses that have been determined to be financially feasible should next be analyzed to establish the use that is most profitable. Higher discount rates should be applied to higher-risk land uses.

Accessibility

The purchase of realty is the purchase of access rights. A principle of land use is that as the accessibility of land to urban "goods" increases, its value also increases. In fact, the locational choice is fundamentally a trade-off between access to a variety of other locations on the one hand and the cost of purchasing or renting real estate at a given location on the other. The role of access as a factor in the evolution of cities has been recognized by Williams:

> Urban locational decisions, indeed the very creation of cities, are the net product of many people trying to become more accessible to one another. The same process that creates cities continues after they are formed.[1]

Pioneers in land economics viewed distance as a barrier to interaction. Distance was a type of social "friction" that needed to be overcome. Friction, of course, was a metaphor for transportation and communication costs. As a general principle, the more accessible a location to the positive elements in the environment, the more valuable it will be. However, different types of land uses call for access to different things. A commercial establishment may seek access to markets that make it easier (and cheaper) for customers to make a buying trip. Likewise, it is easier and cheaper for an establishment to deliver a product if its customers are accessible. As a result, land planners and developers recognize that the more accessible a location, the greater its profit potential. In addition to markets, businesses also seek accessibility to a capable labor force, other businesses, and so forth. The strength of each locational influence varies with the business type. Households also desire accessibility. Individuals want to be near work, recreation, shopping, schools, and neighborhoods with certain characteristics. Residential choice requires individuals to balance some types of access against others and to trade off overall accessibility for lot size or cost per acre. Household travel studies have shown that approximately 34% of suburban household trips are made to work whereas only 7% are made to school. Yet, as most brokers will attest, location near schools is a more valued attribute of residential property than nearness to work. A good school district may add as much as $10,000 to the price of a home. Figure 5–1 shows some ideal access relationship.

Proximity and access are not the same thing. Often, access is limited by social, political, and geographical factors in addition to distance. For example, in most suburban areas, it is the school districts—political cal units—that create access. The Joneses may live only 100 feet from Lincoln School, and the Smiths may live 3 miles away. Yet, if the Joneses are not within the proper school boundaries, their children will be excluded from Lincoln and the Smith children will be enrolled there.

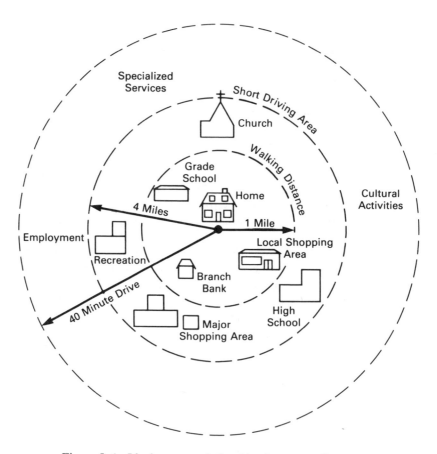

Figure 5–1. Ideal access relationships in metropolitan area.

Political access explains why property values jump thousands of dollars from one side of a street to another. Often, central-city schools are perceived as inferior, and individuals will pay extra for access to the suburban school even though the physical appearance of the districts is identical. The fact that housing prices in one school district are higher than in another means that families living in the more expensive houses will likely have higher incomes. This will reinforce the desirability of the school district because many parents like to have children associate with higher-income families.

Some individuals relocate to improve access. Economists refer to this behavior as "voting with your feet." However, such voting presumes families have the resources to move. Often, less mobile households attempt to create access by changing the institutions or amenities near their residence. The political and social activities of many community groups may be viewed as attempts to improve access. For example, a group that lobbies City Hall for a new park is, in effect, attempting to improve the access of neighborhood residents to recreational facilities.

Time and convenience are important elements of access. Modern transportation networks have made access as much a function of urban infrastructure—types of roads, availability of mass transportation, etc.—as of simple physical distance. There are also social dimensions to the accessibility concept. Fear of crime, for example, has caused many individuals to feel that areas in the central city were not accessible.

Site Value Principles

Several principles of value have been developed in the appraisal literature. They have implications for land use because of the tendency of property to be placed in the most valued use. Thus, site value and land use are linked. Table 5–3 summarizes some appraisal principles that may help determine highest and best use.

PATTERNS OF LAND USE

Two principles regarding land use have been developed. First, there are motives that result in employment of real estate in the most profitable legal use. Second, better accessibility makes properties more valuable locations. Based upon land use principles, several theories have

Table 5–3. Site Value Principles

Principle	Implication
Substitution: If different properties provide similar utility, their prices will be similar and will vary together.	A developer should avoid projects if there are ample properties that can be easily and cheaply substituted for the project under consideration.
Anticipation: Value results from expected future benefits. If expected future benefits increase, price will increase in a well-functioning market.	An analyst should explain the underlying economic forces that will cause a property to appreciate, but those forces may already be reflected in today's price.
Conformity: Value is greater when properties have a reasonable degree of homogeneity, but not architectural monotony.	A proposed land use that does not fit the neighborhood may not be justified and may lower nearby property values.
Regression and Progression: Relative to surrounding properties, higher-valued properties will appreciate less than lower-valued properties.	It is a mistake to overimprove a property and hope to recapture the costs through higher sales price.
Increasing and Decreasing Returns: Up to a point property improvements will add more to value than they cost. Beyond a point improvements will cost more than they will increase value.	Improvements will not necessarily cause value to increase in proportion to costs. Developers should think in terms of the *optimal* extent of improvements.

been developed. Each theory suggests that cities will have a particular segregation of land uses. In spite of the fact that the models provide different pictures of land use, they should not be viewed as competitive. Rather, they all provide insights into land use patterns, and they differ mainly in the degree to which complexities that more accurately reflect actual situations are introduced.

Concentric Circle Theories

Concentric circle theories present urban development as expansion outward from the urban center. What emerges is a view of a city that grows like rings on a tree. While the concentric circle theory is an

abstraction that fits no city exactly, it provides a foundation for understanding some of the forces that influence real estate patterns.

The reason for the formation of concentric circles is that some activities will outbid other activities for land in a particular area. Similar
activities will have similar preferences for access. Hence, homogeneous land use districts will form.

Suppose there were three types of land use as shown in Figure 5–2.
Each use has a rent-bid curve that indicates preference for central
business district locations because these are the most accessible, but
the preference—in terms of willingness and ability to pay— is strongest for major stores, financial services, and similar activities. Thus,
commercial and financial land activities dominate near the center of the
city. The land use patterns that develop from this stylized model tend
to be circular.

Expensive land will also be used most intensively because developers will want to "squeeze" more square feet of rentable space into
expensive land than into cheap land. Hence, we can picture a "density

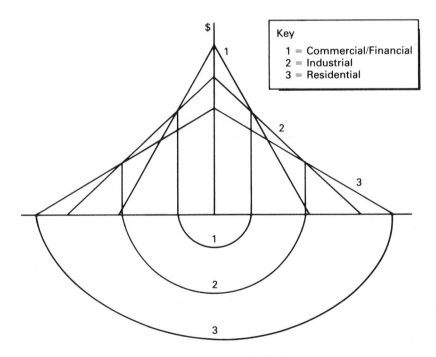

Figure 5–2. Concentric circles.

function" similar to the rent-bid curve. It would show high density near the maximum access point or central city.

Burgess' Empirical Study. Ernest W. Burgess was the first to show that the concentric circle theory applied to "real-world" cities. Largely on the basis of an intensive study of Chicago, he identified the five district areas of a city.

The primary cause of changes in land use, according to Burgess, was growth. As the city developed, interior rings pushed outward and land use was changed from one purpose to another. This was most apparent and created the most problems in the transitional zone because industrial and residential uses are least compatible, but it is a dynamic force that is pervasive within the city.

Complicating the Circles

The concentric circle perspective, based upon the principles of access and highest and best use, provides a general picture of an "average city." But when the theoretical map is compared with the actual landscape of any particular city, the gap between theoretical prediction and observation becomes obvious—and can be a source of embarrassment to anyone who uncritically accepts theoretical predictions. Several additional considerations can narrow the gap.

Axial Theory. The concentric circle model is based upon the assumption that transportation costs are about the same in all directions. The recognition of a highway system requires modifications in the concentric circle model. A location near a main highway is more accessible to other parts of the city than a location not served by good roads. Consequently we would expect land use to be affected by the transportation system. Figure 5–3 is a land use pattern that might exist if two major highways crossed a city. The shape of the rings changes because access qualities of points A and B may be equal even though distances from major markets may vary. Of course, the construction of secondary roads or a beltway around the city would require further modification, but with an understanding of the underlying principles, informed judgments about the effects of new highways can be made.

The realizations that road construction improves access, enhances property values, and determines the city's growth path have led to speculation on the part of some investors when they learn a new highway is being planned. One kind of speculation has been for individuals

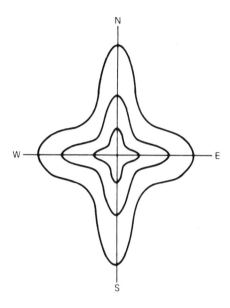

Figure 5–3. Axial development.

to purchase land that will be condemned by eminent domain when the state purchases the right of way. The hope is that the state will offer to pay a price above the current market. Others have been more subtle in their speculation. An investor might purchase a strip of houses that will not be condemned, but will border a new highway. The price of such residential properties will fall when it is known that they will be next to a new highway. After the highway is completed, the properties may be rezoned for commercial use. Indeed, a zoning board would be inclined to grant such a request, since the housing may be poorly suited for residential use. By this process investors have purchased property with good accessibility at low cost. Still other investors have made purchases near the outskirts of a city when it is believed that a new highway will result in more accessibility. Later, the land may be subdivided into prime residential land.

Scale Economies and Lumpiness.   The literal interpretation of the concentric circle theory would imply that some land uses would occupy long, narrow strips around a city. In reality, land use "clumps" appear because of economies of scale and the need for certain activities to be near one another. For example, the balance of cost and access may make a location 2 miles from the city center the most desirable location for warehousing. But because of economies in large-scale railroad terminals—loading and unloading facilities, etc.—there is pressure for wholesale establishments to cluster in circles around the terminal, not around the center of the city. Thus, while the circular pattern may be true for very broad categories, economies of scale change that pattern. Figure 5–4 illustrates a lumpy pattern that might result.

As cities grow, secondary and tertiary centers develop and further distort the concentric circle model. While trips to the central business district (CBD) are occasionally necessary if individuals want to purchase specialty items that require a citywide market, outlying areas are able to support most retail services. Additional development will be attracted to the area because of the advantages of cluster locations, and the retail services will create employment. A market for multiple-family dwellings may develop.

Speculation.   Speculation is a reason for leaving land undeveloped. Speculators often keep large tracts of land in agricultural use in the hope that it will become suitable for more intensive development. Golf

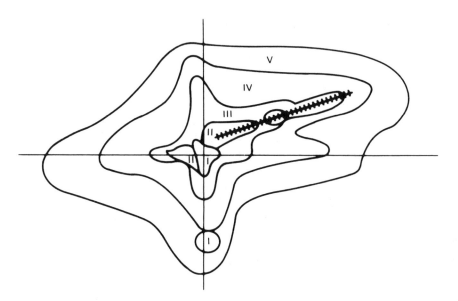

Figure 5–4. Lumpiness and land use.

ranges, horse farms, and small private parks are frequently temporary uses of land owned primarily for speculation. Speculation is a particularly important element in land use patterns in fast-growing cities such as Dallas. Indeed, several major cities have farms within their boundaries because of "leapfrogging" in the development process.

Speculation requires differences of opinion regarding future property values and, ultimately, differences of opinion regarding the underlying economic conditions that affect the value. The speculative real estate market is characterized by frequent transactions as speculators purchase property from each other. Often the transactions provide the *appearance* of price increases. However, Lindeman has shown that the price increases may not reflect changes in land value. Frequently, they simply reflect the fact that the seller is financing the sale and giving favorable financial terms. For instances, if Jones purchased a property for $100,000 cash and sold it to Williams for $120,000, it would appear that the property appreciated. But if Williams financed the purchase by giving Jones a note that carried a below-market interest rate, then the "true" price could be considerably less than $120,000. Creative financing is common in speculative markets because speculators are anxious to leverage their investment and because traditional lenders are often reluctant to lend in speculative markets.

Lindeman noted five characteristics of speculative market financing[2]:

1. The contractual sales price exceeds the cost value of the land.
2. The seller accepts a down payment of less than 30% of the sale.
3. The note is secured by a purchase money mortgage on the property.
4. Interest-only mortgages for initial periods are common.
5. The interest rate on the note understates the true risk inherent in holding the note.

At first the below-market financing supports sales price increases, which stimulates further speculation. The boom may collapse when speculators cannot pay the mortgage notes, forcing a cash sale and a true realization of market value.

Political, Social, and Geographical Factors.   Land use is also affected by characteristics unique to the site. Geologists or geographers have a different perspective about land use than do the analytical presentations based upon the concepts of access and highest and best use.

The geographer might stress the importance of terrain. The subsurface near a lake may not support high-rise construction; a river causes a sharp discontinuity in land use that could not be predicted based upon the principles described above. The historian might cite the importance of a rail spur as the impetus for the first hotel or saloon. Once the initial CBD has been established, it tends to be self-perpetuating. Almost every city has folklore that has little to do with economic principles describing how a particular building site was selected.

The historical and geographical perspectives provide important detail needed to understand the development of a particular city; the more abstract analysis helps us to understand land use patterns in general, but fits no city exactly. However, there is no conflict between the approaches—they all provide important insights into past growth and future trends.

DYNAMIC PERSPECTIVES

The discussion thus far has built upon the tenet that alternative activities will pay varying amounts of rent for the access that each site offers. Through competitive bidding among activities, predictable land use systems emerge. This conceptual view of development aids our understanding of the forces that are involved, but it does not answer all of our questions. Why, for example, does the financial sector outbid other activities for central city land? How will future events affect the locational advantages of alternative locations? In order to answer these kinds of questions, we need to examine the locational requirements of business and households.

First, we ought to ask why financial and commercial activities dominate the CBD. It has been argued persuasively that financial and business activities place the highest value upon quick access to other individuals in related fields. For example, much of the real estate lawyer's time is spent in meetings with other lawyers, developers, and officials of other financial institutions. Telephones may reduce the number of necessary face-to-face meetings, but there appears to be a social aspect to the nature of human beings that makes personal contact an important element in most business transactions. Perhaps this dimension is best exemplified by the business lunch. The individuals who need to be involved in transactions vary on practically a daily basis. The lawyer may need quick access to public records or a law library. Thus, individuals in many related fields find it advantageous to work in the same area. Coupled with the necessity of personal access is that these executives or entrepreneurs are generally highly paid. Their time is valuable, so it would not be economically sound to require them to drive all over the city, from one outlying location to another, for various meetings. People in general and executives in particular are the most expensive commodities to transport because their time has significant opportunity costs. Thus, individuals in financial and related activities are willing and able to outbid other uses in order to avoid these opportunity costs. As transportation costs are altered or the need for face-to-face communication decreases, the locational attraction of the center city will decrease. The increased use of home computers with modems will accelerate this trend.

Retail establishments value customer accessibility. Individuals like to consolidate shopping trips, and therefore they will prefer to shop in an area where they can make other purchases without additional trips. Consequently, the major agglomeration of retail establishments tends to be found near the financial area in Burgess' Zone I. However, a trend of central retail district decline and gains for outlying shopping complexes is apparent in most major cities. Can this shift be understood in the context of the land use principles described above?

One reason for the shift is that the suburban shopping centers are accessible to the affluent segment of the market. Furthermore, access to downtown (relative to outlying) retail centers has been diminished due to failures of mass transit, improvements in intraurban highway networks, and the increasing need for automobile space.

At the same time that some elements in the environment encourage change, there are strong forces that encourage stability and consequently slow down the rate of change. The strength of inertia is especially important in financial and commercial real estate. The long life and fixity of real property is one factor that prevents sudden shifts in land use patterns. If the locational advantage of an area diminishes, rents will fall in the short run, and only in the long run will land use change. An additional factor, of possibly greater importance, is the mutual dependency of economic activities. Let's return to the example of the real estate lawyer to illustrate the point. Suppose she lives somewhere in Zone V, as do hundreds of other individuals with whom she must deal in the course of a year. They might all be better off to rent office space near a subcenter rather than in the CBD. But when the lawyer's office lease expires, she will be reluctant to be among the first lawyers to set up office in the area because all the advantages of the central location will be lost. Others will feel the same way. Since no one will want to be the first to move, none will move, even though many individuals would prefer the outlying location *if* it were established.

The same principle applies to commercial establishments. The downtown commercial district attracts individuals not only because of its location but also because of the variety of stores that are there. All the shop owners might decide to move if they could do so together. But locational decisions are made individually, and no single store would be willing to relinquish the advantages of being located near the other commercial establishments.

The manufacturing plants generally require access to long-haul transportation facilities. During the developmental periods of most cities, this access required proximity to railroads. Since the terminals of the national transportation network were located near the central city, manufacturers have been historically bound to these sites. However, because of the improvements in truck transportation, the dependence of many manufacturers on locations near rail terminals has been diminished. A trend toward outlying manufacturing locations has been reported, particularly among establishments that require the kind of work force most often found in suburban areas. Also, manufacturing is often incompatible with other activities because of pollution, noise, and odor. This fact explains why manufacturers' shifts to the suburbs have been selective. The most offensive activities have remained in the city near the lower-income housing. However, a warehousing district often buffers manufacturing areas from commercial and residential use, thus decreasing effects of land use incompatibility.

Residential land is the predominate urban real estate use. On the surface it may seem strange that the poor live so close to the most valuable property in the city and the more affluent congregate further away on lots that are often less expensive per acre. According to Muth, this outcome is a result of increasing preference for large lots as income rises. This preference for large lots can be expressed most economically in outlying areas. Of course, the costs of commuting also rise—if we assume that the opportunity cost of time spent commuting increases with income. But the preference for those things that are associated with outlying locations more than offsets the cost of commuting.

NEIGHBORHOOD GROWTH AND CHANGE

The spatial area that has the most immediate impact upon the value of an individual property is the neighborhood. A neighborhood represents a set of individuals and institutions to which a property has most immediate access. Conversely, a property is most accessible to other nearby properties. It is difficult to overstate the importance of the neighborhood as a determinant of land use and value. While it is most common to think primarily of residential neighborhoods—and most of the discussion will be in these terms—commercial and industrial neighborhoods also exist, as do mixed land use neighborhoods.

The Concept of Neighborhood

A neighborhood is difficult to define because it encompasses social, physical, and economic dimensions. Social definitions include the vicinity near one's home, an area in which one feels at home, and an area where one lives in proximity to friends and family. Neighborhoods were once the source of strong social and kinship ties and employment, and the place in which individuals lived most of their lives. In these areas, the neighborhood tavern often has a key social role. Yet the social-kinship neighborhood is declining in importance. Urban neighborhoods are becoming more homogeneous in terms of income, but the social-kinship ties have weakened.

The physical environment is a critical factor in delineating a neighborhood because it limits access and thus limits the scope of social contact. The cohesiveness of many neighborhoods has been destroyed by the construction of a highway that severed the existing access patterns. On the other hand, physical impediments are not necessary for neighborhood delineation. Many sharply defined neighborhoods exist in the absence of any physical dividing lines. Classic examples are racial divisions on either side of an ordinary local street.

Several levels of neighborhoods have been identified by Lee.[3] The smallest area is a *social acquaintance neighborhood* which includes only a few streets and is, except for a possible convenience grocery, almost totally residential. Proximity results in a high proportion of individuals knowing each other either directly or indirectly through mutual friends. The *homogeneous neighborhood* has a wider boundary and includes residential houses that are of similar character. Residents may not know each other personally, but they generally have a feeling that they share a common set of beliefs and belong to the same social class. Many individuals feel secure in the knowledge that they are similar to this wider set of neighbors. The *unit neighborhood* includes a range of nonresidential activities. It includes individuals who have little socioeconomic similarity but who attend the same church, shop in the same retail strips, or are in a common high school attendance area.

From the point of view of most real estate activity, the social acquaintance neighborhood is not as important a selling point as the homogeneous and unit neighborhoods because prospective buyers seldom know of the social networks that exist until after they have moved into an area. However, in terms of economic stability, the social acquaintance neighborhood is often important because it is a unit that provides social incentive for maintenance of property. The larger units can be though of as being composed of several social acquaintance neighborhoods.

The homogeneous and unit neighborhoods tend to have the same overall pattern of neighborhood growth and decline. If a homogeneous neighborhood loses economic value, for example, this will have an adverse effect on the unit neighborhood also.

Economic and Demographic Change

Neighborhoods also have economic characteristics in common. Most importantly, neighborhoods have a common change pattern. This common cycle explains why analysis of the neighborhood is an important feature of most estimates of a property's value and why a prospective home buyer will be well advised to examine the neighborhood as carefully as the specific property. Indeed, prospective buyers should walk through the neighborhood rather than just drive by the area. Furthermore, the neighborhood should also be examined at different times of the day and on weekdays as well as weekends to get an accurate idea of the area's character. Many individuals examine property only on Sunday afternoons and consequently get a distorted picture of an area.

Neighborhood Life Cycles.   Appraisers have suggested that typical areas have a life cycle of approximately 100 years.[4] Stages in the neighborhood life cycle include:

1. Development. The first 15–20 years constitute the development period. Relative values peak during this stage as improvements are completed, roads and sidewalks are installed, trees mature, etc. The length of time to maturity depends largely upon the size of the project.
2. Decline. As the properties no longer fulfill the needs of the original buyers, values start to decline. For example, the area may lose some of its fashion or conspicuous consumption appeal. A new class of individuals move into the neighborhood.
3. Transitionary periods. As word spreads that a certain neighbor-

hood is affordable to lower-income groups, prices may rebound slightly, but they will not attain the previous peak levels. Transitionary periods may be repeated several times as the neighborhood passes through different stages. For example, after passing from a middle- to lower-income area—or as one broker put it, a bourbon to beer neighborhood—many houses may be converted to multifamily use.

4. Blight. At some stage a neighborhood may reach a period where abandonment is frequent. Few properties are maintained, and violation of housing codes is common. Investors have low expectations about the area's future. Property values are at their lowest.

5. Rehabilitation. Concerted efforts may have brought about change; the character of land use rises. Often this stage occurs only after the disinvestment process is completed, but occasionally it will occur before the period of blight.

The Department of Housing and Urban Development has used a more pessimistic model.[5] The stages in the HUD model are (1) healthy neighborhood, (2) incipient decline, (3) decline, (4) accelerated decline, and (5) abandonment. The major difference between the life-cycle stages cited before and the HUD model is that the HUD model does not imply that revitalization is a natural stage. The evidence indicates that abandonment is occasionally, but not always, followed by redevelopment.

Filtering.   The residential neighborhood cycle is propelled by a process known as *filtering*. Burgess described metropolitan dynamics as a moving outward of interior land uses. Later, Hoyt emphasized the importance of the movement of upper-middle-income individuals to the periphery along the transportation routes. Lower-income groups follow the path established by the wealthy. From the perspective of the residential neighborhood this is seen as the movement of lower-income families into areas that were once the domain of the next-higher-income class. Alternatively, the dwelling units can be thought of as *filtering down* to the next-lowest use.

Of course the filtering process has been a source of a great deal of misunderstanding and social tension. Some individuals see their neighborhood's changes as the result of being invaded by a lower class rather than as a result of upper-income individuals vacating housing, which then becomes available to lower-income groups. This attitude is especially prevalent among families who, because of financial inability to move, feel trapped in the area.

The importance of the filtering process has been widely recognized as a mechanism whereby housing is made available to lower-income families. Filtering is probably more important than all the low-income federal housing programs combined. However, what has not been recognized is that the filtering process also enables the higher-income groups to move outward into new, more expensive housing. Because the next-lowest-income group provides a resale market for the housing that will be sold, higher-income groups can purchase more expensive housing. The revenues from the sale of a home generally make up the bulk of the down payment for the subsequent home purchase.

As Ring pointed out in his analysis of the neighborhood life cycle, the transition to a lower-income group is associated with a change in the physical nature of the property. For example, a single-family house may be subdivided. Exterior and interior maintenance will be less. The reason for these changes is that the poor tend to consume less of everything—including housing—than the more affluent. Dividing existing units into multifamily units and lowering maintenance expenditures are two ways of providing housing at lower rents without decreasing profits.

Commercial Neighborhoods

We are more used to thinking in terms of residential rather than commercial neighborhoods. Nevertheless, commercial establishments form complementary and competitive clusters. In a sense, these may be thought of as commercial neighborhoods.

The complementary aspect of commercial neighborhoods stems from the desire of individuals to minimize shopping trips. Thus, even at the smallest level, a variety store and a grocery store may find it advantageous to locate together. Each establishment benefits from the customers that the other store attracts, and some individuals who need both groceries and lightbulbs will travel to the two-store cluster area rather than make separate stops first at a grocery and then at a variety store. This may be true even though the total driving distance to the cluster may be greater than the separate stops. The success of small neighborhood shopping centers, as well as large regional shopping centers, depends upon—among other factors—the degree to which individual stores complement one another.

Competitive establishments also have a tendency to cluster together. One reason that similar competing establishments tend to locate near each other has been labeled the *principle of median location*. Figure 5–5 helps to illustrate the concept. Assume that the line repre-

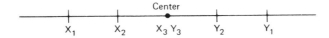

Figure 5-5. The principle of median location.

sents a beach with vacationers distributed evenly along its length. X and Y are hot-dog vendors. They have easily movable stands, and they sell identical products at identical prices. Thus, customers will purchase from the vendor with the nearest stand. Suppose the vendors initially locate along the beach as indicated by superscript 1. Each will sell to one-half of the market because those to the right of the center will purchase from Y and those to the left will purchase from X. However, this is not a stable situation because Y may realize that he can increase his market by moving to the location indicated by Y_2. X will then move and, following the logic of the process, both will end up at the center. At this point neither will be able to gain further advantage from moving. The locational attractiveness of the center would be reinforced if we assumed that the population were concentrated at the center rather than evenly distributed.

The principle of median location is not the only reason for concentration of similar commercial establishments. There is a widely noticed tendency for businesses, such as automobile dealerships, to locate near one another. Why would a Chevrolet dealer locate next to a Ford on the same intersection or along the same strip as a Ford and Chrysler dealer? The answer again is that individuals like to consolidate shopping trips. Most people who shop for cars will want to compare the major brands, so they will be inclined to visit a particular dealership if it is near other, competitive, dealers. This tendency of establishments that sell similar competitive products to locate near one another might be called the showcase effect. Examples of other types of establishments that have this symbiotic relationship include shoe, clothing, and jewelry stores.

MEASURING MARKET DEMAND FOR RETAIL SPACE

The amount of demand for retail space in a particular neighborhood depends upon the underlying demand for retail purchases. The case study you will read in Chapter 8 shows that before a decision to increase the retail shopping space could be made, the real estate analyst had to study the size of the market.

Business location experts have conducted numerous studies to measure the size of a retail market within an urban area. Generally these studies include surveys in which shoppers were asked where they made retail purchases and where they lived. By examining the relationship between where individuals live and where they shop, several generalizations can be made that may help determine the demand for commercial real estate.[6]

1. The number of consumers shopping at a specific shopping area varies with the distance from the shopping area.
2. The proportion of consumers within a particular neighborhood who frequent a shopping center depends upon the size of the shopping area. Larger shopping centers have a larger draw.
3. The distance a consumer will travel to shop for a product depends upon the type of product. Generally more expensive products will induce individuals to travel longer distances.
4. The attraction of a shopping area depends upon the nature of competing shopping areas.

The above rules of thumb can be helpful to real estate developers. However, it may be more useful to have a methodology that can give a more precise estimate of the underlying retail demand. Huff developed a probabilistic model to determine shopping patterns within a metropolitan area. This approach can be used to develop a more quantitative estimate of underlying demand and, ultimately, the demand for real estate.[7]

Assume that the likelihood that an individual located at a particular point, say point i, would shop at a particular shopping center depends upon (1) the distance between the customer and the destination, (2) the number of competing shopping places, and (3) the size (actual or proposed) of the shopping center being studied. Mathematically these ideas may be expressed:

$$P_i = \left(\frac{S_q}{T_q^{\,b}}\right) \div \left[\sum_{j=1}^{n} \frac{S_j}{T_j^{\,b}}\right]$$

where P_i = probability that a person living in area i will shop at the center in question

S_j = size (measured in square feet of shopping space) of competing shopping areas

S_q = size of the shopping center under consideration

T_j = distance between i and each competing shopping center (usually measured in driving time)

T_q = distance between i and the shopping center under consideration

b = exponent usually equal to 2 (to be exact the exponent should be estimated separately in each situation. However, separate estimation requires a great deal of data collection, and so 2 is often used as a rough and ready approximation)

An Application of the Model

In order to see how the model is applied, assume a developer is planning to construct a small neighborhood shopping strip of 10,000 square feet. There are two existing centers, A and B, with areas of 15,000 and 20,000 square feet, respectively. What is the likelihood that an individual located in area i will shop at the proposed center? Area i is 2 units of travel time from the proposed center, A is 3 units away, and B is 4 units away. Applying the retail trade model yields:

$$P_i = \frac{\dfrac{10,000}{2^2}}{\dfrac{10,000}{2^2} + \dfrac{15,000}{3^2} + \dfrac{20,000}{4^2}} = 0.46$$

Thus the probability of an individual in area i shopping at the proposed center is .46. We may interpret this result as 46% of the population in i shopping only at the proposed center, or more realistically, that average shoppers will make 46% of their trips to i.

The estimate of the likelihood of shopping at the proposed center must be supplemented with additional data before the volume of retail trade can be estimated. Specifically,we would need to know (1) the population size of area i and (2) the expenditures per capita. Data on the population size of various areas can be obtained from local sources. Furthermore, areas are often defined as census tracts so that census data can provide an estimate of population. Expenditures per capita can be estimated by direct survey. In addition, estimates on annual household budget expenditures by product category for various levels of income are available from data published by the U.S. Bureau of Labor Statistics. *Survey of Buying Power*, published by Sales Management, contains similar data.

Returning to the task of estimating retail trade at the proposed center, assume that the population of area i is 8,000. Suppose also that we determined that the average family spends $700 per year on the type of retail goods anticipated for the proposed center. Then the amount of trade estimated for the center from i would equal:

$$.46 \times 700 \times 8,000 = \$2,576,000$$

The market estimating procedure indicates only the sales likely to come from individuals in area i. In order to develop a complete estimate of demand at the proposed center, the same procedure would have to be followed for every area.

Share of Space Approach

The probabilistic model described above may require more data collection than is practical. This may be particularly true if the development under consideration is small. Mason and Mayer describe a rule of thumb that assumes that a store will attract customers in proportion to its square footage relative to the square footage of competing shops.[8] They describe six steps:

1. Determine the trade area for the proposed site. In doing so, consider competition, access, and income.
2. Estimate the population of the trade area.
3. Determine the sales per capita as a measure of market potential.
4. Multiply per capita sales by the population of the trade area. This is the aggregate market potential.
5. Calculate the competitive square footage in the trade area. Then calculate the ratio of square footage of the proposed center to that of the competing centers.
6. Multiply the ratio calculated in Step 5 times the aggregate market potential. The result is the estimated sales at the subject site.

Clearly the share of space approach requires less work, and that is a major advantage. However, the results may be less accurate because the share approach does not account for the drop-off due to distance.

SUMMARY

Cities are composed of distinct land use areas. The land uses are not determined randomly, but are a function of underlying economic forces. Cities across the world have similar patterns of land use that suggest a regularity. Furthermore, land use areas change over time in response to the same underlying forces.

Three concepts of land use determination are highest and best use, accessibility, and site value principles. The highest and best use principle states that individuals will put their property in the use that generates the most satisfaction to them, subject to zoning ordinances and other legal restrictions. In order to operationalize the concept, "highest and best" is interpreted to mean the most profitable legal use. Highest and best does not imply the most socially desirable use, nor does it suggest the most intensive use. It is the use that provides the highest present value residual to land. The principle of accessibility states that the more accessible land is to positive activity in the city, the greater shall be its value. (Conversely, access to negative activities such as crime will diminish value.) However, *access* is a multidimensional concept because different activities seek access to different things. Thus, a business will seek access to inputs or markets, whereas households seek access to good schools or congenial neighbors. Site value principles provide ways to analyze the site that may influence highest and best use.

The concentric circle theory of urban development may be derived from the principles of highest and best use and accessibility. The concentric circle theory assumes that land near the center of the city is the most accessible and hence the most valuable. Rents for land near the center are greatest; finance, services, and commercial activity tend to outbid other enterprises and characterize downtown city land use. Residential housing tends to dominate farther away from the center where it outbids other uses. The concentric circle model can be modified to account for roads, scale economies, lumpiness, speculation, sociopolitical factors, and geographical irregularities. The modifications change the theoretical map, but they are consistent with the fundamental theory. The principle of highest and best use also explains why land uses change. It was argued that increases in transportation costs would increase the rent-bid curve near the most accessible locations.

The neighborhood life cycle was described as consisting of five stages: (1) development, (2) decline, (3) transitionary periods, (4) blight, and (5) rehabilitation. The filtering process, where individuals in lower social and economic categories reside in areas vacated by groups moving into better housing, is an important mechanism to the neighborhood cycle.

Commercial neighborhoods also develop as businesses locate near one another in what is often a symbiotic relationship. The complementary aspect of commercial neighborhoods stems from the desire of individuals to minimize shopping trips. Even competitive establishments cluster for this reason. Yet the clustering causes rents to rise, which may discourage some commercial activities.

Techniques to measure retail sales potential are useful because estimates of retail sales are an input into the determination of the demand for commercial real estate.

6

Understanding and Forecasting Urban and Regional Growth

Two characteristics of real estate are long economic life and physical immobility. Because of these two factors, the value of a property is linked closely to the long-term economic prosperity of the area in which it is located. The value of property is largely a function of the future benefits resulting from ownership. Therefore, if the expected future growth prospects of an area decline, the present value of real estate may decline even if there is no change in current income or employment. Certainly the amount of new construction will be affected. Indeed, differences in real estate activity among urban areas are so critical that it is almost always inappropriate to rely solely upon national trends to analyze current or future real estate prospects for a specific city. Consequently, a market study should consider regional growth. The purpose of this chapter is to present the theoretical and quantitative tools necessary to understand the citywide determinants of real estate activity.

Building permits are an excellent index of overall real estate activity in a city because a move by one family into a newly constructed home will induce a series of other relocations via the filtering process. Building activity also indicates price trends. Since construction costs generally rise over time, the newly constructed properties exert a pull on the rest of the market. How can we account for the large variations in building activity? Population change is a partial explanation. But what causes population change? Both demographic and economic factors affect the growth rate. Demographic influences such as migration patterns have a considerable impact on land use. This phenomenon was pointed out by Plattner.[1] He contended that people were migrating to the West and South for retirement as well as for employment reasons. Economic growth or decline affects the availability of jobs. Economic incentives also have an impact on peoples' choice of location. The evidence shows that there has been, and will continue to be, a significant outflow of people from central cities in all regions of the country to the suburban areas. Middle-income families are moving out, while poor families are moving into central cities. This movement is partly attributed to welfare benefits available in the cities. Welfare costs may drive the middle-class families to the suburbs. Plattner suggested that the very wealthy and the poor will live in the cities, and the middle class will move to the suburbs. The Census Bureau reported that over half of interurban migration is accounted for by the poor. This represents movements with a low effective demand for housing.

Economic growth or decline affects the availability of jobs. Growth differentials among localities are determined largely by rates of migration. A report by the U.S. Bureau of the Census concluded that well over one-half of all interurban migration in the United States was job-related.[2] Therefore, an important element in the study of local real estate activity is an understanding of urban economic growth.

THE CIRCULAR FLOW MODEL

A *circular flow diagram* of a local economy is shown in Figure 6–1. This highly simplified model divides the local economy into two conceptual categories: households and businesses. The categories are con-

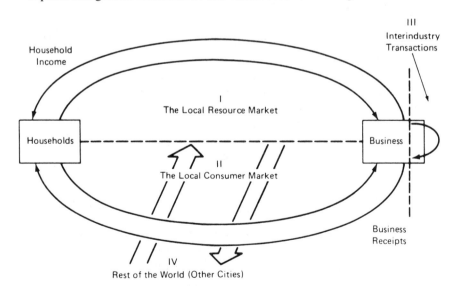

Figure 6–1. A local circular flow and interregional trade model.

ceptual because the same person may run a business and a household. The upper portion of the diagram labeled "The Local Resource Market" shows that business purchases factors of production (land, labor, capital, and enterprise) from households. In return for the factors of production, households receive wages, rents, interest, and profits. If none of the households earn income outside of the community, the sum of payments received by households from local producers will equal total local income. The "Local Consumer Market" encompasses the second set of transactions. This market is shown in the lower portion of Figure 6–1. If we assume no nonlocal customers, local consumers will account for the total business receipts. Third, interfirm sales are an important group of local transactions. Establishments within a city buy and sell intermediate goods and services from one another. For example, a local grocery may purchase canned goods from a local wholesale distributor. These exchanges are depicted by the loop within the local business sector labeled "Interindustry Transactions."

Monetary Flows

Exchange with the rest of the nation and international trade are also important to a locality's economy. Indeed, the key difference between the local model and a comparable national economic model is the extent of outside trade. Monetary inflows and outflows (exports and imports) constitute a very small percentage of economic activity for the United States as a whole, but they are extremely significant for local economies. Exports constitute only about 6% of the U.S. gross national product. Six percent is a significant percentage and implies that international trade is important. For instance, the U.S. imports many critical products—particularly raw materials—not available domestically. On the other hand, outside trade may account for 50–70% of the economic activity in small communities.

The difference between the size of the monetary inflows and outflows is critical to local economic growth. Monetary inflows increase the entire volume of money that circulates within a city. This in turn increases employment. A major source of income for the community is payments for goods produced in the city and sold elsewhere. For example, when a Detroit-made automobile is sold to a resident of Chicago (or more accurately, to an auto dealer who expects to sell to a Chicago resident), income flows into Detroit. Sales of goods and services to nonlocal customers are often referred to as *exports*. Other nonlocal sources of community income include interest payments from outside corporations, government transfers such as Social Security, gifts received, and investments by nonresidents.

Monetary outflows shrink an area's circular flow and consequently decrease local income and employment. For example, when residents of one area increase their purchases from neighboring cities, the outflow represents forgone income to local business—money that could have been paid to households in subsequent transactions. Purchases of goods and services from nonlocal sources are called *imports*. The term *imports* applies to all purchases made outside the city and not just to international transactions. Thus, the resident of Chicago who purchases a car from Detroit causes an outflow of funds from Chicago and, assuming auto retailers maintain their inventories, an inflow of dollars to Detroit.

What is the equilibrium condition of the model represented in Figure 6–1? When monetary outflows equal monetary inflows, community income will remain constant. The equilibrium condition can be proved mathematically, but it can also be grasped intuitively by the bathtub analogy. The amount of water in the tub will remain constant only when the water flowing from the faucet equals the amount that leaves through the drain. However, the condition of equilibrium does not imply stagnation. The composition of the inflows and outflows can change, and new products may be exported or imported. The mix of jobs will change, and some families will enter and others will leave the city. But as long as the monetary exchanges with the rest of the world are equal, the size of the circular flow will remain constant.

The Multiplier

Economic growth in both community income and employment results from increases in the volume of transactions per period of time. As the volume of business begins to expand, multiplier or ripple effects will further increase the amount of activity. In order to illustrate the multiplier, suppose a business earns increased income by selling its products in a nearby state. A portion of the increase will accrue to households as payment for labor and other services involved in producing the output. Households will spend a fraction of the increased earnings in local establishments, thereby expanding the local consumer market and allowing businesses to purchase additional factors of production. However, businesses and households will purchase from outside the area and cause monetary outflows. Therefore, the process of local spending and respending will not continue indefinitely. Figure 6–2 illustrates

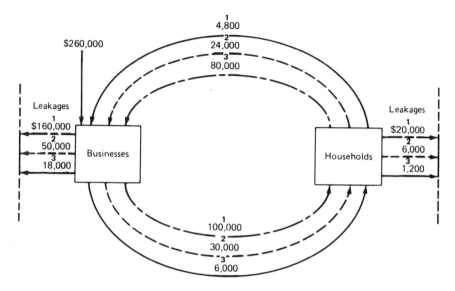

Figure 6–2. A community's income-expenditure pattern.

what might happen if a major convention were held in Star City. Of the $260,000 in increased spending, $160,000 went to outside suppliers and to the nonlocal corporation that owns the major hotel. One hundred thousand dollars of income for local residents who provided services for the conventioneers was created. Eighty thousand dollars of the original $100,000 is spent locally, while $20,000 flows outside the city. Carrying the process further, we can see that of the $80,000 spent at local business, $50,000 is used to replace inventories (purchased outside the city) and $30,000 is given by business to residents as payment for services. The process continues, and after a few rounds the original $100,000 leaks out of the community in the form of business and consumer spending. But because of successive rounds of local spending, $40,000 of household income is created in addition to the initial $100,000. The larger the leakages per transaction, the smaller the total increase in household income.

The multiplier has a different effect if the monetary inflow occurs in a single period or if it is a permanent increase. In order to distinguish between the two impacts, assume local convention business increased permanently by $260,000 annually. An extra $100,000 would be earned every period. Community income would be $130,000 in the second

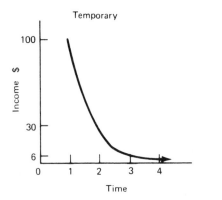
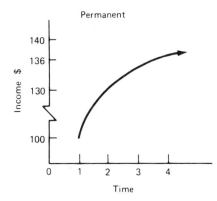

Figure 6–3. Temporary and permanent increases in a community's monetary inflows.

round—the $30,000 shown in Figure 6–2 plus the extra $100,000 earnings. Total income would rise to $136,000 (100,000 + 30,000 + 6,000) in the third round. Thus the increase in inflows would cause community income to rise permanently to $140,000 annually. Figure 6–3 compares the income effects of a temporary and permanent increase in monetary inflows.

THE EXPORT BASE THEORY OF GROWTH

The previous section described the major types of monetary inflows and outflows. However, some monetary inflows are caused by economic growth. They are not likely to increase by themselves. This section describes the most widely accepted causal model of local economic growth and decline. The export base theory is an empirical statement of what kinds of activity cause economic growth and what kinds of activity are the result of economic growth.

The export base theory assumes that local business may be divided into two categories. Businesses in the first category are industries that sell goods and services to nonresidents and, consequently, earn money for the area; these industries are referred to as *basic* or *export* industries. Firms in the second category are the establishments that sell goods and services in the local consumer market to residents. These activities are referred to as *service* or *nonbasic*. Tiebout described the fundamental relationships posed by the export base theory:

Export markets are considered the prime movers of the local economy. If employment serving this market rises or falls, employment serving the local market is presumed to move in the same direction. When the factory (export) closes retail merchants (local) feel the impact as laid-off factory workers have less to spend. Because of this prime mover role, export employment is considered as "basic." Employment which serves the local market is considered adaptive and is titled "non-basic."[3]

The key idea behind the economic base theory is that export (basic) activity is the engine of growth. Income originally earned by the export sector is spent and respent, creating a multiplier effect. Export industries generate the money that flows into the city. A portion of the export-earned dollars are in turn spent locally by the export workers, creating local service jobs.

The export base theory of growth conforms to the model represented by Figure 6–1. Export base theorists believe that income from exports—represented as a monetary inflow in Figure 6–1—is the community income that is most likely to change due to forces outside the city.

The local multiplier concept is also important in understanding the relationship between exports and the community's overall income and employment growth. For each dollar of output that a local firm sells, a fraction is used to purchase supplies and inventories from nonlocal firms. This fraction leaves the local income stream. Another fraction of the sales dollars goes to local households and thus becomes local income. Therefore, unlike a gift from a rich uncle or an increase in Social Security payments, only a fraction of export earnings actually becomes local income. However, given the initial income increase, the spending process—the multiplier effect—is the same as that shown in Figure 6–1. The additional spending then results from the initial increase in export earnings and may be termed *induced spending*.

Local retail stores and service establishments are likely to benefit from induced spending, whereas local manufacturing establishments may sell very little in the local market. Total community income will increase by more than the initial increase in income earned by the exporting industry. Equation (1) is a symbolic restatement of the export base theory of urban growth. It shows the importance of the multiplier, k.

$$\Delta T = k\Delta B \qquad (1)$$

where ΔT = the change in total income
   k = the local multiplier
   ΔB = the change in export (basic) income

Equation (1) states that an area's total change in income will be k times the change in basic income; k is greater than 1 because the change in total income (basic + induced or nonbasic income) is always greater than the change in basic income alone.

In the short run, increased export income may result in higher per capita income. Exporting firms may pay for more overtime work or hire unemployed local residents. Wages may rise as local firms compete with one another for employees. However, the availability of jobs and higher wages will eventually encourage migrants, thus increasing population and decreasing wages.

HOW TO DO AN EXPORT BASE STUDY
AND POPULATION FORECAST

Since an understanding of a local economy's prospects constitutes an important element in real estate market analysis, it will be useful to examine how a base study is conducted in practice. Before proceeding, however, a note of caution is in order. Because each local economy has unique characteristics, and because base studies are commissioned for different reasons by different clients, there is no one correct formula for projecting an area's economic future. Different aspects of community growth may be emphasized depending upon the situation. The techniques presented here can serve as a guide, but modifications will almost always be required to tailor a study to a particular goal.

Export base studies generally use employment rather than total community income as the operational variable. The distinction is important because growth of total income that takes the form of increased income per employee will have a different impact on economic activity in general and housing activity in particular than growth due to increases in jobs with income per worker remaining constant. If income per capita increases while total employment remains constant, there will be less overall real estate activity than if increases in employment resulted in migration into the area. Nevertheless, a labor-scarce city—that is, a city with a very low unemployment rate and many job openings—will probably experience both wage and population increases simultaneously. Migration into a city will occur because of both job openings and higher wages.

The *first step* in a base study is to determine the appropriate geographical area. A neighborhood or small community is too small an area for a successful base study because of the extremely high degree of interdependence with the larger metropolitan economy. Such sub-areas do not have a sufficiently developed internal circular flow, and the local workers are generally not even the same individuals as local residents. Consequently, studies of very small areas should be undertaken in conjunction with larger studies of an integrated area. While the appropriate area depends upon the purpose of the study, cities, counties, or standard metropolitan statistical areas are generally chosen for analysis because such areas are integrated economies, export similar items, and are affected by the same trends.

The *second step* is to describe the local economy and determine the sources of export employment. Various government agencies collect detailed and accurate data on employment and other economic indicators that can help in developing an economic profile. Table 6–1 lists published data sources that can be helpful at this stage. In addition to current statistics, the description should include trends so that both expanding and declining industries may be identified. Additional information can be derived by personally contacting officials in the local Chamber of Commerce or government agencies such as the Bureau of Employment Security or business officials. While such direct methods are good data sources and are often the only way to get some types of information, they can be time-consuming and expensive to attain. Furthermore, reliance upon officials or business surveys requires a high degree of cooperation from local officials.

Table 6–2 presents hypothetical employment data for Star City and comparable information for the U.S. economy. Unadjusted employment data do not convey an idea of which local industries are large or small compared with the same industry in other cities. The location quotient shown in column 4 is a good device for measuring the relative size of industries. It is attained by dividing the percentage of the work force in Star City in each category by the comparable statistic for the U.S.:

$$LQ_i = (e_i/e) \div (E_i/E) \qquad (2)$$

where e_i = local employment in industry i
        e = total local employment
        E_i = employment in industry i in the U.S.
        E = total U.S. employment

A location quotient greater than 1 for an industry implies that Star City has a higher percentage of employment in that sector than is the case for the country as a whole; employment is disproportionately

Table 6–1. Published Sources Useful in Economic Base Analysis of Local Areas*

Source	Variables	Comment	Frequency of Publication
Census of Population, Vol. 1 and 2.	Population by age, sex, race, households, education, and income.	Data are essential to the analyst and are available at almost any library.	10 Years
Census of Manufactures, Vol. 3, Area Statistics.	Manufacturing employment, number of establishments, payrolls, capital expenditures, and assets.	Data are disaggregated by industrial category, i.e., food, apparel, etc., manufacturing only.	5 Years
Census of Retail Trade Area Statistics.	Retail employees, size, and business receipts by type of establishment.	Good disaggregation of various activities for SMSAs—drugstore, grocery store, etc.	5 Years
Census of Service Industry—Area Statistics.	Services industry employment, volume of business, and number of establishments.	Used to gauge potential markets, project and analyze sales, and plan new outlets.	5 Years
Census of Wholesale Trade—Area Statistics.	Wholesale sales, inventories, and establishments.	No employment data. Data on inventories, the flow of goods, and other aspects of wholesale trade provide keys to understanding current economic conditions and anticipating the future.	5 Years
Census of Transportation.	Shipments by type of industry to area of destination.	Data only for states and SMSAs. This is a good source if there is a need to estimate major export markets.	5 Years

Table 6–1. Continued

Source	Variables	Comment	Frequency of Publication
County Business Patterns.	Employment and payroll data for all major employment areas.	A good all-around source, although the level of detail is not as great as in other sources shown above.	1 Year
Sales Management Magazine.	Disposable income and market size.	Estimated data: widely used to determine market potential by advertisers.	1 Year

* In addition to these sources, most states, counties, and cities publish statistics on local SMSAs.

Table 6–2. Employment Data for Star City, 1986

	(1)	*(2)* *% in Star City*	*(3)* *% in U.S.*	*(4)* *Location Quotient*	*(5)* *Estimated Export Employment*
Agriculture	1,628	1.2	6.9	.17	—0—
Construction	9,634	7.1	6.2	1.14	1,221
Furniture, lumber and wood	2,985	2.2	1.8	1.22	543
Primary metals	16,841	10.2	2.0	5.1	14,127
Fabricated metals	13,570	10.0	2.1	4.7	10,720
Chemicals	—0—	—	—	—	—0—
Other manufacturing	10,355	7.6	25.0	.30	—0—
Transportation and communications	2,342	1.72	7.6	.22	—0—
Wholesale and release trade	27,783	20.4	18.9	1.07	2,000
Finance, insurance and real estate	11,700	7.2	4.4	1.6	5,799
Services	38,925	25.0	21.6	1.15	4,614
TOTAL	135,763				44,024

Total Population for Star City (1976) = 336,700

concentrated in Star City. If an industry has a location quotient greater than 1, it is usually assumed that exports, rather than unusual consumption patterns, account for the larger than average levels of employment. Conversely, a location quotient of less than 1 indicates that the product is imported.

The location quotient technique is useful as an approximation. For example, Milwaukee, the "beer capital of the world," has a location quotient of 4.6 for the "beverage" category. In general the location quotient accurately reflects export industries. However, the technique has been criticized for failing to take into account differential consumption patterns. A city that has a high level of per capita beer consumption will have a high location quotient even if it exports no beer because a high percentage of the labor force will be employed in beer production. Another important criticism has been called the *product mix* problem. Milwaukee, although a major producer of beer, also imports and exports the product at the same time. A significant number of residents prefer beer produced in other areas and thus it must be imported. Therefore, a location quotient of greater than 1 does not necessarily imply that importation does not exist.

An estimation of the actual number of employees producing goods for export, and consequently earning monetary inflows, is also an important element in the description of a local economy. Under the assumption that a location quotient of 1 implies neither importation nor exportation, export employment for a product can be estimated by:

$$Exp = e_i - e\left(\frac{E_i}{E}\right) \tag{3}$$

where Exp = estimated export employment and all other symbols are as in Equation (2)

The logic of Equation (3) is straightforward. The term $e\left(\frac{E_i}{E}\right)$ is the expected local employment in industry i if the area has the same percentage as the nation. Subtracting this term from e_i—the actual local employment in industry i—equals the extra, or export, employment.

The *third step* in a base study is to determine the local multiplier. The question to be answered is: If basic employment increases by a given amount, how many additional jobs will be created in the city as a whole? What is the value of the multiplier, k, in Equation (1)? Since, depending upon type of work and income, spending habits of workers may vary considerably, we need to explain the value of k for a typical or average worker. Let us therefore assume that each new export employee will support as many nonbasic workers as the current average. In other words, the ratio of the change in total employment to the change in basic employment is equal to the ratio of total to basic employment: $\Delta T/\Delta B = T/B$. From Equation (1), $T/B = k$, and therefore $\Delta T/\Delta B = k$. Since the economic profile discussed in the second step provided information needed to estimate both T and B, the employment multiplier can be estimated. In the example of Star City, the multiplier is 3.08. On the average, for every new export job created, two additional nonbasic workers will be required.

The Star City multiplier is slightly larger than what would be expected in a medium-sized city. Generally, local multipliers range between 1.2 and 3.5. This range is much smaller than the multiplier for the United States as a whole, which ranges between 4 and 5. The reason that the national multiplier is larger than local multipliers is because the monetary outflows or leakages from any (one local) economy are greater than the leakages in a larger economy. Generally a multiplier will be larger in isolated, large, and low-income cities, since each of these characteristics is conducive to purchasing locally rather than traveling to another city to make a purchase.

The *fourth step* is to forecast changes in the local economy. Given the export base theory of development, the fourth step may be divided into two key questions: (1) What are the likely changes in export activity? (2) What additional nonbasic employment will be induced as a result of changes in the export activity? Forecasting changes in export employment is the stage where the judgment of the researcher is most critical and where the possibility of error is greatest. Therefore, it often is useful to develop ranges of estimated employment changes.

A frequently employed estimating technique is to apply national trends to the current local employment levels. For example, if the machine tools industry is growing at 4% annually, the analyst might assume that the exports of the machine tool industry in Star City will grow at 4%. This technique is feasible for local industries that can be expected to grow at the national rate, but some areas may experience an increasing or decreasing share of national employment. For example, textiles were a major export from Boston during the 1950s. Yet, Boston's share of national employment in textiles decreased rapidly during this period. In cases such as these, adjustments to national trends or to national forecasts are essential. Local business and government leaders can be helpful, even essential, when making adjustments to national trends in the export sector.

Table 6–3 is a checklist of questions that ought to be considered when projecting exports.

Once the export employment has been forecast, the multiplier is used to determine total changes in employment. In our example the Star City multiplier is 3.08. If the 10-year forecast is for an increase of 5,000 jobs in the export sectors, then the total change in employment can be estimated as 3.08 × 5,000, or 15,400 jobs. In other words, 10,400 additional jobs could be created and supported in the service sector by the original 5,000 new jobs in exporting.

The *fifth and sixth steps* are to make population and household forecasts based upon the employment estimates generated in the fourth step. By adding the estimated change in total employment ($\Delta \dot{T}$) to the current level of employment (T), future total employment ($\dot{T}$) is derived.[4] Equation (4) states that the relationship between employment and population is determined by the employment participation rate.

$$\dot{T} = r\dot{P} \tag{4}$$

where $\dot{T}$ = total employment
r = employment participation rate
$\dot{P}$ = population

Since $\dot{T}$ was derived in Step 4, all that is needed to estimate population is r, the participation rate. In the example of Star City, the employment participation rate for 1986 is (135,700/336,700), or about .40 ($r = T/P$).

Table 6–3. Export Projection Checklist

Have transportation costs changed new highways, and so forth?

Has the employment in various sectors grown at a significantly faster or slower rate than for the nation?

How do wages compare with national averages?

How do wages compare with the cost of living in the community?

Have any major new plant locations been announced? Anticipated?

Are nonlabor inputs available?

Are current plants and equipment modern or obsolete?

What do demographic-based population projections indicate?

Are major government projects planned for the area?

While r is often assumed to be stable over long periods of time, it is subject to short-term variations during stages of the business cycle. When unemployment in an area rises, r will decrease. In the long run, unemployed families will move, thus tending to restore r to the long-term average. On the other hand, when jobs are easy to find, many individuals may be induced to enter the labor market, thus temporarily raising r. The value of r also can be affected by social ideas. For example, the women's movement has been cited as a factor causing r to increase nationally. The structure of the local economy may also have an important bearing. Chinitz hypothesized that women are less likely to be in the work force if the employment opportunities are dispersed throughout the city because of extra transportation problems that arise. Furthermore, if the industrial structure is such that one family member has to work rotating shifts on weekends, this may also discourage participation, thus lowering the employment participation rate.[5]

Because of the possibility of variations, it is best to use the average of the employment population ratios for the past several years when estimating r. Another advantage of calculating r over a several-year period is that it enables the analyst to look for systematic trends in the employment participation rate; if a trend is evident, it could be extrapolated into the future.

An alternative method for estimating population is to rely upon demographic projections. Such forecasts rely upon birth and death rates of age-sex groups rather than on economic factors to estimate population. Demographic patterns are important determinants of population change. While the economic approach is generally more accurate for local forecasts, particularly in the long run, it is important to realize that certain segments of the population are not as affected by employment opportunities as others. Thus, under some circumstances it may be advisable to use a cohort survival method to estimate the population.

Finally, a *sixth step* is needed to make the application to housing explicit. The number of housing units that will be needed in the future can be estimated from population projections. While this last step is not necessary for an economic base study, it is often included because of the importance of housing to most local economies. Of the total future population, a portion will be housed in group quarters. This segment includes individuals needing long-term medical care, students, and prisoners, among others. Since such individuals often have no direct effect upon the private housing market, it is recommended that they be excluded from the rest of the population.[6]

Unless there is evidence to the contrary, it is generally assumed that the proportion of the population living in group quarters will be the same as that shown in the latest decennial census. The population not in group quarters can be estimated in the following manner.

$$N\dot{G}QP = q\dot{P} \tag{5}$$

where $N\dot{G}QP$ = nongroup quartered population
q = percentage of population not in group quarters
$\dot{P}$ = estimated population [see Equation (4)]

Once $N\dot{G}QP$ has been estimated, the total number of housing units needed will depend upon the average number of persons per household, f. This figure (f) also can be derived from past census reports, since both household and population statistics are available. $N\dot{G}QP$ divided by the number of households equals f. However, care must be taken because the long-term trend has been toward smaller household size. Because of the national trend toward smaller family size, a value of f calculated using 1980 census data may be slightly greater than the value of f in the year for which a projection is being made. A study by Schussheim suggested that although the rate of growth of the population is slowing, the need for housing is increasing.[7] The reason for this is twofold. First, there is a bumper crop of persons reaching adulthood, and second, these people are moving out of their parents' homes and establishing their own living quarters. This spreading out of people has meant that more housing units are required to accommodate an increasing population. Therefore, an estimate of the number of households based upon a historical $NGQP$ to household ratio is likely to be slightly high, but of course, local areas vary in the degree to which they reflect this national trend. Nevertheless, through careful examination an appropriate ratio may be derived. The future number of households can be estimated as:

$$H\dot{H} = N\dot{G}QP \div f \tag{6}$$

where $H\dot{H}$ = estimated number of households
f = the average number of persons per household

Not only is $H\dot{H}$ important in forecasting housing need, but f can serve as an indicator of space requirements per household. A large f is an indicator that a larger number of bedrooms or more square feet per unit are warranted.

Some Caveats

The most pressing warning to a practitioner of the techniques described above is to avoid extreme rigidity in application. One workable technique was outlined in this chapter, but it was not intended to be a formula that can be applied without regard to circumstance. Any research plan aimed at analyzing future conditions must be flexible. In reality, almost every economic base study has unique features.

It is also important to keep in mind that the numbers represented by r, q, and f are assumed to be constant over time. This assumption is correct only as an approximation. For example, if a new university with dormitory facilities were established in a city, the value of q, the percentage of the population not in group quarters, would change. This problem is of course true of any estimating technique, but it is necessary to be cognizant of the fact in order to make adjustments when necessary. Successful economic base studies require a knowledge of the details of a locality. Thus, interviews and personal legwork supplement data found in published sources.

Finally, several additional steps are necessary to move from an estimate of the number of households that will be formed to an estimate of the actual demand for new housing in an area. Specifically, there is need to distinguish between demand, which indicates a willingness and ability to buy, and need. The number of households is a measure of need or willingness, but many may not be able to afford housing by themselves. Living with a friend or more commonly with relatives is a frequent response for families that cannot afford a separate household.

Furthermore, the demand for new housing is partly a function of the existing housing stock. For example, a city with a substantial vacancy rate could absorb more new households without the need for additional construction than a city with a very low vacancy rate. The effect of buying power and of the existing stock of housing on real estate is discussed in Chapter 7.

Location of Individual Establishments

The importance of industrial location to urban development and the implications ultimately for real estate activity should be evident from the study of the export base theory. For reasons of practicality, most export base studies make projections based upon trends in industries and groups of industries or upon future plans of specific establishments already located in the city. Nevertheless it will be worthwhile to examine the locational decision from the perspective of an entrepreneur contemplating the location of a new establishment.

Profits for individual firms are the major constraint on location. Other things being equal, an entrepreneur will choose the most profitable location. However, surveys of businesspersons reveal that, while many corporate locational decisions are based upon careful calculations of profits in alternative cities, independent entrepreneurs often mention personal factors as the reason for location. For example, many establishments are located where they are because it is the hometown of the founder. Nevertheless, even in cases where personal reasons seem to predominate, profits are critical for two reasons. First, an individual may start by asking what kind of establishment would be profitable in the area where he or she wanted to locate. Thus, even though the entrepreneur might feel that personal geographical preferences were most important in the decision, profits are still the key. Second, if a business were initiated in an unprofitable location, it would not survive. Therefore, competition in the market causes locations to be in profitable places.

Exactly what factors determine whether a location is profitable? The pioneers of location theory believed that transportation costs were the critical factor. They distinguished between (1) the *market* for the product, (2) *localized inputs* available only at specific locations, and (3) *ubiquitous inputs* available almost everywhere. The location decision was posed as a choice of either building a plant at the site of the localized raw material and shipping the output to the market, or locating at the market and transporting the inputs.

While there are several simplifications in this one-market–one-input model, it illustrates the tendency of some goods to locate near markets. Soft drinks are a good example. The cost of transporting the localized inputs, such as sugar, is low. However, because water, the ubiquitous input, adds significantly to the weight and bulk (therefore increasing transportation costs), soft drinks tend to be produced near the market. With reference to the export base theory, strictly market-oriented activities are nonbasic or service. Transportation cost savings that result from combining the production process at a common locality have been termed *agglomeration economies*.

Thus far, transportation costs have been considered as the principal locational force. Many firms do locate principally on the basis of transportation costs, although such a model of the choice of an industrial location is not enough for most purposes. Agglomeration economies will be examined in this section. Agglomeration economies may be defined as: "a cheapening of production or marketing which results from the fact that production is carried on to some considerable extent at one place. . . ."[8] Although the concept has been widely discussed, urban-regional theorists have not finalized the concept or fully explored the ramifications. However, Edgar Hoover has classified agglomeration economies into three types[9]:

1. *Large-scale economies* within a firm, consequent upon the enlargement of the firm's scale of production at one point.
2. *Localization economies* for all firms in a single industry at a single location, consequent upon the enlargement of total output of that industry at that location.
3. *Urbanization economies* for all firms in all industries at a single location, consequent upon the enlargement of the total economic size (population, income, output, or wealth) of that location, for all industries taken together.

The first type refers to economies resulting from increasing the size of an establishment. Thus a firm will find it more efficient to have one large plant than several plants even though the small plants could be scattered in such a way as to minimize transportation costs. Localization and urbanization economies are external to the firm. If lower production costs arise from an agglomeration of establishments in the same industry, then localization economies exist. The disproportionate concentration of the fashion industry in New York is an example of a localization economy. Some establishments need the advantages of a large or diverse labor force, ready access to specialized services, and public services that more likely are found in urban areas. These types of activities may prefer urban locations even if the minimum transportation point site is a rural area or small town.

Many economic activities are more sensitive to input costs than to transportation costs in selecting the most profitable location. The influence that these cost factors exert depends upon their relative importance in the production process and the factor cost differential. In order to illustrate the point, assume a hypothetical production process that uses the following inputs per unit of output:

Electric energy	300 KWH
Labor (unskilled)	2 hr
Steel	2 tons

A locational decision is contemplated, and the choice has been narrowed to two cities that are alike in every respect except they have different input costs as shown below:

	City A	City B
Electric energy	.01/KWH	.02/KWH
Labor (unskilled)	2.00/hr	2.00/hr
Steel	3.50/ton	2.50/ton

Assuming no difference exists in other locational factors, in what city will the firm locate? Per unit cost is calculated by the cost of each input times the amount of input used. Thus for A, cost per unit equals $(300 \times .01) + (2.00 \times 2) + (3.50 \times 2) = 14$. The per unit costs are $14 in A and $15 in B, so that, *ceteris paribus*, location will be in A. The lower steel costs in B are more than offset by the higher costs of energy.

Next, suppose a technological change occurs such that the required electrical inputs decrease from 300 to only 100 KWH per unit of output. Will the optimal location be affected? Yes, the per unit costs would now equal $12 in A but only $11 in B. The change in input requirements affected the most profitable location. Thus, the proportion of inputs required in the production process is as important to the locational decision as the kinds of inputs. In the above example it was assumed that the proportion of inputs was fixed. While this assumption is correct in some instances, it is not generally true for all industrial processes. If we allow for different proportions of factor inputs, or if we substitute oil for electric energy, then the locational decision becomes more complicated.

Blair and Premus compared locational determinants since 1970 with the factors that were considered important before 1960.[10] These results are shown in Table 6-4. They concluded that industries have become more footloose. Locational choices are governed less than in the past by access to markets, labor, transportation, and raw materials. While these traditional locational factors still exert an influence, the list of important locational determinants has been extended to include taxes, education, business climate, availability of skilled labor, public infrastructure, and quality of life.

Finally, many types of economic activity that contribute to the base of a community are made by nonprofit agencies. For example, the location of an IRS National Office in Kansas City or a naval base in San Diego contributes to the export base and brings in monetary inflows,

Table 6–4. Locational Determinants

Prior to 1960	Today (since 1970)
Markets	Labor
Labor	Markets
Raw materials	Transportation
Transportation	Raw materials
Taxes	Energy
Financial incentives	Productivity
	Taxes
	Education
	Unionization
	Personal reasons
	Attitudes toward business
	Familiarity with local economy

but the locational factors are often political rather than economic. Many small cities have experienced upheavals because of the closing of a government shipyard or military base. Thus, political factors are becoming an increasingly important locational factor.

This discussion has only skimmed the surface of the locational decisions that determine the future of real estate within a general area. Nevertheless, an understanding of the basics of location theory coupled with specific knowledge about the economic advantages and disadvantages of a particular city can help lessen the uncertainties of a real estate investment decision.

Criticisms of Export Base Studies

In recent years, export base studies have received a good deal of criticism in scholarly journals. It is important to review the criticism in order to understand the limitations and to avoid misinterpretations of the results. In general, the objections can be divided into those that concern technique and those that disagree with the underlying theory.

Many researchers believe that the categorization of all economic activity into two broad categories—basic (export) and nonbasic (service)—is too shallow. A modern urban economy is an extremely complex system, and industrial interdependencies differ among the various subcomponents. One group of critics of export base studies claim it is more important to know the *differential impact* that each individual industry will have than to know an *average multiplier* for all industries.

For example, the expansion of a steel mill will have a different impact on a local economy than the expansion of a food processing plant. Furthermore, a change in export activity of any one industry will have a differential impact on other local industries. In an expansion in steel production, trucking enterprises may be affected more than textile producers. Therefore, analysts who argue that interindustry detail is requisite to adequate planning claim that the base study does not provide enough information. Thus, the technique of the traditional base study is criticized as lacking in detail, although there may be no disagreement with the idea that exports are the key to local growth.

In an effort to examine the local development process in more detail, input-output tables have been developed for several large cities. Table 6–5 is a basic table for Star City.

Since a typical urban or regional input-output table will have in excess of 40 rows and columns, the Star City illustration is an abridgment that serves only to illustrate how such an analytical tool can be used. With the exception of the "Total" row and column, each cell shows the annual dollar volume of sales purchased, by the sectors listed at the top, from the local industries listed on the left. The cell where the "Manufacturing" row intersects the "Trades" column shows that local manufacturing firms sell $100 per year to area wholesale and retail trades. The "Final Demand" sectors include "House-

Table 6–5. Input-Output Coefficients

Sectors Selling \ Sectors Purchasing	Agriculture	Manufacturing	Trades— Whole and Retail	Households	Exports	Trade Gross Output
				Final Demand		
Agriculture	100	50	70	75	75	370
Manufacturing	50	50	100	10	40	250
Trades	20	10	20	100	100	250
Households	40	50	60	30	10	190
Imports	160	90	0	25	0	275
Total gross outlays	370	250	250	240	225	1,335

holds" and "Exports." The "Exports" column shows the monetary inflows due to export sales of industries on the left. While the "Households" column shows local consumption, the "Households" row shows payments by the industries across the top for factors of production—primarily labor—purchased from local households. The "Imports" row shows purchases from outside the area; therefore values in this row represent monetary outflows.

An input-output table is an excellent descriptive model of an economy, but it is not as useful as a table of direct coefficients for making projections. If each cell of Table 6–5 were divided by the total gross output of the purchasing sector, the data could be calculated on a per unit basis as shown in Table 6–6.

As an example of how Table 6–6 was calculated, let's again examine the cell in Table 6–5 that shows sales of manufacturing to wholesale-retail trades. Since the total gross output of trades is 250, we may conclude that for each dollar of output by wholesale-retail trades, 40 cents ($100/$250) is purchased from local manufacturing establishments. By carrying out such a calculation for each sector, the Table of Direct Coefficients (Table 6–6) was derived. For purposes of forecasting, the assumption is usually made that for each $1 of increased exports, the increase in interindustry requirements will be constant.

Table 6–6 provides the analyst with a tool for estimating the impact that an increase or decrease in one sector will have on each of the others. What would be the impact of a $100,000 increase in manufacturing output on agriculture? A $1 increase would cause agriculture to increase its output by $.20, and so, assuming a constant relationship between the industries, a $100,000 increase in manufacturing output should cause a $20,000 (.20 × $100,000) increase in agriculture's sales to manufacturing.

Table 6–6. Table of Direct Coefficients

Sectors Selling / Sectors Purchasing	Agriculture	Manufacturing	Retail and Wholesale Trades
Agriculture	.27	.20	.28
Manufacturing	.14	.20	.40
Trades	.05	.04	.08

The study of interindustry linkages is often carried a step further. It was shown that an increase of $1 in the output of trades will cause manufacturing establishments to increase output. But if manufacturing firms are to increase their output, they in turn will purchase more from agriculture and trades. Thus, a whole chain of repercussions is set in motion. An increase in the sales of any one sector causes other sectors to increase output directly, as shown in Table 6–6, and indirectly due to the induced increase in other activity. The culmination of the entire process can be calculated and is termed a *table of direct and indirect coefficients*. Table 6–7 shows the direct and indirect requirements per $1 of increase in output that each sector listed across the top will have for the output from the sectors listed at the left.

An input-output study provides a more detailed description of a locality's growth. It can be particularly helpful to persons in industrial real estate since it provides a technique for estimating additional expansion and new industrial locations that may be induced as a result of a location of a specific industry. Since different industries have alternative real estate needs, the disaggregation provided by the analysis can be very useful. For example, from the simplified table of direct and indirect coefficients shown in Table 6–7, an analyst can determine that a $10,000,000 increase in basic manufacturing activity may ultimately induce a $1,700,000 increase in the sales of the trades sector (.17 × $10,000,000). This increase may have major repercussions for future land use as well as market studies of various retail endeavors. Useful as it is, input-output analysis does not in itself provide a theory of growth. It provides no insights into the forces that set off the growth

**Table 6–7. Direct and Indirect
Coefficients**

	Agriculture	*Manufacturing*	*Retail and Wholesale Trades*
Agriculture	1.48	.30	.38
Manufacturing	.38	1.26	.49
Trades	.27	.17	1.10

Note: not derived from Table 6–6.

process. Even by using input-output techniques, some change in exports is assumed to be the factor that stimulates growth. Therefore, input-output applications rely upon the export base theory to explain the initial cause of development.

A major reason input-output analysis is not used more widely is that the effort and expense of developing such a table are significantly greater than the previously described base study. Whereas a simple base study can be computed by one or two individuals in several months, construction of an input-output table may take a large staff and several years. Most practitioners consider primary data necessary for an input-output table. Therefore, a survey of local firms is essential, and this accounts for most of the time and expense. However, for analysis interested in general trends, the extra expense is probably not justified.

Whereas input-output analysis answers criticism about shallow categorization, a more fundamental criticism has been levied against the theory that underlies base studies. It has been suggested that the emphasis on exports is leading to an imbalanced approach. Contrary to export theorists, the critics claim that the traditional service sectors are the engine of growth. For example, the real estate sector can be seen as responsible for developing industrial land and finding the necessary tenants. It may therefore be a cause of industrial growth. Therefore, according to this view, many of the service sectors are really responsible for urban growth. As Thompson stated, important factors of area growth are[11]:

> The creativity of its universities and research parks, the sophistication of its engineering firms and financial institutions . . . and all the other dimensions of infra-structure that facilitate the quick and orderly transfer from old dying bases to new growing ones.

The nature of the service sectors may well be critical variables for determining a city's ability to generate export industries and for explaining why some cities, such as mining towns, never recover from the loss of an export industry whereas other cities tend to generate new exports. Boston, Massachusetts, is a good example of a city that suffered a loss of many of its low-wage industries—textiles and shoes—to the South, but was able to create a new export base in electronics and computers. However important the service sectors may be, few can argue that a city needs exports to remain viable. The type of export industry and the area's ability to attract new industrial locations may well depend on the service sector. Consequently, services may be an element in making projections concerning the growth in exports. Nevertheless, the link between exports and growth is clear.

Applications to Specific Real Estate Questions

An export base study is considered a tool that provides information applicable to other purposes. In the case of real estate, the implications of such a study can be easily applied to housing demand. First, it is fairly easy to derive a population projection from an employment projection. Since most cities have a fairly constant employment-to-population ratio, total population can be derived. The economic approach is a good complement to the standard demographic projections that are based upon birth and death rates. Another valuable input into housing forecasts that can be derived from an export base study is income levels. If the export sectors that have been projected to expand are high-wage industries such as machinery and metals, then community income will rise. Finally, if export employment is expected to grow at a slow rate or decline, unemployment and population loss have unfavorable implications for housing construction.

Because of the obvious applications to housing demand, the application of export base studies to other areas is often overlooked. The future of export activity has a direct bearing upon commercial and industrial land use. What type of industrial facilities will be required if industry A expands in an area? What changes in zoning ordinances ought to be made? How many new restaurants or theaters should be built and where? Of course, as we show later, answers to these questions require other data as well, but the base study is an extremely useful and versatile tool.

SUMMARY

This chapter describes the theory and tools needed to understand and forecast urban and regional growth. Property values are closely tied to the long-term growth of an area because real estate has a long life and is immobile.

A model of growth is the circular flow diagram. It conceptually divides a local economy into business and households. Households give business factors of production, and households receive goods and services from business. Interindustry transactions and exchanges with the rest of the world also are important factors in the model of urban growth.

The export base theory of growth contends that the sale of goods and services outside the local economy is the engine of growth. An increase in exports will cause a multiplier effect in the local economy, thus creating secondary jobs to provide services for the export workers. The duration of the multiplier impact depends upon whether the export increase is temporary or permanent.

The export base theory can be linked to population and household forecasts. The steps in a forecast are:

1. Determine the appropriate geographical area
2. Describe the local economy, and determine the sources of export employment
3. Estimate the local multiplier
4. Estimate changes in the local economy
5. Forecast population as a function of employment change
6. Estimate households on the basis of the population forecast

The export base theory has been criticized on two grounds. First, many researchers believe that the categories, basic (export) and nonbasic (service), are too gross. Input-output analysis is one way to increase the detail of industrial studies. Second, it has been argued that emphasis on exports leads to a neglect of the service sector. The service sector is important in creating export jobs. Both critiques have validity, but the link between exports and growth is nevertheless a key to understanding and forecasting urban development.

7

National Economic and Social Influences

All investment decisions are affected by the larger economic environment. The macroeconomy refers to total or aggregate economic activity. The purpose of this section is to describe the relationship between the real estate industry and the United States economy as a whole. As Stevens stated:

> Historically, the housing industry has been characterized by recurring upswings and downswings which generally have been associated with fluctuations in overall economic activity. A sizable fluctuation in new home construction has been associated with each of the officially defined business cycles of the past thirty years. [1]

Because real estate (including construction) is a large subsector of the U.S. economy—and it is important to realize that we are describing a model of simultaneous causation—the events in the real estate sector affect the total value of goods and services produced as well as other variables such as the interest rate and employment. At the same time, the economic conditions that prevail in the economy as a whole affect the real estate market. As previously noted, the real estate sector is especially sensitive to changes in interest rates, but other factors such as per capita income and expectations of future income are also important determinants of real estate activity.

BUSINESS FLUCTUATIONS

The business cycle has been compared to the ebb and flow of an ocean—but such a comparison may obscure rather than enlighten. In fact there is a rough regularity to economic activity, but there are several types of cycles, each with an effect and timing of its own.

However, the word *cycle* may lend an air of regularity to business fluctuations that is not supported by historical evidence. As C. Lowell Harris pointed out:

> Another warning: We must not expect the future to repeat the past with enough similarity to give . . . a reliable basis for anticipating just what will happen and when. The word "cycle" may convey a uniformity of movement in the economy resembling the rhythms of the seasons or the cycles of a motor. Such an impression would mislead an investor, a businessman, or an assessor, *none of whom should act on the assumption that there is a regularity in movements of the national economy.*[2]

The most notable peaks of prosperity and depths of depression occur when the various cycles that affect business activity simultaneously reach turning points. The interaction of the cycles is expressed by the words of Lewis Richardson:

> Great whirls have little whirls
> that feed on their velocity;
> and little whirls have lesser whirls
> and so on to viscosity.

Four types of economic fluctuations that bear upon real estate investment decisions are: (1) random fluctuations, (2) seasonal fluctuations, (3) business cycles, and (4) secular trends. Figure 7–1 presents two idealized portraits of economic activity and also illustrates the four types of economic fluctuations.

Random fluctuations are short-term irregular changes in business activity. Such fluctuations also are difficult or impossible to forecast because they have no pattern and their cause is usually known only in retrospect, if ever. Poor weather in a crop-growing region of the world may cause food prices to rise temporarily. This in turn may affect employment in related sectors. However, unless they are extremely severe, random fluctuations seldom affect the underlying conditions of a modern economy.

Seasonal fluctuations are regular and reasonably predictable. Disruptions are minimized because individuals, as well as the economy, are able to anticipate price increases. Real estate construction is greatest in the fall, summer, and spring; produce prices dip in the late summer when supplies reach the market; and unemployment rates peak after spring graduations. In fact, most industries have seasonal runs. Managers account for these fluctuations in their planning so that

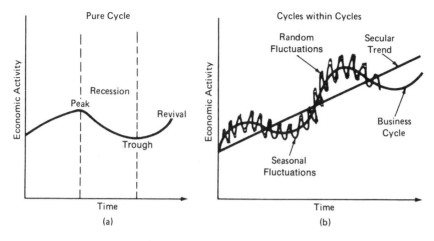

Figure 7–1. Business cycles.

periods of boom or bust are avoided. It is the sum of all of the industrial fluctuations that creates seasonal price levels and production cycles in the economy as a whole.

The business cycle is a fluctuation that affects the aggregate economy. Wesley C. Mitchell, a pioneer in the study of business cycles, has divided a business cycle into four phases: (1) expansion, (2) recession, (3) contraction, and (4) revival. The cycles are recurrent, and regular enough to be termed periodic. The business cycle may vary in length from 1 year to 10 or 15 years. A recession is defined as the period from the peak to trough.[3]

It is useful to distinguish between major and minor business cycles. Minor cycles are mild and temporary adjustments from the normal economic growth path. Minor cycles are normally sparked by inventory adjustments, so they are temporary cutbacks in production until inventories are depleted. The business cycle, because of its ability to disrupt normal economic processes, is the center of most of the attention from government and private-sector policymakers. Governmental economists are often concerned with appropriate monetary and fiscal policies. Unfortunately, inappropriate policy has, on occasion, exacerbated the problem. Business economists are concerned with the business cycle because it is more powerful, is less predictable, and has more severe impacts on their industries than seasonal fluctuations.

Secular trends represent the underlying economic conditions that may influence generations. These long-wave movements are also referred to as *Kondrotieff cycles* (they are named for the Russian economist who first documented them). The construction of the railway system, which opened much of the West and stimulated additional development, is an example of an investment outlet that created a long wave of prosperity. More recent long waves were the automobile and the accompanying investments in highways, gas stations, motels, drive-in theaters, and suburban housing developments. Currently, many people believe that the increasing scarcity of nonrenewable resources may be the reason for a long period of stagnation. Just as the period between World War II and approximately 1970 may be known as the Age of the Automobile, many economists believe that the period we are entering is a Kondrotieff cycle which is characterized as "postindustrial," "postaffluent," or "slow growth."

Causes of the Business Cycle

Many economists, spanning all ideologies from Marx to Friedman, have tried to determine the cause of the business cycle. Although economists do not agree on an explanation, each theory provides useful insights.

Early writers believed that the business cycle was caused by *physical phenomena*. Good weather, for example, produces periods of prosperity, and bad weather has an adverse effect. Biblical cycles of feast and famine are weather-related. Sun spots are a widely ridiculed physical theory of cycles. In an age of fewer economic interdependencies, physical changes probably had a more direct impact on the family economy. Currently, the diminution of energy resources is cited as a cause of economic problems. *Psychological theories* claim that business and consumer optimism or pessimism change and cause economic swings. Psychological theories can help explain the length and extent of recessions and expansions. Once a particular view of the future dominates thinking, there may be a snowball effect and other opinions may be denied credibility. Unfortunately, psychological theories generally fail to explain why business attitudes shift from optimism to pessimism or vice versa.

John M. Keynes described the role of *savings and investment* in the business cycle. Savings and investment, he claimed, must always be equal because they are the same thing—income that is not spent. However, planned savings and planned investment need not be equal. Some savings are forced rather than planned. When forced savings are significant, an economic downturn may result. For example, if inventories accumulate because consumers attempt to save a higher proportion of income, producers will be forced to save in the form of increased inventories. Production will decline, unemployment will result, and incomes will be lower than otherwise. By similar reasoning, if businesses decide to increase investments by an amount greater than what individuals plan to save, then employment will increase. If full employment exists already, prices will increase. Individual incomes will be above expectations, and therefore savings will increase. Thus, while planned saving and planned investment may be different, actual (or, as the economists say, *ex post*) investment will be equal to realized savings.

There is a link between savings and investment and psychological theories of business fluctuations. One of the reasons that surveys of business confidence and planned investment are indicators of future business activity is that investment is a stimulant to further spending and a creator of ripple effects. Lack of confidence on the part of business or rapid accumulation of excess inventories due to lack of consumer confidence will result in less investment in the future.

Figure 7–2 is a hypothetical sales/inventory relationship. In Stage I, an economy may be in a recovery as shown by increasing sales. Inventories are low because of lack of investor confidence and tend to decline even further in the early stages of a recovery as sales outpace production. In Stage II sales continue to increase, confidence builds, and business also wants to increase inventories. Sales start to decline in Stage III, but inventories that may have been ordered weeks in advance accumulate to a level in excess of the desired sales/inventory ratio. In Stage IV orders are canceled, investment plans are changed, and inventories decline. The bottom of the cycle occurs when inventories are still declining while sales are turning upward. Figure 7–2 also represents a very common local and national housing cycle. When sales peak, construction may continue for over 6 months because of the long delay between initiation of a project and completion.

Monetary theories of the business cycle are particularly appealing in a period of inflation. They are, however, consistent with other explanations. Monetarists, as proponents of this view are called, believe that changes in the money supply will affect the interest rate. The interest rate in turn will stimulate or depress business investment. For instance, as the prime interest rate approached 20%, business borrowing and investing dropped sharply. Monetary theories are often contrasted with *fiscal theories* of business fluctuation. Fiscal theories contend that government spending determines business activity directly and indi-

Figure 7–2. Sales/Inventory cycle.

rectly through the multiplier effect. Both views regard aggregate demand as an important variable. When either the money supply or the level of government spending increases too rapidly, inflation will result as aggregate demand increases more rapidly than the productive economy. Proponents of these two views disagree about the best way to affect aggregate demand.

Cycles may have many simultaneous causes, so there is room for more than one explanation. Lack of confidence, for example, may be caused by a streak of bad weather that may lead to a shrinkage of credit as bankers cut back on agricultural loans. In this example physical, psychological, and monetary theories interact. Furthermore, some explanations explain particular cycles better than others. Finally, some industries are more sensitive to some variables than others. Thus, variations in real estate activity are extremely sensitive to changes in the interest rate.

REAL ESTATE AND THE AGGREGATE ECONOMY

Although both the degree and timing of the impact vary, most types of economic activity are affected by business fluctuations. The real estate business is especially sensitive to the vagaries of the business cycle for four reasons. First, construction activity is sensitive to expectations of the future because realty is an asset with a long economic life. When sections of the economy slow down, long-term expectations of the future become uncertain or pessimistic or both. Plans for major spending on durable goods are canceled or postponed. (Spending on food and

clothing is difficult to postpone.) The importance of psychological expectations on housing decisions should not be underestimated. During
periods of rising prices, on the other hand, individuals will hurry to
purchase property before prices go up again. The adaptability of real
estate is the second reason for its sensitivity to macroeconomic fluctuations. Real estate can normally be repaired or renovated readily. Consequently, individuals will postpone new home purchases during periods of uncertainty. Remodeling the attic may suffice; a newly married
couple may live with one of the parents until the economy improves.
Third, most real estate projects require debt financing. Lending institutions become cautious when they contemplate making long-term loans
secured by an asset that may fluctuate in value. Lenders will also have
less confidence in the future earning ability of borrowers. Financial
institutions' reluctance to lend may be even more evident on income-
producing properties because the value of such properties is determined partly by estimating the discounted value of future returns. During a business recession, vacancy rates may be high as families
"double up." Thus, NOI will be below normal. Yet because of pessimism, analysts may consider the depressed operating income normal.
Current value estimates therefore will reflect current rather than long-
run or stabilized rents and vacancy rates. Finally, the small construction firms that characterize the housing industry generally lack the
resources necessary to survive a severe downturn in activity. Therefore, construction employment is sensitive to the business cycle.

Many of the same factors that depress real estate activity during
business downswings stimulate the industry during economic expansions. For example, when the aggregate economy is expanding, most
lenders are more willing to lend. Likewise, potential buyers are less
reluctant to borrow because they believe they will be earning more
money in the future. Repayment will be easier and housing prices will
increase, so why wait to buy?

The link between real estate activity and the aggregate economy has
been discussed largely in terms of construction. However, the impact
of business economic fluctuations pervades all sectors of the real estate
business. If new construction declines, few people will be vacating
existing homes, so it will be more difficult for those with inadequate
housing to find better housing on the market. Intraurban relocation will
decline. Economic slowdowns also restrict business relocations. Thus
brokerage commissions from the sale of existing homes normally fall
during a recession. Real estate salespersons, especially those who are
new to the business, have high dropout rates during recessions. Like-

wise, consulting firms will have fewer clients, syndicators will find it more difficult to attract investors, appraisers will have less work, mortgage companies will experience declines in volume, and title insurance companies will issue fewer new policies.

Timing

Construction and real estate development cycles do not match the average cycle for the economy as a whole. Housing starts generally peak before the aggregate economy peaks, and bottom out before the rest of the economy does. Thus, housing starts lead aggregate economic activity in both the downswing and upswing phases of the business cycle. Consequently, housing starts or housing permits issued are often used in predictive models of the aggregate economy. When business forecasters see housing starts decline for several periods in a row, they will suspect that the rest of the economy will slow down later. Figure 7–3 shows fluctuations in privately owned housing starts for 1965–1984. The shaded areas represent periods of business recession from peak to trough. Housing starts lead the business cycle peaks.

There are at least three reasons why real estate is a leading economic indicator. First, it is one of the first sectors to experience the effects of declines in consumer and investor confidence. Few individuals want to lock themselves into a long-term obligation if they are unsure of their future ability to pay. Second, real estate is one of the first sectors to be hurt by rising interest rates. As activities with expansion plans compete for funds, interest rates will rise. Real estate activities, most of which are interest-sensitive, will tend to be outbid for the use of the loanable funds. The interest sensitivity of real estate development is due to its heavy reliance on long-term debt finance. For instance, an increase in the interest rate from 10% to 12% will increase the monthly mortgage costs of a $75,000 home (assuming 10% down and a 30-year term) by about $100 per month; this will drive marginal buyers from the market. The problem will be compounded because savers will withdraw their money from savings and loan associations, which traditionally loan to home buyers—and invest directly in private or government securities. Higher interest rates also will increase the costs of construction because developers borrow to build. Furthermore, loans and profit potential of new projects are evaluated on the basis of the present value of future returns. Increases in the interest rate will decrease the present value of proposed projects. Again assuming an increase in the interest rate from 10% to 12%, the value of a

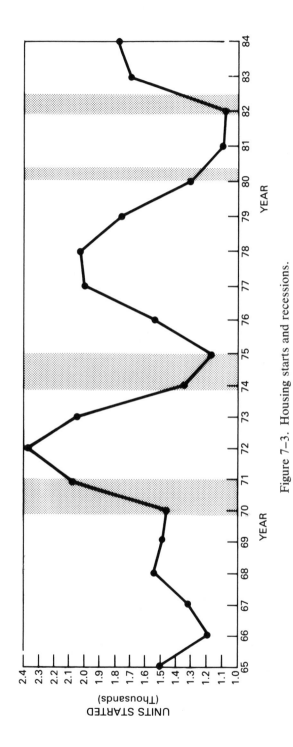

Figure 7-3. Housing starts and recessions.

rental project with an economic life of 30 years and an NOI of $1,000,000 will drop by about $1,500,000.

Third, a slowdown in real estate development depresses other areas of the economy. Because real estate development is such an important part of the aggregate economy, it has a more significant influence on other sectors than do most activities. Furniture sales, for example, will decrease if housing starts decrease, since furniture and new housing are complementary goods. Not only will the direct ripples take a toll, but employees throughout the real estate industry will themselves purchase less. It has been estimated that the loss in economic activity that resulted from the development slowdown in 1980 had an impact equivalent to the bankruptcy of three Chrysler corporations.

The discussion has thus far focused upon national economic trends. It is important therefore to reiterate a theme of several previous chapters. Real estate activity is closely tied to local as well as national market conditions. Occasionally a real estate business prospers in one locale even though the national economy is lethargic. Conversely, a few areas may be in a virtual depression when the national economy is prosperous.

Real Estate Cycles.   Clayton Pritchett, a New York–based real estate consultant, contended that real estate investors have not paid enough attention to national real estate cycles.[4] Practitioners have emphasized the significance of local markets or aggregate economic cycles. Consequently, they have downplayed the significance of national markets. However, institutional investors are increasingly concerned about national real estate cycles. Pritchett argued that there is a national real estate cycle.

The timing of real estate cycles is different for industrial, retail, and office construction. Office development is the largest component of investment-grade real estate—over $4 million valuation—so Pritchett focused on office developments. Figure 7–4 shows a typical cycle. It has four stages.

1. *Rising:* The quantity of space demanded is above the quantity available. And demand is rising. Construction adds to the supply. During this stage vacancies are, at first, high, about 10%, and then decline as supply catches up. Toward the end of this phase, vacancies are 5–6%, roughly a normal level.

2. *Top:* Demand starts to weaken and decline. During the early stage of this phase, new demand is still greater than additions to sup-

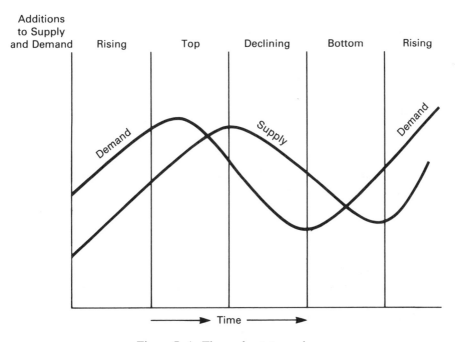

Figure 7–4. The real estate cycle.

ply. Later, the additions to supply continue to increase while the quantity demanded falls. Vacancies start to rise as a result. Rents will weaken as well.

3. *Declining:* Incremental supply and demand are both decreasing. Developers are pessimistic, expecting vacancies to climb to 10–15%.

4. *Bottom:* Additions to supply continue to drop while demand stages a turnaround. Vacancies typically peak between 10% and 15% and then decline during this stage.

Brown also traced a national real estate cycle.[5] He claimed the cycle is about 18 years in duration from the start of one cycle to the start of another cycle. Usually, Brown noted, financial panics have come within 2 to 4 years after building activity peaks.

The real estate model described by Figure 7–4 has several implications for real estate developers and investors. First, extra caution is needed when making plans at the top of the cycle and in the early declining phase. Developers should become conservative while popular sentiment is bullish. Second, the most advantageous time to buy or build is near the bottom stage of the cycle. Both construction and purchase prices will be lower. Furthermore, a new property started toward the end of the bottom phase will be able to rent units quickly if they become available at the start of the rising stage. However, Pritchett reminds readers of the saw, "No one rings a bell at the bottom of the market." Third, the top of the cycle is the most opportune time to lease.

Since we cannot directly observe the gaps between the quantity supplied and the quantity demanded, a market study must rely upon a variety of approximation techniques to determine the particular phase of the cycle. Vacancy rates are one of the most useful indicators of the real estate cycle.

Suburbanization. Manson and his associates presented evidence that the process of metropolitan decentralization depends upon the national and real estate cycles.[6] The rate of suburbanization accelerates during expansions in the national economy and declines when the construction industry is sluggish. Thus the central city experiences relative decline during national construction upswings because most of the new constructions occur outside the city.

Cities may face another problem related to the national business cycle. A high percentage of inner-city production facilities tend to be older and therefore less efficient than suburban facilities owned by the same company. Inner-city plants may be the first closed when the economy is in recession, and they are reactivated only when needed near the end of the recession. As prosperity continues, newer suburban facilities are built, further compounding the problem for the next cycle.

In order to understand the source of many housing forecasts, it will be useful to review several major techniques of macroeconomic forecasting.

Economic Forecasting and Econometric Studies

There are several techniques employed in economic forecasting, and each technique can be complicated or relatively simple. Regardless of the technique employed, forecasting still contains major elements of judgment, interpretation, and luck. In addition, experience indicates that forecasting models are more accurate when the economy is moving along a stable trend line. Predictions of turning points—peaks and troughs—are much less accurate, and yet the turning points are of interest to investors. Also, when fundamental structural shifts occur in an economy, statistical models cannot predict well. For example, in 1974 the Arab oil embargo and the subsequent high energy prices were not foreseen by economic forecasters. In fact, they lack tools to make such forecasts, and so it would be unfair to blame them for not taking such factors into account. Yet the change in energy supply set off a worldwide recession.

There are several types of economic forecasting, ranging from subjective intuitions to totally quantitative forecasts that exclude variables that cannot be mathematized. Three types of forecasting techniques that will be discussed are mathematical modeling, indicator analysis, and attitude surveys. The mathematical models often are held in awe by nonmathematicians. The most sophisticated forecasting techniques are the computer simulation models such as the FMP (Federal Reserve–Massachusetts Institute of Technology–University of Pennsylvania) model, which is a system of over 200 interdependent equations. The FMP and other forecasting models attempt to estimate interrelationships between various sectors of the economy.

Fromm recently evaluated the reliability of 11 of the most sophisticated models for their usefulness in predicting real estate activity. His conclusions concerning the accuracy of the forecasts were fairly harsh. First, he claimed that they failed to distinguish between various types of housing and location of housing. Second, Fromm contended that, *without exception,* statistical models have proved unreliable for forecasting purposes. Analysts who use the models have found it essential either to ignore the objective mathematical forecasts and develop their own estimates independently or to adjust the projects on the basis of other information.[7] The implication of Fromm's study is that statistical models are at best a guide to developing estimates of economic trends and fluctuations. Wilson has also criticized econometric studies that are totally "self-contained." "Intuitive forecasts might prove more valid and useful than those based on quantitative methods; this is because data can only reflect relationships in the past, and it is almost certain the relationships will change."[8]

Many analysts place more confidence in surveys that indicate consumer and business intentions. This approach might consist of direct questions, such as: "Do you plan to make a major purchase in the next six months?" or "Do you plan to move in the near future?" or indirect questions designed to probe less conscious opinions: "Do individuals have more opportunities to advance today than twenty years ago?" Study of attitudes provides an alternative and complementary perspective on the economic environment compared with the traditional forecasting models.

The most significant problem with the survey technique for forecasting real estate activity is that it examines only part of the market. The demand is a function of ability as well as willingness to buy. Questions about attitudes may measure willingness, but only when the individual actually enters the market and examines interest rates and housing prices can demand actually be measured. Furthermore, even if surveys provided an accurate description of demand, they often do not reflect supply.

The use of economic indicators is a popular and fairly easy technique for getting a rough idea of economic trends. Variables that tend to precede aggregate economic change are called *leading indicators*. When 90% of the leading indicators suggest that the economy will expand, then confidence can be placed in the projection. Unfortunately for housing analysts, most housing-related variables are leading indicators. Thus, housing tends to be one of the first variables to turn around from expansion to contraction. Since turning points are difficult to predict, housing forecasts go awry. However, as mentioned earlier, interest rate changes are a rather reliable leading indicator of home construction.

THE INTEREST RATE

One of the most important interfaces between occurrences in the economy as a whole and the real estate sector is the capital and money markets. The money market refers to the borrowing of funds for short-term periods, and the capital market refers to the long-term credit market. Almost all phases of real estate are affected by changes in the interest rate. Arcelus and Meltzer found that interest rates not only influenced the demand for housing, but, along with labor costs, are a major determinant of construction cost and therefore the supply of housing.[9] Consequently, a low interest rate affects both the demand and the supply of housing. More accurately, however, we should refer to interest *rates* rather than interest *rate* because the cost of borrowing varies with the characteristics of the borrower and the type of loan. Many statistical studies include 10 or more measures of interest rates. Nevertheless, interest rates generally rise and fall together. Consequently, a change in the yield of 3-month Treasury bills will correspond to a change in the interest rate paid on a 30-year mortgage note. It is important for real estate practitioners to understand the factors that influence the cost of money.

Interest Rates and the Business Cycle

The interest rate is both a cause and an effect of the business cycle. When the economy is doing well and is expected to continue to grow, interest rates rise because businesses are anxious to invest when they expect continued or accelerating prosperity. A higher percentage of planned projects seems profitable under conditions of full employment and rapid economic growth than when recessionary periods are envisioned. Conversely, during recessionary periods interest rates fall because there is a dearth of profitable projects.

Control of the Money Supply

The institution that has the greatest influence on the money supply and the interest rate is the Federal Reserve System. The Federal Reserve System, or the *Fed* as it is commonly called, constitutes the central banking authority in the United States. It is largely responsible for monetary policy. Thus, through control of the money supply, the Fed attempts to ensure full employment, economic growth, and stable prices. Each of these variables is affected by the interest rate and the money supply. Unfortunately, goals are seldom compatible. For example, decreasing unemployment normally calls for large increases in the money supply and simultaneously lower interest rates. However, "easy" monetary policies also result in more rapid price increases. Regarding the effect of housing trade-offs in monetary policy, Stevens observed:

> In view of this alleged link between interest rates and housing, aiming government policies at keeping interest rates low and stable in order to encourage home building seems appropriate to many individuals. The pursuit of such policies, without regard to monetary aggregates, however, probably will lead to periodic economic recessions and inflation—both of which have damaging effects on housing.[10]

Federal Reserve officials must also be concerned with the future direction of the economy because monetary policy initiated by the Fed impacts different parts of the economy after a time lag. If the rate of inflation is too high, interest rates may rise and investors may decrease borrowing for investments. Consequently, the rate of inflation will decrease. Unfortunately, the aggregate economy is not always self-correcting. On the other hand, if the Fed determines that the self-correcting forces are insufficient and attempts to decrease the money supply (or more realistically, slow the rate of increase), the dampening effects may be too great. The economy could experience unexpected high levels of unemployment. The fact that the Fed, like other investors, must *anticipate* a wide variety of economic factors explains why it has contributed to the development of forecasting models. The fact that federal policies influence key variables, especially the interest rate, explains why it is useful for investors to be able to interpret federal activities.

The Money Creation Process. The Fed has several tools that can affect the money supply. The major devices are: (1) open market operations, (2) the discount rate, (3) reserve requirements, (4) moral persuasion, and (5) selective credit controls. However, before discussing each tool it is necessary to understand the money creation process.

If we define money as cash and demand deposits (money in checking accounts), then the role of the banking system in money creation becomes clear. An individual may deposit, say, $1,000 in a checking account. What happens to the money? The bank will keep part of the deposit as a reserve against the possibility of withdrawal. Since, on any given day, most banks will take in more deposits than will be withdrawn, they normally could get by with no reserves. But as a precaution against withdrawals, banks keep a fraction of each deposit as a reserve. The rest is lent to individuals in the normal course of business.

In our illustration of money creation let's assume that $200 was held in reserve and $800 was lent to another individual. The borrower may spend the $800, and the merchant who made the $800 sale may put the money in her checking account. Of the $800 deposit the bank will again keep a fraction in reserve and lend a fraction. The process will continue as money that is lent either directly or indirectly is deposited in a demand account and a fraction is lent. Table 7–1 illustrates the money creation process under the assumption that 20% of each deposit is kept in reserve.

Several caveats about Table 7–1 will make the presentation more realistic. First, it does not matter if the deposits/loans are at only one bank or several banks. The fractional reserve system is not affected. Second, the monies need not pass from one individual to another in tidy lumps as depicted in the example. For instance, the initial $800

Table 7–1. The Money Creation Process

Deposits	Loans	Reserves
1,000	800	200
800	640	160
640	512	128
512	409.60	102.40
409.60	327.68	81.92
327.68	262.11	65.57
262.11	209.68	52.43
209.88	167.74	41.93
167.74	134.19	33.54
.	.	.
.	.	.
.	.	.
.	.	.
$5,000	$4,000	$1,000

loan could have been spent at more than one store, and each of the merchants might have deposited the money in different banks. Again, the money creation process will not be affected. However, there are leakages in the system that will affect the money supply. Since these leakages cannot be predicted with a high degree of accuracy, there is always uncertainty in the money creation process. Suppose that some of a loan is simply kept in cash under a mattress or that funds are deposited in a savings account. These "leakages" will decrease the total amount of money created. Finally, banks will differ in the amount of reserves they keep. The greater the reserve ratio, the smaller the increase in the total money supply.

Open Market Policies.   In discussing the money creation process illustrated in Table 7–1, one might ask the source of the original $1,000. From where did it come? One possibility is that the Federal Reserve Open Market Committee decided to purchase bonds from private buyers. The Fed can pay for the bonds with money that it prints. Thus, when the Fed buys U.S. Government securities, the money supply is increased. When the Fed sells securities, the money supply is decreased.

Open market operations affect the relationship between the money supply, the interest rate, and the price of bonds. A bond, or security, can be thought of as a promise to pay X amount of dollars in the future.

The difference between the price of the promise and the future amount is what determines the interest rate. For example, if a promise to pay $100 in one year sold for $95 today, the interest rate would be 5%. The higher the price of the bond, the lower the yield or interest rate. When the Fed buys bonds, it increases the demand for bonds on the market, and therefore bond prices increase and interest rates decrease. Open market operations are the most frequently used tool of the Federal Reserve System. The Fed attempts to fine-tune the money supply with this device. Over the long run, the Fed is a net buyer of securities. Thus, if the Fed is concerned about a slight possibility of inflation, it will sell a smaller quantity of bonds than it would if inflation was a more severe problem. Conversely, if the economy requires stimulation, then the Fed will buy bonds, raising the price of securities and lowering the interest rate.

The Discount Rate.   Member banks may borrow from the regional federal reserve bank and often use the promissory notes that they receive when they make loans as security. The interest rate paid by member banks is called the *discount rate*. Since banks may lend the money they borrowed from the Fed, a low discount rate can be stimulatory if it encourages member banks to borrow and then lend the funds.

In reality, changes in the discount rate are not a powerful tool because even when the rate is low member banks are reluctant to borrow. There is a feeling that such borrowing is a bad banking practice since it often is used when institutions have inadequate reserves, and inadequate reserves indicate poor management. However, the discount rate is often employed as a signal of the attitude of the Fed and the likely course of future events. An increase in the discount rate, for instance, is generally interpreted as an indication that the Fed will pursue a tight money policy.

The Reserve Requirement.   The Federal Reserve Board of Governors has the authority to set the fraction of deposits that member banks must keep in reserve. If, for example, the Fed set the reverse ratio at .20, then at least $20 must be kept in reserve for every $100 in demand deposits. Raising the reserve requirement decreases the amount that banks may lend and consequently decreases the money supply.

The reserve requirement is the determinant of the multiple by which banks can lend and is therefore a very powerful tool. It is used rather infrequently because it is so powerful. Changes in the reserve requirement are more appropriate when drastic adjustments are needed rather than when just fine-tuning is warranted.

Moral Persuasion and Other Regulations. *Moral persuasion* refers to the ability of the Federal Reserve Banks to persuade members to operate in a manner that may help the economy as a whole. For example, they may warn member banks of the dangers of excessive contraction of the money supply, if there is fear of impending interest rate increases. Moral persuasion may also be used to encourage banks to lend on certain types of projects that have high public priority. For example, in spite of the inflationary pressures of the Korean war, the Fed urged curtailment of only nonwar-related lending.

Interest Rate Determination Reconsidered

The Federal Reserve System, through its control of the banking system, has significant influence on the money supply and the rate of interest. As we mentioned earlier, it is probably the single most influential institution. However, it is necessary to realize that other actors also influence interest rates. The U.S. Treasury, for example, sells bonds directly to the public. Many other federal agencies, especially those involved in real estate such as the Federal Home Loan Mortgage Corporation and the Government National Mortgage Association, also issue notes that affect the interest rate.

The interest rate, as we mentioned, is a price for money's use. But there is no clear definition of the money supply. In addition to cash and demand deposits, some monetary theorists have argued that such things as passbook accounts, short-term Treasury notes, and liquid corporate securities ought to be considered "money." Indeed, over a dozen definitions of money have been discussed in the literature. The broader the concept of "money," the less control the Federal Reserve System has on the money supply. For example, if the value of passbook accounts is included in the money supply, then savings and loans become important sources of money creation. Thus, the actions of the Federal Home Loan Bank Board—the primary regulatory agency of federally chartered savings and loans—become important to monetary policy.

Finally, because private borrowing is important to the money creation process, there is often little that the Fed can do to stimulate the economy if private individuals will not borrow. Even at low interest rates, individuals may lack the confidence to borrow during a recession. Excess reserves will accumulate in bank vaults or as a credit in Fed accounts and will not become part of the money supply. The difficulty of creating money during such periods has been summarized by the colorful phrase, "You can't push on a string."

The Term Structure of Interest Rates

The rate of interest varies with the length of the loan. Generally, the longer the period to maturity, the greater the rate of interest because consumption must be postponed; the more distant the payment, the greater the risk. The pattern of interest rates as a function of length to maturity is called the *term structure*. The solid graph in Figure 7–5 illustrates a typical interest rate structure.

When interest rates rise or fall, they normally shift together. Both the long-term and short-term rates will ordinarily rise, and they will both fall in a recession.[11] However, the short-term rates normally vary over a significantly wider range than longer-term rates. The expectationist theory of interest determination explains why the long-term rate is more stable than the short-term rate.

What are the implications of interest rate structure for real estate? The short-term rate affects the cost of constructing a project, since the construction funds are normally borrowed. Interest payments are a significant cost of construction. Once the project is completed, the long-term interest rate will affect the sale price because potential buyers will probably borrow long-term money to finance the purchase. Thus the lower the interest rate, the more a buyer can pay for a property and yet keep the monthly payments constant.

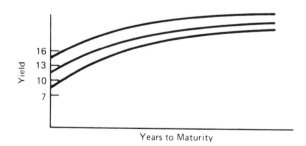

Figure 7–5. The term structure of interest rates.

FISCAL POLICY

Fiscal policy refers to government spending and tax policies to affect the level of output and employment. Increases in government spending and decreases in taxes tend to stimulate the economy by increasing the demand for goods and services. Spending cuts and tax increases tend to reduce the level of demand, thus cooling the economy. An initial change in taxes or spending will have repercussions throughout the economy due to the multiplier effect.

Demand management has been the primary fiscal policy tool for generating economic stability since World War II. The primary policy of Keynesian theories is that demand can be increased either by cutting taxes or by increasing government spending. By such actions aggregate demand will be stimulated and output will increase.

Recently "supply-side" economists have criticized the demand management approach. They claim that in the long run workers and business may become accustomed to governmental demand increases. Thus they may be less restrained in seeking wage and price increases, knowing that if they raise prices, the government demand-side stimulation will ratify their previous increases. Eventually demand management will fail to produce real output increases because all of the increase in aggregate demand is used to support wage-price increases.

Another criticism of Keynesian economics is that government spending intended to stimulate demand is wasteful. Such funds could be better spent in the private sector.

President Reagan has generally supported supply-side approaches to economics and has rejected demand management. Supply-side economists are concerned with increasing output by increasing the ability of the economy to produce goods and services. Tools of the supply-side approach are incentives to business to invest and produce and reductions of governmental regulations that may increase the cost of business. Their expectation is that if the economy is stimulated through the proper incentives, the federal deficit will be reduced even while government spending is increased and taxes are reduced. Critics doubt that supply can be increased in the short run.

The mix of supply-side policies and outside events has resulted in a moderate inflation, low inflationary expectations, and a high real interest rate. (The real interest rate is the actual interest rate less the inflation rate.) The price for these benefits has been job growth too slow to lower the unemployment rate much below about 7 percent.

TRENDS AND SPECULATION ON THE DECADE AHEAD

The 1980s has been a decade of relatively slow real economic growth and rapid price increases, although inflation moderated in the latter part of the decade. Table 7–2 shows trends in several key economic variables. But what of the 1990s? Obviously we can only speculate, but many futurists claim that 80% of the future is already determined. Certainly we can anticipate several factors that will influence the real estate sector.

The Economy

Two potential problem areas are apparent and will have to be addressed in the 1990s. The way that these problems are addressed will affect real estate prospects. First, the federal deficit has been around $200 billion per year since about 1982. There are no solid prospects for this trend to change. Unless the deficit is reduced, it will continue to absorb significant amounts of investment dollars that otherwise would be available for use by private investors, including real estate investors. The deficit is one of the factors that has kept the real interest rate high. Although the interest rate has fallen from the highs of the early 1980s, so has inflation, and so the real interest rate has remained high. High real interest rates combined with low inflation will be negative factors in real estate investment decisions.

The U.S. balance of trade is a second potential problem that will have to be addressed during the 1990s. Currently we are buying more from the rest of the world than we are selling. The question is: What will foreigners do with the dollars they are earning? Currently those dollars are being reinvested in the U.S. This foreign investment helps keep interest rates from being higher then they otherwise would be. Also foreign investors have been heavy purchasers of real estate with the export dollars they have earned. Thus the balance of trade problem has indirectly supported U.S. real estate prices. The danger is that the patterns of foreign investment will not continue unless U.S. interest rates are increased. Another possibility is that the value of the dollar will fall further, making foreign goods more expensive and contributing to inflation.

There are several other unresolved economic problems such as labor productivity, relatively high unemployment, the farm crisis, and reindustrialization (or deindustrialization). We are often tempted to ignore these futuristic problems because the outcomes are speculative.

Table 7–2. Trends in Key Economic Variables

	1960	1965	1970	1975	1980	1983	1984
Median income	5,620	7,143	8,734	11,800	12,686	20,873	22,415
Gross national product (billions)	506	688.1	993	1,549	1,718	3,305	3,663
Personal savings (billions)	17.6	30.3	55.8	94.3	82.5	118.1	156.1
Consumer Price Index (1967 = 100)	88.7	94.5	116.3	161.2	170.5	298.4	311.1
a. Rent	91.7	96.9	110.1	137.3	144.7	236.7	249.3
b. Homeownership	86.3	92.7	123.6	169.7	179.0	344.8	361.7
M_1	N/A	N/A	217	291	310	528	559
M_2 (billions)	N/A	N/A	628	1,023	1,164	2,189	2,372
Interest rates							
a. Prime commercial paper (3-month)	3.85	4.38	7.76	6.25	5.24	8.88	10.10
b. Conventional new home mortgage	6.20	5.89	8.52	9.10	8.99	13.43	13.80
Gross private domestic fixed investment (billions)	72.7	102.5	147.4	224.4	263.0	437.7	544.4
Federal government expenditure on housing (billions)	N/A	N/A	853	1,059	810	1,080	N/A
State and local government expenditure on housing (billions)	N/A	N/A	1,319	1,821	1,396	2,921	N/A

Source: Statistical Abstract of the United States, 1986.

233

Unfortunately, when rents for a real estate development are forecast into the distant future, developers must at least be conversant with long-term economic prospects.

Demographics

Demographics is the statistical study of characteristics of the population. Changes in the size, composition, and life-styles of the American population have significant implications for real estate because demographic factors are an integral component of demand. Another reason that it is important to understand demographics is that, compared with other variables, it is relatively easy to forecast changes in the size and composition of the population. Other demographic features involving values and life-styles are more difficult to forecast.

Two demographic trends, it is generally believed, will have an important impact upon real estate: (1) the increase in one-person households and (2) the maturing population. A brief examination of each trend is in order.

The number of persons in single-person households constitutes about 10% of the U.S. population. And the proportion of single-person households has grown rapidly, increasing 60% between 1970 and 1980. Several factors are probably responsible for the increase: (1) longer life expectancies, (2) increased divorce rates, (3) the tendency to postpone marriage, (4) the decline in the birth rate (childless couples are more likely to become single households), and (5) attitude changes that emphasize independent living.[12]

There are several implications of this trend for developers. Most obvious, the market for one- and two-bedroom units will increase compared with other units. Furthermore, these accommodations can be equipped with scaled-down food and and sanitary facilities. However, many single-person households may have less money that multiperson households, and so the need for smaller units may not translate into effective demand.

Better health, nutrition, and environments have resulted in longer life expectancies. Government and private pension plans have increased the amount of discretionary income available to the elderly. Persons between 55 and 64, many of whom have retired early, spend 30% more than the national average on vacations and are 50% more likely to have a second home. Between 1970 and 1980 their income grew 25% faster than the U.S. average.[13]

The implications of this change in regard to real estate include amenity-oriented communities, second-home communities, and limited-care facilities. These changes will occur at the expense of long-term public commitments for roads, schools, and other public facilities not used by the elderly.

Trends That Are Not: There are many demographic myths—things that everyone knows are true, but are not. Just as it is important to identify trends, it is important not to make decisions based upon myths. Robey described major demographic myths[14]:

Myth	*Reality*
1. We are in the midst of a baby boom.	1. The World War II baby boom is over.
2. The family is dead.	2. Americans believe in the importance of family.
3. The typical family has four members.	3. Most families do not have four members, and the average size is declining.
4. We are a nation of elderly people.	4. The median age is about 30 years.
5. Singles are young and swinging.	5. Many singles are over 65, and the values of singles are similar to those of the rest of the population.
6. Americans are moving back to the cities.	6. Americans continue to move to the suburbs and ex-urbs.
7. The sunbelt is growing at the expense of the frostbelt.	7. The sunbelt is growing, but not due to significant plant relocations.
8. Americans are becoming wealthier.	8. The median family income is rising slowly and only recently passed the level in 1973.

Additional Speculations

The Futurist, a publication of the World Futures Society, published several pages of forecasts for the future, and many of them have at least indirect implications for development.[15] For instance:

1. By the end of the next century a single city may have more than 100 million inhabitants. In the more distant future cities of a billion residents are anticipated.

2. More than 13% of the U.S. population will be 65 years old by the year 2000, twice the percentage in 1940.

3. Lightweight materials can reduce the cost of manufacturing airplanes, making personal planes possible. A plane in every garage?

4. Home computer usage will explode. Special architecture to accommodate computers is likely.

5. By the turn of the century, 25% to 35% of all paid work will be done in the home.

6. The bathroom of the future will become a social center. The two-person bathtub will be common, as well as bathing pools for family bathing. The bathroom may be designed to accommodate exercise equipment.

7. Network families such as church groups or Alcoholics Anonymous will become more important as the single family grows smaller.

8. Water shortages, already a problem in many areas, will increase within two decades.

9. Algae may provide a low-cost fuel substitute, helping to replace the depleting fossil fuels.

10. The market for access-controlled security systems will triple. They will include biometric devices that identify people by hand, voice, or eye "prints."

Values.   Economic values and priorities are expected to shift. Willis Harman believes that rejection of material and social status goals will open new areas for self-development and integration between work and leisure. The shift in values has caused many individuals to be concerned with the "social limits to growth." A recent poll indicated that three out of four Americans agree with the statement: "The trouble with most leaders is that they don't understand that people want better quality of almost everything they have rather than more quantity." All the shifts in attitudes appear to constrain the growth in per capita income.

The impact of any of these or other changes on the real estate sector is a matter for speculation and not for definitive statements. Yet they represent the features that will influence the economic environment of the decade ahead.

INFLATION AND REAL ESTATE

Since World War II, one of the salient characteristics of the American economy is the prevalence of price increases. Prices are increasing for a variety of reasons, and while there may be disagreement over the rate of future price escalations, the long-term economic outlook is for continued inflation. Therefore, it will be worthwhile to consider briefly the impact of inflation on real estate.

General inflation is a rise in overall prices. It should be distinguished from price increases in specific products. Real price increases can be thought of as an increase in exchange ratios. Some prices will rise and others fall even in a noninflationary economy. As an illustration of the same distinction in an inflationary economy, assume that an index of all consumer prices increased by 6% over a year. The price of a three-bedroom house in the Hilltop section of Middleville increased from $30,000 to $33,500 during the same period. Of the $3,500 increase, only $1,700 represents an appreciation in purchasing power of the house relative to other goods. Because only a fraction of total price increases is due to increased relative value, it is possible for an investor to earn a monetary profit and experience a real loss in value. In the above example, if the property had sold for any amount less than $31,800, it would have decreased in real value.

Why does the resale price of housing normally increase when the resale price of other goods—appliances, clothing, cars, etc.—normally decreases in monetary value? There are two reasons why housing appreciates in value: (1) well-established resale markets and (2) slower rates of depreciation. Many used goods fail to bring as much in resale as they could because "used" markets are generally not in the main market economy. Perhaps there is also a stigma attached to some used goods that is not associated with housing. Both real estate and other goods depreciate over time and through use. However, because real estate has a longer economic life than most other goods, its annual rate of real depreciation is only 2–4%. Since inflation has been more rapid than the rate of depreciation, resale prices tend to increase. For example, if a $50,000 property depreciated at 4% annually, it would be worth only $48,000 after 1 year. However, if inflation is 7%, the real estate will sell for ($48,000 × 1.07) $51,360. In recent years, however, housing prices in most parts of the country have risen in value more than other prices. Thus, there is a *specific* price increase in addition to the *general* price increase factors. The combined effect of these two conceptually distinct types of price increases may be expressed[16]:

$$P_n = P_1 \times [(1 + GI) \times (1 + SP)]^n$$

where P_n = sale price in year n
 P_1 = sale price in base year
 GI = rate of general inflation
 SP = rate of specific inflation (real price increase)
 n = years

Assume that a property was purchased for $150,000 and sold 1 year later for $200,000. If the general level of inflation were 7%, what is the rate of specific price increase? Solving the formula: $200 = 150 [(1.07)(1 + SP)]$; $SP = .25$. Thus, the real rate of value increase is 25%. While this is a significant rate of appreciation, it is less than the 33% increase in monetary value.

Figure 7–6 illustrates the relationship between general price increases, real price increases, and depreciation. Figure 7–6 assumes that the specific price increase is 0. In a "no inflation, no specific increase" world, we would expect improved real estate to diminish in value to the extent of locational, functional, and physical depreciation. In this example, the actual value of the property does not increase as rapidly as does the general price level because depreciation has a dampening effect. For example, if the general price level were increasing at 6% and the actual rate of depreciation of a property were 1% per year, then the actual price increase should equal 5%.

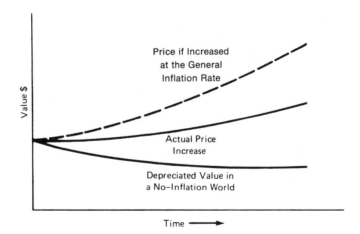

Figure 7–6. Elements of price changes.

Real estate investments are frequently described as an excellent hedge against inflation. Often this concept is accepted uncritically or is wrapped with cliches such as "land values must always rise as population increases" or "everyone must live somewhere." These views often ignore the complexity of value determination and the fact that there are many types of real estate investments. Different types of property and alternative ownership forms may be affected differently by general inflation and increases in specific properties.

Undeveloped Land

The value of undeveloped land is determined by the residual of the value of the completed property minus the costs of construction. If land is in agricultural use, the cost of raising the product should be subtracted from the value of the output to determine the annual net yield. Market value under many circumstances will be discounted value of the income flow. General inflation will increase both the costs of development and the revenues by the same amount. Thus, the difference between the two will also increase by a similar percentage. Table 7-3 presents an example of the value of agricultural land. The same figures could be used to analyze land held for development. In that case, gross income would constitute gross inflows, and costs would be the operating expenses plus capital amortization.

In the example the value of land kept pace with the general price level. While the land held its relative value, relative value was not enhanced by inflation. However, the example assumed that everything remained constant other than general prices. Several other changes that are associated with inflation warrant consideration. First, during a

Table 7-3. Undeveloped Land and Inflation

	Base Period	After 6% Inflation	
Gross income	$ 5,000	($5,000 × 1.06)	$ 5,300
Minus costs (nonland)	1,000	($1,000 × 1.06) −	1,060
Net return to land	$ 4,000		$ 4,240
Land value capitalized at 8%	$50,000		53,000

Value of land comparison: $50,000 × 1.06 = $53,000

Value of land in base period dollars: $53,000 \times \frac{100}{106} = \$50,000$

period of rapid inflation there are few investments that will hold value. Most real goods depreciate in value in spite of inflation. Consequently, investors may be willing to pay a premium for land. In other words, they may pay more than the discounted present value of future returns warrants. Thus, undeveloped land prices may rise as has been the case during recent years. Second, the interest rate tends to rise when inflation is anticipated because of increased reluctance to save. Loss due to inflation is one of the major impediments to savings. An increase in the discount rate will tend to decrease the present value of land. If gross income rose by \$300, as in our example, but the discount rate simultaneously rose from 8 to 8.5%, the value would remain virtually unchanged (\$4240/.085 = \$49,882). Other things being equal, a larger increase in the capitalization rate would actually decrease value.[17]

During the 1970s, aggregate land values rose more rapidly than most measures of the general price level. This was true in spite of the fact that interest rates rose significantly.

The Development Phase. Exposure to risk is perhaps greatest during the planning and construction phase of development. Gibbons described a scenario in which inflation brought sizable losses and bankruptcy to investors in large-scale projects.[18] While his examples were hypothetical, they accurately depict what happened to numerous projects that were initiated prior to the 1974–1975 period of rapid price increases coupled with a slow real economic growth. In Gibbons' view, the type of inflation of the period was cost-push. Rapid increases in the cost of materials forced construction expenditures above original projections. Lumber, masonry, and petroleum-based products experienced rapid price increases. In addition, labor unions demanded higher wages because of increasing prices for food and other basic consumer goods.

In order to slow the rate of inflation, a series of price ceilings was enacted under presidential authority. These ceilings resulted in shortages of basic materials. Labor strikes—attempts to keep up with living costs—resulted in further delays. As a result, many projects took 6–10 months longer to complete than anticipated. The extra time was costly because the interest meter—on funds actually lent and on commitments—was continually running.

Even after extreme delays, Gibbons showed that the completion of construction did not alleviate investor problems. First, operating costs rose more rapidly throughout the period than did rents. This was largely because of the specific increases in taxes and fuel costs. Since demand did not increase enough to compensate the projects, net operating incomes fell, and, consequently, value fell. Even investors who planned to sell projects rather than operate them had their plans thwarted. Inflation caused the interest rate, and hence the capitalization rate, to increase. The high capitalization rates caused a decline in the present value of future income streams. In addition, many financial institutions started scrutinizing properties more carefully or requiring larger down payments as money became tight. This action created marketing problems for some properties; the longer the gap between completion and sale, the greater the total interest payments.

Gibbons' analysis merges concepts of general and specific inflation. It also includes sociopolitical as well as economic repercussions of inflation. His broad perspective provides insights absent from many analyses. At the same time, the problems he described were not uncommon during the period of rapid inflation experienced throughout the 1970s. Individuals who invested in projects similar to those described by Gibbons might vigorously dispute broad generalizations about the benefits of inflation to real estate investors.

Ownership of Developed Real Estate.   It is helpful to distinguish between impact of ownership per se and the related but conceptually distinct consequences of the means of finance. We shall focus first upon the pure ownership factors.

Perhaps small real estate investors experience the impact of inflation most immediately through its effects on properties they already own. "I've made $15,000 in three years on this property" is a frequently voiced (boasted?) claim. Ricks concluded that a California homeowner would have realized an 18½% annual rate of return on a $26,500 house purchased in 1965 and held for 10 years. But the gains were largely due to general inflation.[19] In this case it is also necessary to distinguish between general inflation and specific or real price increases. If general inflation causes both gross income and operating expenses to increase at the same rate as the general price level, then NOI will keep pace with inflation. However, inflation can be risky. Interest rates will rise and have a depressing effect. Also there has never been a "pure" general inflation, and it is difficult to know whether costs or income will increase more rapidly. During recent years, existing properties have also been affected by increases in new construction that outpaced general cost-of-living increases. Because individuals are willing to substitute existing houses for new housing, the price ratio between the two will remain reasonably constant over short periods of time.

For an individual interested in the use value of housing, ownership offers a chance to protect an important part of the family budget from inflation, since the cost of renting will probably continue to rise. Thus, homeownership offers a hedge in a protective, rather than a money-making, sense. However, not all costs of housing are sheltered from inflation. Taxes, maintenance, and insurance may continue to rise at a rate equal to or greater than the general price level. But the homeowner normally has the monthly mortgage payments more or less fixed.

The single-family housing market also appears to have been affected by inflationary expectations as well as by inflation itself. Many buyers would have lower monthly payments if they rented rather than bought. However, because of escalating prices, homeownership has proved to be a financially successful investment for most families. It is partly because of the expected continuation of inflation that individuals are willing to pay the higher monthly outlays associated with ownership. In addition, the ability to deduct interest and taxes from federal income taxes is an incentive to homeownership.

Many investors have wondered whether prices in particular markets are "artificially" high and based upon unrealistic future inflationary expectations. Will there be a shakeout if expectations are not realized? Will the financial benefits that owners have derived reinforce the nonfinancial values traditionally associated with homeownership? When will the spiral ever end? These and other questions have arisen from recent inflationary experiences.

Leverage.   Leverage provides one of the most effective investment tools during inflationary periods. It is through the operation of leverage that most owners of existing properties benefit from inflation. Even if capitalization rates rise with inflation so that the property's value increases less than the general price level, a highly leveraged investor can earn an extraordinary return. For example, if an investor purchases a property with a 10% down payment, the rate of inflation is 10%, and the property increases in value by 6%, then the monetary rate of appreciation will be 60% (.06/.10). The *real* rate of appreciation will still be 90% of the monetary rate, or 54%. This is an excellent *real* rate of return in an inflationary period when one considers that a typical bank or bond will yield negative real rates of return.[20]

Lienholders.   Normally lienholders suffer from inflation because the lien is a debt expressed in current dollars. If the debt is repaid in current dollars, inflation will have diminished the purchasing power.

While there are several types of liens, in another sense lienholders may find their position enhanced. If inflation causes real estate prices to increase, owners of property will be less likely to default. Thus inflation indirectly enhances the security of real property liens.

Housing and Inflation: Victim or Villain?

Gillogly suggested that housing is well suited as a stabilizing sector of the economy.[21] Housing is a good stabilizer because: (1) it is more sensitive than other sectors to monetary and credit changes, (2) it accounts for 25–30% of all credit funds, so housing is large enough to be significant, (3) the expenses associated with home-building—appliances and other contingent goods—provide additional leverage, and (4) it is a local industry, so that the impact will be similar among the various regions of the country.

Attempts to stabilize housing create problems elsewhere in the economy. The institutions that support the secondary mortgage market, the Federal National Mortgage Association, Federal Home Loan Bank Board, Government National Mortgage Association, and others, are stimulating the economy by lending funds (purchasing mortgages). Yet the Fed is undertaking restrictive monetary policies by borrowing funds (purchasing securities). Therefore the housing-support institutions may operate in ways that thwart the policies of the open market committee.

SUMMARY

The level of overall economic activity affects the success of real estate investments, and, at the same time, real estate investments influence the macroeconomy. The major types of economic fluctuations are: (1) random fluctuations, (2) seasonal fluctuations, (3) business cycles, and (4) secular trends. Real estate activity is most affected by seasonal fluctuations and business cycles. The most important theories of business cycles are physical, psychological, savings and investment, monetary, and fiscal theories. The fact that there are several explanations suggests that cycles may have more than one cause.

There are four reasons why real estate is more sensitive to the business cycle than most other activity. First, construction activity is sensitive to pessimistic outlooks. Second, real estate may be repaired and remodeled rather than replaced. Third, lending institutions may be reluctant to lend. Finally, many small construction firms let the industry dissolve during slow periods.

While housing cycles are affected by overall economic conditions, the business cycle does not coincide with fluctuations in construction activity. Housing starts generally peak and bottom out before the rest of the economy. Real estate is a leading sector because it quickly experiences the impact of a slowdown in consumer spending on the downside and it is more sensitive to increases in the interest rates during expansions. Several techniques have been developed to forecast business activity, although judgment of the analyst is still critical.

The interest rate is one of the most important links between the money market and the real estate sector. The interest rate is set by the interaction of individuals and institutions borrowing and lending money. The interest rate may also be thought of as the price of bonds. The institution with the greatest influence on the interest rate is the Federal Reserve Board, which is often said to control the money supply. Its control is significant but not total. The main tools of the Fed are open market operations, discount rate adjustments, the setting of reserve requirements, moral persuasion, and other regulations.

Real estate is greatly affected by inflation. Realty tends to increase in value because of the well-established resale market and the slow rates of depreciation compared with other assets. Individuals who own mortgaged property have done well as a result of inflation because property values have increased while the mortgage debt remains a fixed-dollar-value obligation. Furthermore, real property values have generally increased more than the general price level. However, even during inflationary periods, not all real estate investments are successful. Lienholders normally suffer. If costs and revenues increase at the same rate as inflation, NOI will also only keep pace. Changes in the capitalization rate could reduce value. Expectations of future inflation are just as important as inflation. Many investors have been willing to accept fairly low rates of return in order to purchase a real asset.

SECTION III

Assessing the Planning Process Using Case Studies

The following chapters present case studies extracted from actual reports. The purpose of this section is to illustrate the process and procedures used in the development of the market and feasibility studies in the real world. The focus of this section will be directed toward the methodology and practices employed by those who have conducted the studies. The studies have been chosen because they represent a range of various land uses and demonstrate different approaches to development problems. The reader should also be able to discern the strong and weak points of each study by comparing the actual approaches with the idealized methodology presented in Chapters 1 to 7. Due to the proprietary nature of much of the material, where appropriate, names and some of the data have been changed. These changes, however, do not change the methodology or outcome of the process.

8

Case Study: Industrial Park Development

The industrial park is located in Wyoming and is presently considered to be a successful land development. The developer was a successful businessman and was involved with the industrial development of the state of Wyoming. He was concerned with the future growth of the state and believed that one of the drawbacks to increased industrial development was the lack of improved land for industrial use. He owned a large ranch near the city of Cheyenne, Wyoming, and decided to investigate the possibility of developing a portion of the ranch for industrial use. The site chosen was adjacent to the city of Cheyenne but was not within the city boundaries. Figure 8–1 is a regional location map. The developer set aside an area in excess of 1,000 acres for potential development.

Before contacting the consulting group, the developer had already made land sales to several firms wishing to move into the area. This was being done in the absence of any overall market analysis or land use plan.

The consultant chosen was a large Denver-based AE&P firm. The firm offered a complete line of land development services. A meeting was held to discuss the scope of services required. During the initial meeting between the consultant group and the developer, the developer's objectives, project concept, and internal constraints were all discussed.

CLIENT OBJECTIVES

The developer felt that the state of Wyoming badly needed industrial development and that one principal constraint was the lack of planned and developed industrial sites. He mentioned that the Governor of Wyoming and key members of the legislature were in complete agree-

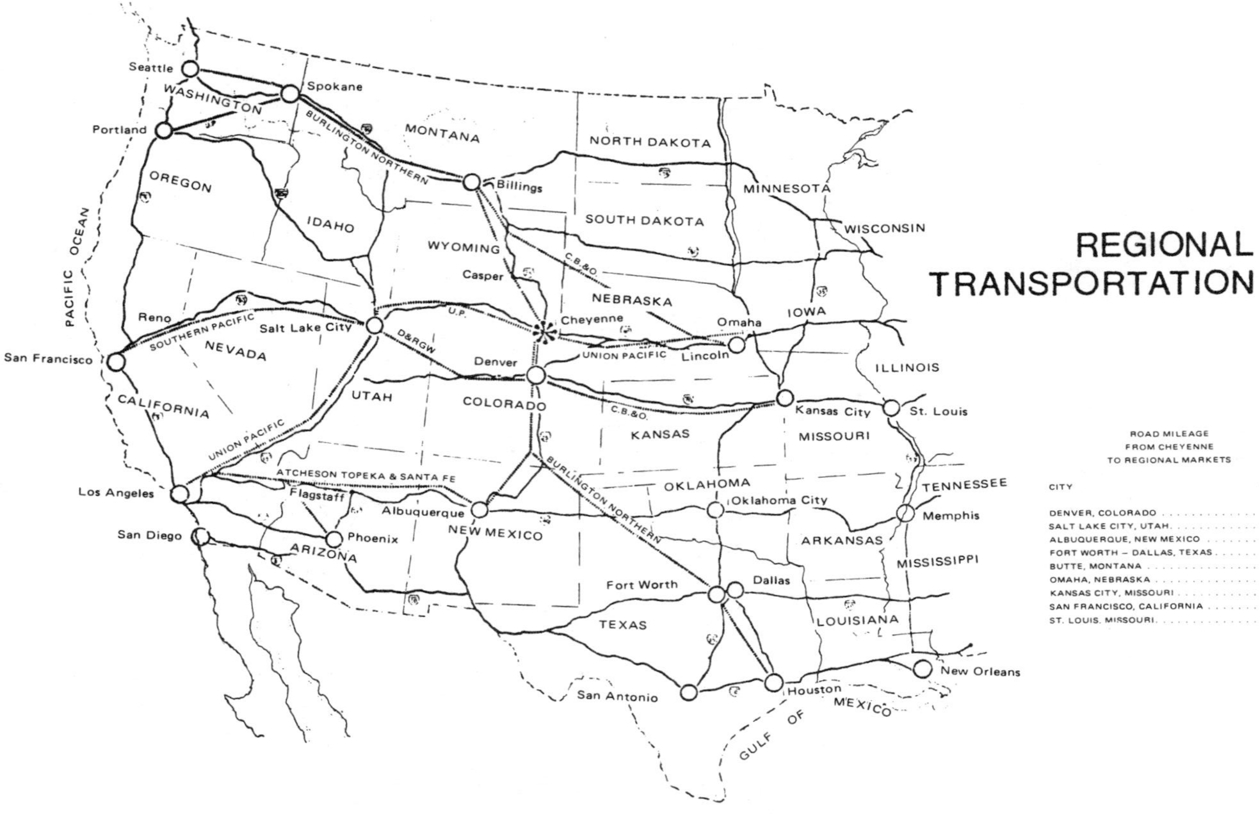

REGIONAL
TRANSPORTATION

ROAD MILEAGE
FROM CHEYENNE
TO REGIONAL MARKETS

CITY	MILES
DENVER, COLORADO	97
SALT LAKE CITY, UTAH	435
ALBUQUERQUE, NEW MEXICO	555
FORT WORTH – DALLAS, TEXAS	872
BUTTE, MONTANA	705
OMAHA, NEBRASKA	507
KANSAS CITY, MISSOURI	600
SAN FRANCISCO, CALIFORNIA	1,181
ST. LOUIS, MISSOURI	851

Figure 8–1. Regional transportation.

ment with him. His only interest was in developing the land for industrial use. He defined the area to be planned and imposed certain constraints on the physical dimensions of the site. He felt this was essential to maintain the integrity of the ranch.

He indicated that he was only interested in industrial land development and sales. He was not interested in speculative building construction or any type of operational involvement. He also stressed that he wanted the potential of agriculturally linked industrial operations thoroughly investigated, since he felt that these types of activities would be the most likely prospects. With the preliminary objectives established, the initial phase of the market analysis was begun.

THE MARKET STUDY

Indirect Economic Factors

Site inspections were made by the consultant company planners, economists, and civil and transportation engineers. Pannilization, i.e., erecting ground controls for aerial photography, was initiated. Meetings and interviews were held with Cheyenne area businesspeople, public officials, and environmental groups, all concerned with the area's development.

No apparent political, attitudinal, or regulatory constraints were imposed on the project as a result of these discussions. All groups were very optimistic about future growth, and had no reservations about the ability of the city's present and planned urban subsystems to handle an increased population resulting from increased employment.

On-site inspections did not turn up any major physical constraints to development. Given the surrounding land use, crossing rail lines, and occasional odors due to the prevailing winds and the proximity of the petroleum refinery and the sewage plant, the planning area was believed to be well suited for industrial development.

The remainder of the market analysis dealt with economic factors.

Direct Economic Factors

The consultant defined the principal objectives of this portion of the investigation as:

1. The determination of the present and potential effective demand in the Cheyenne area for industrial land use.

2. The delineation of that portion of aggregate demand which could be attracted to the planning area. Demand would be translated into total potential developable.
3. The identification of the types of firms that represent the best prospects for locating on the site as an aid in marketing efforts and estimating the developmental planning costs.
4. The establishment of a basis for development programming.
5. The provision of projected revenue and cost data for the feasibility analysis.

In organizing his market study of the direct economic factors, the analyst structured the following basic outline:

  I. Basic Elements of Overall Demand
        Population characteristic
        Employment potential and stability
        Income trends
 II. Economic-Sector Analysis
        Primary sector
          Agriculture
          Mining
          Forest products
        Secondary sector
          Manufacturing
          Construction
        Tertiary sector
          Transportation
          Finance
          Warehousing
          Tourism
III. Land Use Trends
 IV. Existing Supply
  V. Recommendations

The market study pointed out that the immediate availability of improved land for industrial expansion is becoming an increasingly significant factor in locational decisions. A firm's decision to locate in a region is partially based on such factors as proximity to markets, quality and quantity of the available labor force, costs of natural resources used in the firm's production process, and transportation. Once a regional decision has been made, individual plant site selection will depend to a large degree on the availability of planned and improved sites.[1]

The market study also indicated that potential industrial land requirements may be determined by estimating, from the point of view of various industries, the effective demand existing in the region for their products. This determination is based, in part, on an analysis of those economic elements of an area that make up aggregate demand. The principal components of demand are population, employment, and income. Other areas that require investigation include existing, and possibly nonexisting, sectors of economic activity in the region. The effect of individual sectors on aggregate supply and demand conditions, as well as on their present and potential growth rates, provides the basis for determining those types of industries most likely to successfully locate in the area. These firms are referred to as "*best fit.*"

Population Analysis.   The study of the direct economic forces began with an analysis of the population characteristics of the area (see Table 8–1), followed by an analysis of the community's income and employment patterns.

The study found that the most significant population factor in Wyoming has been its rate of net migration.

The population section of the study concluded that Cheyenne appeared to have reached a position of equilibrium and was exhibiting definite signs of population growth and economic expansion. The con-

Table 8–1. Population Characteristics, City of Cheyenne

Year	Total Population	Population Change	Percentage Change from Previous Period	Average Yearly Change Percentage
1900	14,087	—	—	—
1910	11,320	−2,767	−19.6	−1.9
1920	13,829	2,509	22.2	2.2
1930	17,861	3,532	25.5	2.5
1940	22,474	5,113	29.5	2.9
1950	31,935	9,461	42.1	4.2
1960	43,505	11,570	36.2	3.6
1970	40,914	−2,591	−6.0	−.6
1980	47,283	6,369	15.5	1.5

Source: U.S. Department of Commerce, Bureau of the Census, *Census of Population: Wyoming, 1980,* U.S. Government Printing Office, Washington, D.C.

Table 8–2. City of Cheyenne, Population Projections, Selected Studies

Study	1970	1975	1980	1985	1990
Cheyenne master plan[a]	52,500	56,600	62,600	69,100	76,400
Mineral study[b]	42,617 (1972)	—	55,009	—	76,122
Land use survey[c]	48,000	51,100	54,800	58,400	—
Water plan[d]	55,380	—	67,380	—	79,380
Prior market study[e]	67,000	71,000	75,000	—	—
Consultant projections[f]	40,914	47,000	54,500	62,500	71,250

Notes:
[a] *Cheyenne-Laramie County, Comprehensive Plan 1970–1990.* These are figures for Laramie County. Cheyenne in 1970 was approximately 73% of Laramie County.
[b] *Wyoming Mineral Industries, Review and Forecast,* Cameron Engineers, Denver, Colorado, 1969.
[c] *Land Use Survey,* Cheyenne Planning Commission, 1966.
[d] *The Cheyenne Water Supply Plan,* J. T. Banner and Associates, 1961.
[e] *Land Use and Marketability Study,* Cheyenne, Larry Smith and Company, Inc., 1967, county figures.
[f] Projections developed by the consultant using a cohort survival model, modified by estimates of future employment.

sulting company developed population projections and compared the projections with five other population studies that had been recently completed. The consultant's figures, demonstrated in Table 8–2, were more conservative than the other five, and therefore the company could not be accused of being overly optimistic.

Employment and Income. During the population analysis, the area's employment and income were also being investigated. The more salient points, uncovered in the employment and income categories, were the causes of the consultant's conservative population projections.

The number of persons in the Wyoming labor force from 1962 to 1970 declined. During this period relative per capita income also declined. The economic sectors primarily responsible for this decline were agriculture, contract construction, transportation (which includes communications and utilities), and manufacturing. The sectors that expanded their labor force were mining and government, while wholesale and retail trade services and finance remained relatively constant.

The most recent estimate of unemployment in the state at the time of the study was 3.1%, which was slightly over one-half of the national average. This low rate of unemployment was due, in large parts, to the out-migration of unemployed persons. This out-migration, combined with Wyoming's higher labor participation rate, kept the unemployment rate low.

Wyoming's labor supply was very mobile. Their educational level and technical skills were such that they had little trouble relocating to areas where employment was more readily available. Since 1930 Wyoming had exported skilled workers. However, the analyst believed that demand for labor in the state was exceeding effective supply in some areas. Wages paid in manufacturing in Wyoming were 4–8% above the national average. Personal income, it was noted, increased by 10% during 1971.

In concluding the employment and income section, the analyst made employment and income projections to 1981. In comparing his projections with those made by the Employment Security Commission of Wyoming, it was apparent that his were the more conservative figures. This was subsequently reflected in the adjustments made to the consultant's overall population projections, in Table 8–2.

The researcher noted that any significant renewed growth would depend, to a large extent, on continuing government employment and a determined effort by communities to develop more diversified economic bases and to aggressively search for new industrial firms. This in turn would require the provision of industrial land.

Economic-Sector Analysis

In addition to the analysis of the major components of areawide demand, i.e., population, employment, and income, Wyoming's economy was disaggregated into three major sectors. The primary sector, which was of critical importance to the state of Wyoming, was the first one to be examined. The primary economic sector generally included the activities involved in the extraction of natural resources—agriculture, forestry, and mining. The secondary sector encompassed manufacturing and construction operations, and the tertiary sector involved the sale and distribution of goods and services.[2]

Primary Sector—Agriculture. The market study indicated that due to the extensive nature of Wyoming agriculture production, little agglomeration or industrial concentration had taken place. This, in turn, held back significant development of processing plants and agricultural support centers.

Primary Sector—Mining and Mineral Production. The market study indicated that Wyoming's extraction industries ranked 12th in the nation in the production of primary fuels, although total Wyoming production amounted to less than 2.5% of national production. Even though major increases in the production of coal, uranium, oil shale, and some specific nonfuel mineral industries were predicted, the analyst did not expect Cheyenne to receive any direct benefits from predicted expansions.

Primary Sector—Forest Products. The analyst did find some potential for development in the primary sector. Employment in forest products in the state was small. However, the projected future national demand for lumber and other forest products suggested the possibility of substantial growth in Wyoming's production. Estimates indicated that Wyoming's forest resources could support an industry twice its present size.

The types of firms identified from the primary sectors include meat-processing, feed-milling, livestock-feeding, irrigation systems distribution or manufacturing or both, and particleboard and hardboard plants. Although these types of firms exhibited growth potential and their general locational factors were compatible with the Cheyenne area, they remained part of slow-growth industries at both the national and the regional level.

Secondary Sector—Manufacturing. Examination of Cheyenne and its economic base indicated a similar picture to that of the state; i.e., Cheyenne had very little manufacturing. However, unlike the state, Cheyenne was not dependent, directly, on the primary sector. The biggest strength of Cheyenne's economic base was government.

The analyst found that the manufacturing sector provided the most potential for industrial development. The majority of Wyoming's manufacturing activity was geared to processing natural resources. There were several valid reasons to account for the lack of diversified manufacturing activity within the state. However, the researcher pointed out that these obstacles—lack of market, lack of support services, transport costs and financing difficulties, and little improved land—were becoming less and less of a barrier, particularly in Cheyenne.

Given these conditions, the analyst concluded that those "best-fit" industries that had the greatest potential benefit for the Cheyenne area are these manufacturing firms in the secondary sector. Firms with the highest potential are those typically classified as "footloose," i.e., those not particularly market-oriented. These types of firms usually have a high value added to transportation costs and view their markets from a regional and national perspective. Their locational decision factors are primarily labor market considerations, favorable tax climates, readily available land, good access to regional markets, community attitudes, land prices, and management's personal preferences.

The market analyst made a study of principal locational factors for major industrial groups in the U.S. and their regional growth trends. Secondary data were used exclusively for this part of the research. The research indicated that 22 types of manufacturing operations had the potential of being attracted to the Cheyenne area within the ensuing 5–10 years. These firms were listed in a grid arrangement demonstrated in Table 8–3.

Secondary Sector—Construction. The construction industry was indicated to be in a good position in Cheyenne. Projected increases in population, renovation work on the missile sites, development of several firms in the area, and the new state office building would cause the present rate of construction to triple within the next year. The demand for steel reinforcing bars generated some interest in the potential of a mini steel mill. However, the analyst felt that the locational criteria for this type firm would most likely rule out Cheyenne. This projected growth in the construction industry indicated a potential for cement and prefab modular home manufacturing.

Tertiary Sector—Trade and Services. The tertiary sector included distribution and sale of goods and services, and accounted for nearly two-thirds of both total employment and total civilian income in Wyoming. The growth of the tertiary sector of any economic system depends in large part on the primary and secondary sectors.

The analyst concluded that adequate space was available in the Cheyenne area for any short-run expansions of retail operations. This space was a result of the general downturn in the late 1960s, which caused many retail outlets to close their doors and left large amounts of commercial space available.

Tertiary Sector—Transportation. Employment in transportation was projected to increase with the location of major trucking firms in the area and anticipated increases in warehousing activities. It was

Table 8–3. Locational Factors Assigned Values

"BEST-FIT" FIRMS	Environmentally Sound	Regional Market Compatibility	Local Market Compatibility	National Growth Trend	Regional Growth Trend	Labor Market Fit	Production Process and Available Supplies	Compatibility with Transportation System	Utilities	Value Added to Transport Cost	Local Money Market Compatibility	Intraindustry Stability	Regional Competitive Position	TOTAL
Petrochemical	3	4	1	5	3	3	4	3	2	5	2	5	3	43
Transportation operations	5	5	2	4	4	5	2	5	5	4	3	4	5	53
Candy mfg.	4	4	2	4	3	3	4	3	2	4	3	3	3	42
Cement	3	2	4	4	4	5	5	4	4	3	4	3	3	49
Textiles	5	3	3	2	2	4	3	5	4	3	4	2	3	43
Jewelry	5	4	2	4	3	4	4	5	5	5	5	3	3	52
Toys	5	3	2	4	3	4	3	5	5	4	3	3	3	49
Cosmetics	3	4	2	5	4	4	3	5	3	5	5	3	2	48
Abrasives	5	3	3	3	3	5	5	5	4	4	5	3	3	51
Snowmobiles and small engines	5	5	2	4	5	5	2	3	4	4	3	4	3	49

Skis and related products	5	5	3	5	5	4	3	4	5	5	3	3	55
Firearms	5	5	2	4	4	3	2	4	5	5	4	2	48
Vending machines	5	4	1	5	4	3	3	3	5	4	3	3	47
Photographic equipment	5	5	3	4	4	3	2	5	5	5	4	4	54
Fertilizer	3	3	2	3	2	5	5	3	3	3	3	2	41
Feedlot	2	4	2	5	4	4	5	3	4	3	4	4	49
Crop processing	4	3	1	3	3	3	1	3	3	4	3	3	35
Paper products	4	5	3	4	4	5	4	3	3	4	3	4	51
Warehousing and distribution	5	5	2	5	3	5	5	5	5	3	4	4	54
Prefab housing, mobile homes and modular	5	5	3	5	4	5	4	3	5	3	4	3	54
Feed manufacturing	5	3	4	3	5	5	2	3	5	5	3	3	45
Glass and fiberglass mfg.	4	5	2	4	3	5	4	4	5	5	4	4	52

(continued)

Table 8–3. Continued

"BEST-FIT" FIRMS	Environmentally Sound	Regional Market Compatibility	Local Market Compatibility	National Growth Trend	Regional Growth Trend	Labor Market Fit	Production Process and Available Supplies	Compatibility with Transportation System	Utilities	Value Added to Transport Cost	Local Money Market Compatibility	Intraindustry Stability	Regional Competitive Position	TOTAL
Electronics assembly and mfg.	5	5	2	5	5	4	4	5	5	5	5	5	4	59
Irrigation systems	5	4	4	3	3	5	2	4	5	4	5	3	3	50
Plastics	5	4	2	5	4	2	4	4	5	5	5	5	4	54
Wood hardboard and particleboard	4	4	2	3	3	5	4	3	4	3	5	4	3	47
Plywood and veneer mills	4	3	2	3	3	5	4	3	4	2	5	3	3	44
Medical hardware mfg.	5	4	1	4	4	3	2	4	5	5	4	4	2	47
Meat packing and processing	3	3	2	3	2	3	5	4	2	3	5	3	2	40

known that four major trucking firms had contacted Cheyenne representatives with the intention of locating in the area. They were looking for appropriate sites.

Tertiary Sector—Finance. The analyst noted that, until recently, it was virtually impossible to obtain significant amounts of capital for new manufacturing ventures in the state. However, the organization, in 1968, of the Wyoming Bancorporation, which then held 80% interest in five Wyoming banks and was moving to acquire a majority interest in four additional banks, helped to reduce this problem. Even so, the report indicated that the total resources of the state's financial community were small compared with those of most states. These resources, however, were adequate to handle 90% of the types of firms identified as having the best potential for locating in Cheyenne.

Tertiary Sector—Warehousing and Distribution. To determine the warehousing and distribution potential of Cheyenne, the analyst reviewed the experiences of the cities of Reno and Sparks, Nevada, and Clearfield, Utah. Clearfield is presently the largest warehousing and distribution center in the nation, with 6,000,000 square feet of covered space; Reno and Sparks have over 1,000,000 square feet of warehouse and distribution floor area.[3] Investigations were also made into warehousing and distribution in the Denver area. Interviews were held with managers of both public and private facilities, as well as with industrial development, distribution, and transportation specialists, in Reno, Sparks, Clearfield, and Denver.

Investigations pinpointed 11 principal location factors. Three major classification groups were developed from the 11 factors. The major groupings are as follows:

1. State and local tax laws, geographical location, nearness to market, and transportation facilities ranked highest in importance.[4]
2. Freight rates, state and local laws and regulations, and labor were the three factors ranked in the center of importance.
3. Site, power, fuel, water, living conditions, and climate were felt to be important, but ranked below other factors.

Review of these major groupings in relation to the Cheyenne area indicated that state and local tax laws were very favorable compared with those of other Western states. Wyoming had the most favorable corporate tax structure of the eight major Rocky Mountain states. The state was also among the lowest in terms of sales and use tax and had no personal income tax.

The geographical location of Cheyenne places it in an excellent position to service the Denver regional market on an overnight basis. Cheyenne is also within a 2- to 4-day delivery time to Salt Lake City, Utah; Albuquerque, New Mexico; Ft. Worth-Dallas, Texas; Butte, Montana; Omaha, Nebraska; and Kansas City, Missouri.

The transportation system developing in the area gave a tremendous boost to the potential of Cheyenne as a regional warehousing and distribution center. The development of Interstate 80 running east and west and of Interstate 25 going north and south was mentioned as an important factor to three firms presently in the process of locating in Cheyenne. Cheyenne was also located in an excellent position with regard to rail traffic, being on the main lines of the UP and CB&Q. In addition to the excellent location of Cheyenne with respect to the interstate highway system, all major trucking lines were authorized to operate in the area. Ring Trucking Company was planning on locating a new regional facility employing 200 people in Cheyenne, and discussions with four other firms were underway at the time of the study.

The airfreight capability in the Cheyenne area was limited, but this type of shipping was not expected to be significant to warehousing and distribution operations. In the Reno, Sparks, and Clearfield operations, airfreight amounted to less than 1% of total shipments.

It was found that the majority of the firms in warehousing and distribution (W&D) occupied less than 50,000 square feet of space, with 50% occupying less than 25,000 square feet and 20% occupying less than 10,000. The majority of firms employed less than 25 workers,[5] although not evenly divided between those firms involved in distribution and those in manufacturing. These types of operations were definitely compatible with the local Cheyenne area labor supply.

In summary, the analyst suggested that the Cheyenne area exhibited characteristics which were conducive to the location of W&D operations. These operations would be primarily of a regional nature with overnight service capability to retailers and wholesalers in the Denver metropolitan region. Cheyenne had a competitive advantage in attracting firms that may wish to manufacture, mill, process, and reassemble products for out-of-state shipments, since the Colorado freeport law did not allow this. There was also some possibility of firms locating in Cheyenne to serve the Southwest market.

Tertiary Sector—Leisure Activities.   The market analyst also investigated leisure activities and found that tourism accounted for more
than 15% of Wyoming's total exports. The most direct influence of
tourism was on retail sales, the sector which employed nearly 22,000 of
the state's total labor force of 150,000. Given the fact that Wyoming's
per capita income was then slightly below the national average and the
state ranked 49th in population density, it seemed reasonable to attribute Wyoming's highest per capita retail sales in the nation to the influence of tourist expenditures. Summer tourism could be expected to
increase at 5% per year to 1990, primarily increasing the demand on
retail establishments, and consequently increasing the demand for
commercial space.

National and regional leisure activities were predicted to increase
significantly over the next 10 years—a 17% increase per year in skiing
activity alone in the Rocky Mountain area. The principal manufacturers of products used for winter leisure activities in the Rocky Mountain
area are ski, snowmobile, and related clothing firms. These firms were
felt to be excellent prospects for location in the Cheyenne area, and
were classified as manufacturing in the secondary sector.

The 29 types of firms identified in the primary, secondary, and tertiary sectors were placed on a grid comparing 13 locational factors and
assigned unweighted values from 1 to 5 (see Table 8–3). These assigned
values appeared to be subjective, but were based on the analyst's
knowledge and sensitivity to the subject developed during the study.
This method was used only as an aid to serve in the initial identification
and selection of land use possibilities based on the 13 major locational
factors. The "best-fit" firms were then ranked by locational factor
scores (see Table 8–4).

Projected Industrial Land Use Requirements

Analysis of Cheyenne's land use categories from 1961 to 1971 provided
indicators which were deemed significant and reinforced findings from
the sector analysis. A review of residential land use data indicated an
increase between 1961 and 1966 of 40%. Between 1966 and 1971, total
residential land use changes amounted to 4.8%. This agreed with findings that an acute housing shortage existed in the area due to low
construction rates and an expanding population. Of particular significance was the rate of increase in industrial land use. During the period
1961–1966, this area increased by 45.5%; from 1966 to 1971 industrial

Table 8–4. Ranking of "Best-Fit" Manufacturing

Operation	Locational Factors Score from Table 8–3
Electronics assembly and manufacturing	59
Skis and related products	55
Warehousing and distribution	54
Prefab housing, modular, and mobile home	54
Plastics	54
Transportation operations	53
Glass and fiberglass	52
Jewelry	52
Abrasives	51
Paper products	51
Irrigation systems	50
Cement	49
Toys	49
Snowmobiles and small engines	49
Feedlot	49
Cosmetics	48
Firearms	48
Wood hardboard and particleboard	47
Medical hardware	47
Feed	45
Plywood and veneer mill	44
Petrochemical	43
Textiles	43
Candy	42
Fertilizer	41
Meat packing and processing	40
Crop processing	35

land use increased by 64.4%. Of all major sectors, only industrial and transportation land use had a positive rate of increase, 19.1% and 21%, respectively. A clearer picture of the rapid rate of increase in industrial and commercial land use is shown in Figure 8–2.

Projected industrial land use requirements were based on four considerations: (1) the economic-sector analysis and estimated spatial requirement of "best-fit" firms, along with W&D operations, (2) an analysis of land use trends in Cheyenne over the 10-year period 1961–1971, (3) known acreage requirements of firms existing on the site and firms that had expressed an interest in locating on the proposed site, and (4)

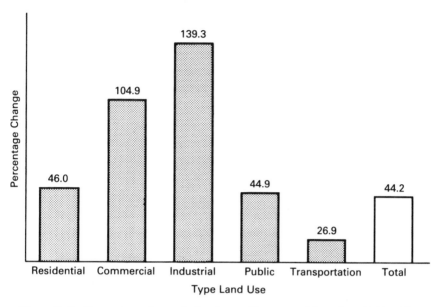

Figure 8–2. Percentage change in land use, Cheyenne, Wyoming, 1961–1971.

interviews with planners, businesspeople, economic development specialists, and industrial park managers involved in the region's development. These figures are demonstrated in Table 8–5.

Projection 1. First, assuming minimum acreage requirements for
each of the "best-fit" firms, including four small to medium trucking
concerns, in conjunction with piggyback and docking operations, a
required net industrial acreage of approximately 420 was estimated.
This estimate was exclusive of any meat packing and processing, crop
processing, feedlot operations, and operations requiring over 25 acres.

For purposes of analysis, it was assumed that only one each of the
"best-fit" firms would locate in the area. Only those firms indicated
were considered. It would not be unrealistic, however, for "best-fit"
firms to use considerably more land than estimated. The demand for
industrial land by 1981 could exceed projections, with the development
of significant warehousing and distribution operations, one or two large
transportation-oriented firms, and concerns other than those indicated.

The market study indicated that the regional market could support
1,000,000 square feet of warehouse space by 1981. Assuming that

Table 8–5. Industrial Land Requirements

Type of Estimate	Estimated Acres Required to 1981
1. Minimum acreage requirements for "best-fit" firms from Table 8–4	465
2. Land use trends	
a. (Constant rate of growth)	555
b. (10% increase in rate of growth)	635
3. Existing and interested firms	
a. (18 acres per firm)	540
b. (21 acres per firm)	630
4. Interviews	1,000
5. Analyst's estimate (figure used for developmental programming)	575

buildings occupy 50% of the net acreage requirements, this would mean approximately 45 additional acres for W&D purposes only.

Projection 2. Analyzing industrial land use trends in Cheyenne over the past 10 years and assuming that the present rate of increase would remain constant, an additional 555 acres of industrial land would be required in Cheyenne by 1981. Assuming a modest increase of 10% in the rate of growth of industrial land, 635 acres would be required.

Projection 3. Examination of structural space requirements and acreage desired, by firms already located on and interested in locating on the property, indicated that the area was attractive to extensive land-use-type operations. The average space requirement for firms that planned to locate on the property was in excess of 18 acres. Using an average of 18 acres and assuming 30 of the "best-fit" firms would locate in the area over the next 10 years, a net acreage of 540 would be required.[6]

Typical lot sizes in smaller industrial districts ranged from 1 to 5 acres, with building sizes of 10,000–50,000 square feet. Analysis of industrial areas with sites of 10 acres or more, however, indicated the average was 20–22 acres. Assuming this average for the "best-fit" firms, approximately 630 net acres of industrial land would be required.

Projection 4. Individual and group interviews were held with area planners, bankers, businesspeople, economic development specialists, utilities representatives, railroad representatives, and industrial park managers in Cheyenne and Denver. The general feeling among this group was that the above estimates for potential industrial land were conservative. Their various estimates ran as high as 500 acres by 1976 and 1,000 by 1981.

Projection 5. The final estimate by the analyst was based on his observation of all the market data. The market data included a review of all existing industrial parks in the region, including their absorption rates and presently available acreage.[7] Table 8–6 indicates that the annual average absorption rate would be approximately 57 acres per year during the 10-year planning horizon. The sale price estimates escalate from $10,000 per acre in 1972 to $15,500 in 1981.

The following recommendations, based on results of the market study and initial sketch plan, were made to the client.

Recommendations for the Developmental Program

1. Establish a developmental program for a total of 575 acres in two phases. The total acres are expected to be absorbed by 1981. A third phase, not recommended for planning at this time and situated between Phases 1 and 2, should be programmed for possible use after 1981.

2. Promote development of the first phase from the west (in the vicinity of the existing and planned industries) to the east in order to take advantage of access, utilities, availability of rail service, and minimum topographic problems.

Table 8–6. Total Industrial Land Use Projected for Site 1976–1981 by Analyst

Land Use	1972–1976	1976–1981	Total to 1981
Industrial	275	300	575
	1972	*1981*	
Projected sale price per acre	$10,000 → (escalating at 5% per year)	$15,500	

3. Establish firm commitments, mutual switching agreements, and time schedules on the development of lead tracks which will provide rail access to the site. The general alignments of rail spurs and lead tracks were reviewed and approved by CB&Q and UP.

4. Establish a development schedule which is coordinated with construction of Interstate 80 and the Cheyenne Bypass.

5. Request the Wyoming Highway Department to include the frontage roads that serve the first phase as part of the first construction element of Interstate 80. If construction of the roads will be delayed, investigate the feasibility of the developer's building the roads with reimbursement from the state.

6. Consult with existing developments on or adjacent to the site to determine future vehicular access where Interstate 80 will interrupt present access.

7. Establish close contact with municipal and private utilities to ensure the provision of adequate supplies of water, gas, electricity, and sewage treatment. It is imperative that construction of the sewage treatment plant be coordinated with the industrial development because the present plant operates at or near maximum capacity.

8. Establish the realignment of the section of Crow Creek which flows through the site in order to increase the amount of usable land and to avoid possible flooding problems.

9. Differentiate between the grading and fill to be done by the developer and by the Wyoming Highway Department.

10. Employ a qualified person or firm to develop and manage a marketing program.

11. Conduct detailed engineering studies of the first phase in order to provide clients with specific data on grading, utility easement locations, and costs.

12. Draw up a minimum set of covenants and operating standards for the development based on criteria discussed in this report. Environmental standards should be stressed.

13. Promote the relocation of the gas line to avoid any future infringements caused by land development. It is recommended that a location along the northern boundary of the site be investigated.

14. Establish contacts with the Bureau of Reclamation in Denver to establish procedures for approval of any construction within the power transmission easement.

15. Contact the owners of all other easements (e.g., telephone easements) located on the site before allowing development on or adjacent to their right-of-way.

16. Consult with rail companies for assistance in promotion, development, and operation in order to obtain the best possible rail service.

17. Encourage industrial clients to conduct soil tests before construction on individual sites.

18. Consider the development of a landscaping plan by a qualified landscape architect.

19. Organize promotional efforts in concert with area railroads, the state of Wyoming, and local development groups to attract warehousing and distribution operations.

20. Consider construction of a speculative building to promote warehousing and distribution operations.

21. Schedule an inventory of approximately 80 acres to maintain a viable marketing program in order to allow industries locational choices.

THE FEASIBILITY ANALYSIS

Although multiple land use potential was indicated in the market analysis, the client decided to restrict all development and financial planning to industrial land use only. However, the final development plan reserved those areas best suited for future commercial operations. The client maintained his position that he was interested in land development and sales only; he wanted no operational involvement.

The financial structure of the development was relatively simple; the estimated value of the land was to be considered as equity investment, while all development funds were to be borrowed at the time required.

Several preliminary sketch plans were drafted and reviewed with the client. Preliminary engineering cost estimates were made and a static pro forma analysis developed. The developmental and financial planning reviews were not conducted in a formal presentation but rather were done in informal meetings with the developer's financial team and the consultant company's planners, engineers, and market analysts. The decision to move ahead was based on a series of pro formas incorporating differing cost estimates and revenue projections. Preliminary estimates indicated that the project should return a reasonable profit if the predicted absorption rate and pricing policy were relatively accurate. These are discussed in the economic feasibility section.

The next step was to structure the formal development plan so that more accurate cost estimates could be determined.

The layout and development of the industrial park were dictated by several factors. Natural physical features, the availability and location of utilities, land easements, existing and proposed access to major transportation routes, and existing development adjacent to and within the site all influenced the physical layout and design of the industrial park.

Design of the Industrial Park

The major elements which determine the appearance of an industrial park are the physical design and the protective restrictions. These planning elements must recognize the restrictions and limitations introduced by the existing natural and urban factors discussed in the previous section.

The Physical Layout.   The principal layout considerations of the subject industrial park were:

Phased development
Block planning
Building and lot sizes
Streets
Rail leads and spurs
Utilities
Landscaping
Restrictive covenants

Phased Development.   The most important criterion for development of an industrial park is to provide as much flexibility as possible in the layout and plan. The entire park was planned as a comprehensive whole developing in economically feasible stages by using phased development. This approach saves capital and allows for changes in future layout by taking advantage of new development alternatives and policies.

Two development phases were planned for the industrial park. The first phase was 280 acres, and a total of nearly 300 acres was projected for the second phase. While a portion of this acreage would be a continuation of the first phase, most of second-phase growth would occur north of the Campstool Interchange. This area was physically separated from the first-phase development, but it would be more desirable to truck-oriented industries because of its direct access to and from Interstate 80. The second phase of development would increase the amenities and drawing power of the industrial park by providing accessibility from two I-80 interchanges.

The area remaining between the two development phases was planned for use beyond the 575 acres required by 1981. (See Figure 8–3.)

Block Planning.   Another method which provided additional flexibility in developing the industrial park was block planning, as illustrated in Figure 8–4. Blocks are delineated by streets, by rail spurs, by easements, and, where the foregoing divisions do not exist, by designated block lines. Under block planning, the overall size of the block is determined, but side lot lines within the block are established later to meet the requirements of individual industries.

Building and Lot Sizes.   The first-phase plan illustrated lot sizes ranging from 2 to 13 acres, with an average lot size of 5.5 acres. By eliminating selected secondary streets, lots of over 40 acres could be developed. Figure 8–5 illustrates typical building development schemes with buildings ranging from a minimum of 10,000 square feet to approximately 100,000 square feet.

Streets.   Traffic circulation throughout most of the industrial park is provided by the Interstate 80 service road complex, namely Campstool Road and the south frontage road. Secondary loop and cul-de-sac streets branch from the major circulation roads, providing access into large land tracts and increasing the number of blocks and lots. Any of these secondary streets can be shortened or eliminated if a potential industrial development requires a lot larger than those shown in Figure 8–4.

Parking and loading would not be permitted on industrial park streets. Adoption of off-street parking and loading standards assured that these requirements would be accommodated adequately on each industrial site.

The location and distribution of industries should be closely coordinated and programmed according to their intensity of rail service requirements. The proper distribution of industries using heavy and light rail service along a spur also should be planned. Intensive rail-use industries should have sufficient spur footage on their property to handle their needs without blocking main spurs. Officials of the railroad companies were available to assist in coordinating and programming these and other matters in order to minimize construction expense and to promote efficient operation of rail service.

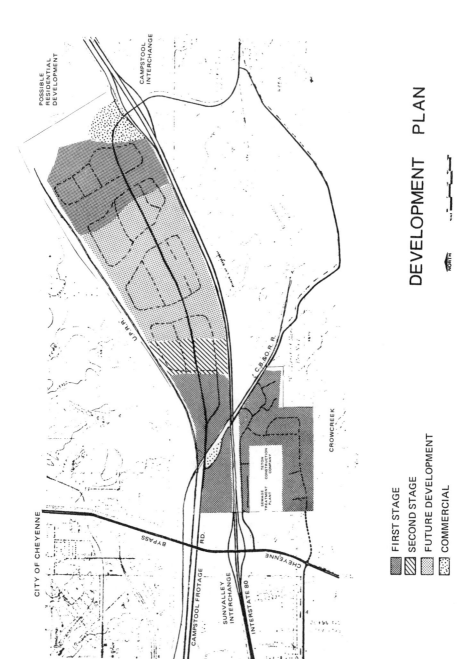

DEVELOPMENT PLAN

NORTH

FIRST STAGE

SECOND STAGE

FUTURE DEVELOPMENT

COMMERCIAL

Figure 8–3. Development plan.

270

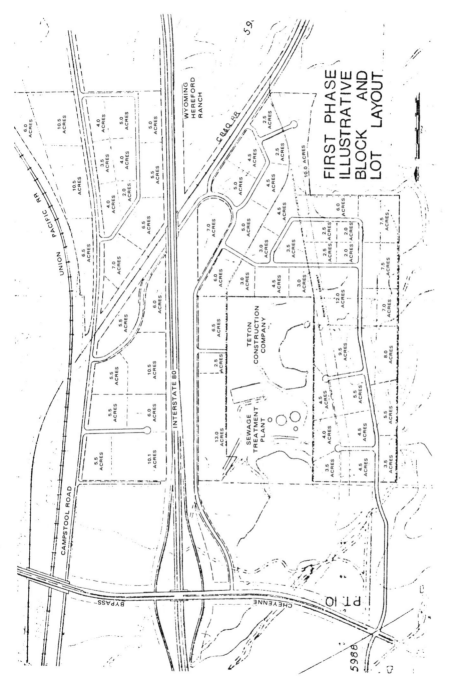

Figure 8–4. First phase illustrative block and lot layout.

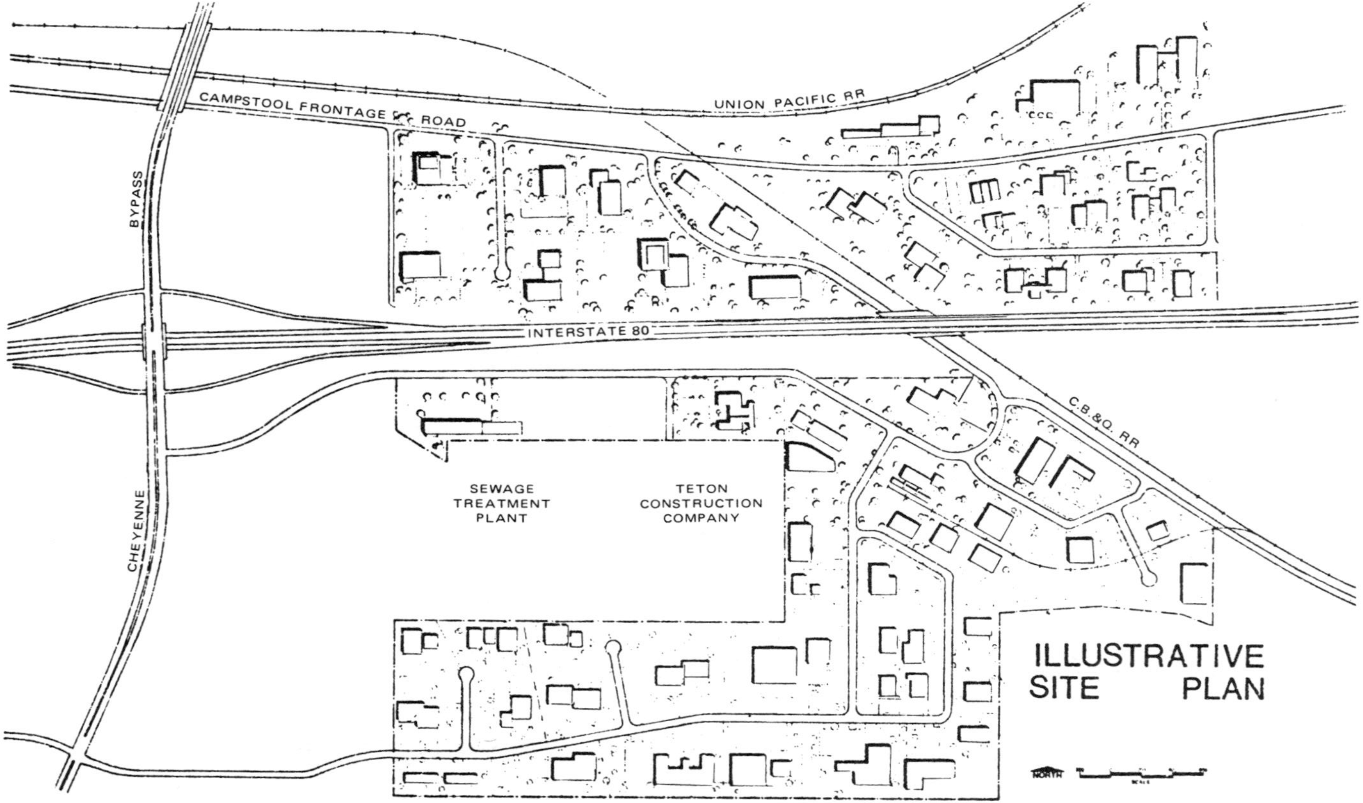

Figure 8–5. Illustrative site plan.

272

Utilities. Planning for water, sanitary sewers, storm drainage, electric power, and gas and telephone service was for capacities larger than those associated with residential and commercial uses. Easements for these utilities were programmed to be placed within streets or railroad rights-of-way or to the rear of lots. Water pressure must be high and steady enough to operate sprinkler systems and maintain favorable fire insurance ratings, and sanitary sewers must be adequately designed to handle the needs of anticipated industrial operations.

Landscaping. The proposed landscaping plan for the envisioned industrial park provided planting areas at the entrances of the industrial park, at street intersections, and along property lines of individual sites. The developer was to provide the basic landscaping as an encouragement for the landscaping of individual sites by park occupants. Specific standards in the restrictive covenant governed landscaping and maintenance requirements, as well as site and building plans, to ensure that park occupants meet designs consistent with the image and continuity of the industrial park.

Restrictive Covenants. The development policies and operational standards of the industrial park were established by restrictive covenants, which specified limitations on the use and development of industrial tracts. The covenants were to be included within deeds or leases and were designed to control nuisances, land use, building lines and site coverage, outdoor storage, building construction and design, off-street parking and truck loading, signs, and other provisions.

Cash Flow Analysis

Results of the cash flow analysis indicated that the project was potentially profitable. Results are illustrated in Table 8–7. A cash flow analysis weighs heavily in the final determination of project feasibility, i.e., whether or not the profit level is great enough to warrant development expenditures. The reliability of a cash flow analysis, in turn, is based on the method of determination and assumptions required for input data.

In Table 8–7, under the first major heading of "Development Costs" are land purchase, streets and roads, utilities, site preparations, and engineering and planning. These cost estimates were made by the consultant company engineers and were based on the finalized Development Plan. However, they were not produced after the fact, but rather were developed as a process of the Development Plan. The engineers

Table 8–7. Cash Flow Analysis—Industrial Park Development
(Thousands of dollars)

Description	1972	1973	1974	1975	1976	1977	1978	1979	1980	1981	TOTAL
Development costs											
Land purchase	664										664
Streets and roads	452				493						945
Utilities	372				405						777
Site preparation	175				191						365
Subtotal	1,662				1,089						2,751
Engineering and planning	150				163						313
Total development costs	1,812				1,252						3,064
Operating expenses											
Real estate taxes	8	7	7	5	4	3	2	1	1		40
Sales expense	30	53	66	81	91	89	87	84	81	62	725
Total operating expense	38	60	73	87	96	93	89	86	82	62	765
Financing											
Proceeds	1,148				1,252						2,400
Principal payments		230	230	230	230	480	250	250	250	250	2,400
Interest payments		138	110	83	55	178	120	90	60	30	864
Total debt service		367	340	312	285	650	371	341	311	280	3,264
Revenue											
Acres sold	30	50	60	70	75	70	65	60	55	40	575
Unit price in dollars	10,000	10,500	11,025	11,576	12,155	12,762	13,400	14,071	14,774	15,513	
Total revenue	300	525	662	810	912	893	871	844	813	621	7,250

Cash flow statement

	1	2	3	4	5	6	7	8	9	10	Total
Total revenue	300	525	662	810	912	693	671	844	813	621	7,250
Less operating expenses	38	60	73	87	96	93	89	86	82	62	765
Less debt service		367	340	312	285	658	371	341	311	280	3,264
Pretax cash flow	262	98	249	412	531	143	411	418	420	278	3,221
Less federal income tax	49	29	76	129	173	120	151	167	181	151	1,228
After-tax cash flow	213	69	173	283	358	23	260	251	239	127	1,994
Cumulative cash flow	213	281	454	737	1,095	1,118	1,378	1,628	1,867	1,994	

Tax statement

	1	2	3	4	5	6	7	8	9	10	Total
Pretax cash flow	262	98	249	412	531	143	411	418	420	278	3,221
Plus principal payment		230	230	230	230	400	250	250	250	250	2,400
Less BK value of acres sold	160	266	320	373	400	373	346	320	293	213	3,064
Net taxable income	102	61	159	268	361	250	315	349	378	315	2,557
Income tax at 48%	49	29	76	129	173	120	151	167	181	151	1,220

	1	2	3	4	5	6	7	8	9	10	Total
Disc. rate of return on equity @12% on cumulative cash flow	29%	37%	55%	82%	113%	115	132	148	161	167	
Disc. rate of return annually @12% on equity	29%	8%	19%	27%	31	2	18	15	9	6	

Equity value

	1	2	3	4	5	6	7	8	9	10
At 6%	201	262	407	631	899	915	1,087	1,245	1,386	1,457
At 7%	199	259	400	616	871	887	1,048	1,194	1,324	1,388
At 8%	197	256	393	601	845	859	1,011	1,146	1,265	1,324
At 9%	195	253	387	587	819	833	975	1,101	1,211	1,264
At 10%	194	250	380	573	795	809	942	1,059	1,160	1,209
At 12%	190	245	368	547	751	762	880	981	1,067	1,108
At 15%	185	237	351	512	690	700	798	880	948	979
At 20%	177	225	325	461	605	613	685	744	790	810

worked closely with the planners in determining alternative development approaches and least-cost positions. These estimates are illustrated in Table 8–8.

The $664,000 for land purchase was a client input and was consid-
ered to be the equity in the project.[8] This was approximately $1,000 per
gross acre. Total development costs in 1972 were $1,812,000 including
land purchase. In 1976, an additional $1,252,000 was required in devel-
opment expenditure for Phase II.

Operating expenses are real estate taxes and sales expense. Real
estate taxes were based on a millage rate of 15 at 80% of the valuation.
This was applied only against those acres remaining to be sold. The
analyst noted that in the initial stages of a development it is extremely
difficult, if not impossible, to determine the future assessed valuation
of the remaining undeveloped property. The consultant felt that if any
tax assessor were to give the analyst a figure, it would simply be a
guess. Given these constraints, present and future tax assessments
were applied against the present market value of the property. That
value, decided by the client for his undeveloped property, was $1,000
per acre.

Sales expenses were brokerage fees, sales commission, and general
overhead. This figure was developed from discussions with the client
about the type of sales staff envisioned and from discussions with local
realtors. The figure of 10% of gross sales revenue was deemed to be
appropriate.

Financing was considered in two phases. The first development loan
of $1,148,000 was to be acquired in 1972 and $1,252,000 for Phase II in
1976, for a total of $2,400,000. Principal and interest payments were
indicated separately, with each loan being amortized over the sellout
period of the particular development phase. The total interest to be
paid at 12% was $864,000, with the total debt service being $3,264,000.

The two key items under "Revenue" in Table 8–7 are acres sold and
unit price. In an effort to lend some quantifiable accuracy to these
items, a computer program was developed using a stepwise regression
technique. The purpose of the model was to predict the absorption rate
and sales price per square foot for developed industrial land in the
planning area. The data for the model were developed from analyzing
all the industrial parks in the region, as indicated in the market study.

The predicted absorption rate indicated a rate of 5% the first year of
sales, rising to a peak of 13% of net acreage in the fifth year, and
thereafter declining to 7% in the last year. This is a rather typical
absorption rate found in most industrial districts across the United

Table 8–8. Preliminary Development and Engineering Cost Estimates

Item	Quantity	Cost[b]
Phase I		
Streets @ $30/lin. ft. (W/C&G)[a]		
West of CB&Q R.R.	10,400 ft.	$ 315,000
East of CB&Q R.R.	4,500 ft.	135,000
	Total 15,000	450,000
Utilities @ $8/lin. ft.		
Water	26,800 ft.	$ 214,400
Sewer	26,800 ft.	214,000
	Total 53,600	428,800
Site Preparation @ $550/acre		
N.W. of I-80, CB&Q grade sep.	64 acres	$ 35,200
S.W. of I-80, CB&Q grade sep.	170 acres	93,500
N.W. of I-80, CB&Q grade sep.	100 acres	55,000
	Total 334	183,700
Engineering @ 15% of total		160,000
Total cost of Phase I		$1,222,500
Phase II		
Streets @ $30/lin. ft. (W/C&G)		
West area	3,500 ft.	$ 105,000
East area	13,500 ft.	390,000
	Total 17,000	495,000
Utilities @ $8/lin. ft.		
Water	21,750 ft.	$ 174,000
Sewer	21,750 ft.	174,000
	Total 43,500	348,000
Site preparation @ $550/acre		
West	80 acres	$ 44,000
East	250 acres	137,500
	Total 330	181,500
Engineering @ 15% of total		153,600
Total cost Phase II		$1,178,100
Total cost Phases I and II		$2,400,600

Total Acreage Breakdown

Phase I	Phase II
354 gross acres	330 gross acres
275 net acres = 82.3%	300 net acres = 90.9%
59 acres lost land = 17.7%	30 acres lost land = 9.1%

Total
664 gross acres
575 net acres = 86.6%
89 acres lost land = 13.4%

Notes: [a] Street costs are with curb and gutter.
[b] Uninflated 1971 dollars.

States. There is a slow start-up period, and then a rapid increase and a slow decline as development costs and land prices increase and the less salable areas are left.

The model was helpful in serving as a guideline in predicting the price per square foot. It should be noted, however, that its usefulness could only be applied during the first year due to changing conditions affecting the independent variables. The predicted price was 25 cents per square foot, or approximately $10,000 an acre. The price was expected to appreciate by 5% per year. The total revenue is the expected annual absorption or acres sold times the price per acre.

The cash flow statement in Table 8–7 indicates the total projected revenue less operating expenses and debt service to produce a pretax cash flow. The cash flow model calculated all taxable items internally and gave the total federal income tax bill based on a rate given by the client. In this case, the tax rate used was 48%. The after-tax cash flow is given on an annual basis. The cumulative cash flow is a summing of the annual after-tax cash flow.

To the pretax cash flow, principal loan amounts are added, and from this total the book value of the acres expected to be sold is subtracted. The book value, calculated internally within the computerized model, is the sum of land costs and development costs on a per acre basis. The result is net taxable income from which income tax of 48% is calculated.

The discounted rate of return is one of the most important determinants in a cash flow analysis. Conceptually, it is a type of annuity capitalization in which future income is discounted to account for the opportunity loss of a given rate of interest on either total investment or equity investment. In this case study, a discount rate of 12% was used to determine the return on equity, the $644,000 original land purchase agreement.

The discounted rate of return is calculated on the cumulative cash flow as well as annual cash flow. The original equity investment, discounted at 12%, is returned in full between 1975 and 1976.

An additional index of profitability is the project's present worth (net present value). This is the accumulated after-tax cash flow discounted by a given interest rate to determine the value in today's dollars. The developer can then determine what he would be economically justified in paying for a given cash flow discounted by some interest rate compatible with alternative investment opportunities and risk. In this instance, the developer, at a discount rate of 12%, would be justified in paying $1,108,000 for the cumulative 1981 cash flow of

$1,994,000. The project passes this index of profitability, since the developer's equity investment was $664,000.[9]

As an index of profitability, the discounted rate of return and project's present worth indicate that sufficient potential for an economic profit existed and also that adequate debt coverage was generated, that is, the amount of total revenue generated above that required to cover the debt service. The amount required by banks and other lending institutions will vary depending on the loan officer's analysis of all risks involved, including the developer's and consultant's track records. Generally, 1.25 times the required debt service is necessary. In this case study, in the second year (the first year of debt payment) the coverage was 1.4 and increased thereafter.

SUMMARY: ANALYSIS OF THE MARKET AND FEASIBILITY STUDY

The market and feasibility study summarized above was a major undertaking for the consulting group involved. Industrial land development is a less frequent real estate activity than commercial and residential development. For that reason the consultants involved are less likely to have the depth of experience normally expected in a residential market analysis.

The market study portion was comprehensive and generally well done. The indirect economic factors were covered in a responsible manner. One unusual and perhaps fortunate aspect of the study was the uniform acceptance of the project by all levels and sections of the local community. Had there been opposition from some local or state special-interest group, the study and the project might have been thrown onto an entirely different track. In this respect the planning process was unhindered and the project was never in question after the profit potential was determined. The surrounding land uses were also compatible with industrial development, and zoning problems were avoided.

The site analysis was conducted in an exemplary manner. If one advantage of dealing with a large consulting company can be cited, it is the variety of in-house skills available to the market analyst. Aerial photos were made of the site which were valuable both in the initial site analysis and in the eventual land use plan. There were also many technical questions regarding water, sewage treatment, soil conditions, drainage, slopes, and rail line and road configurations that could only be dealt with by qualified engineers. Because the market analyst had access to the technical ability of the engineers, the market and feasibility study was able to deal effectively with these technical problems.

The portion of the study dealing with the elements of overall demand, i.e., population, income, and employment, was fairly well handled. The population projections made by the analyst were reasonably consistent with the five other studies used as a comparison in Table 8–2. This is more evidence than most market studies present. However, the analyst alluded to the use of a "cohort survival model, modified by estimates of future employment." This evidence was not presented in the body of the study nor in any appendix. This is a shortcoming.

The economic-sector analysis also seemed to be very well researched. The research used a combination of analyzing all available secondary source data on the sectors and interviewing—by mail, telephone, or personal visit—key individuals in the principal industries within each sector. This can be a very effective method for both developing a current picture of the economic activity within each section and, at the same time, assessing the prevailing views for the future outlook for each industry. One practical problem which was not evident here is that the extensive interview process is time-consuming and thus expensive.

The sector analysis produced several firms, referred to by the analyst as "best-fit" firms, likely to locate in the area. The analyst then made an attempt to rank those firms by assigning numbers to certain locational criteria and then summing the numbers. The numbers assigned were subjective in nature and their value questionable. As near as can be determined from reviewing the study, the ranking of these industries was not used in any manner in the projecting of absorption rates or land use planning. It could possibly be used in some sort of marketing strategy although it was not presented in this manner.

The analysis of the existing land use patterns was seemingly well conducted but presented very poorly. The analyst indicates that nearly 100 industrial districts across the United States were surveyed by mail and telephone and that all industrial parks in Colorado and Wyoming were surveyed. This is entirely appropriate and essential if the analyst is to understand completely the existing competitive supply side of the market. The problem is that most of the data were not organized and included in the body of the study; they were only alluded to where necessary. This may make it difficult for the developer to use the study, in a convincing manner, to obtain additional investment funds.

Investors or financial institutions would not be able to adequately assess the supply side for themselves because much of the information was not in the body of the report. This is a general failure, and a characteristic of too many market studies.

The land planning and general design of the park were exceptionally well handled. It was apparent that a team effort was involved between the market analyst, land planners, and engineers. However, the cash flow component did not appear detailed enough to be useful as a complete decision-making tool. The cost estimates should be more detailed, and the real estate taxes should be based on value under the cost-to-develop approach or recent sales prices. The first year or two should have been presented on a monthly basis to give a more balanced picture. The absorption rate and estimated sale prices seem to be well justified.

However, the analyst again failed to include the quantitative evidence used in the determination of these critically important figures. The result of the surveys of competing industrial districts was not included in the report. The analyst also indicated that regression analysis was used to assist in the determination of sale price and absorption rate, but failed to include the actual data in the body of the report or the appendix. These omissions are a decided weakness in the study but, unfortunately, not unusual in practice. Many consultants believe that if they include such material in a study the client would usually ignore it or quite possibly feel that the consultant was being too esoteric and not dealing with the more relevant practical facts.

It should be apparent from the above case example that market and feasibility studies for industrial land development are extremely complex studies and should be undertaken either by or under the direction of those having an extensive education in business and economics and a broad range of experience in analyzing real estate markets.

SELECTED BIBLIOGRAPHY

Grubb, R. C., "Release Provisions in Office and Industrial Park Development Loans," *Real Estate Review* (Winter 1979).

Hogan, B., Ed., *Guide to Federal Resources for Economic Development,* Northeast-Midwest Institute, Washington, 1979.

"Park that Reversed a Brain Drain: Research Triangle Park," *Fortune,* vol. 95 (June 1977), pp. 148–153.

"Science Parks: Cambridge Goes Commercial," *Economist,* vol. 272 (August 4, 1979), pp. 67–69.

Seymour, C. F., "Appraising Industrial Parks," *Appraisal Journal,* vol. 47 (April 1979), pp. 165–175.

Society of Industrial Realtors (DorDick, Beverly), *Industrial Real Estate: An Annotated Bibliography,* Washington, D.C., 1982.

Society of Industrial Realtors (Educational Fund), *Industrial Real Estate,* 4th ed., Washington, D.C., 1984.

Stafford, Howard A., *Principles of Industrial Facility Location,* Conway Publications, Atlanta, Ga., 1980.

Walker, David, Ed., *Planning Industrial Development,* John Wiley & Sons, New York, 1980.

Whaler, V. G., "See How They Grow: A Survey of Industrial Park Development Trends," *Industrial Development Handbook,* vol. 147 (July 1978), pp. 13–14.

Williams, Edward A., and Massa, A. K., *Siting of Major Facilities,* McGraw-Hill, New York, 1983.

9

Case Study: Shopping Center Renovation

Shopping centers have become a mature land use. The rapid increase in the number of centers, the emergence of superregional complexes, and the recent emphasis on downtown commercial revitalization have created pressures for change in many established shopping centers. Developers have become redevelopers. This case is an example of a redevelopment investment decision. However, the same principles of market and feasibility analysis that are pertinent to redevelopment apply to new projects. The methodology presented here can be applied with only slight modification to an analysis of a new shopping center.

IDENTIFICATION OF PROBLEMS AND OBJECTIVES

At the time of the grand opening in 1963, Northeast, a 30-unit plaza, was considered the premier center in the northern part of a major Midwestern city. Its prospects appeared bright not only because it was new and could attract shoppers from a wide area, but also because its primary market included one of the most affluent residential areas in the city. After 3 years of operation, Mitroff Investments, the New Jersey-based development firm that owned the center, had a successful project. By 1978, however, several shopping centers had opened in surrounding communities. Although those were generally smaller strip centers, each center cut slightly into Northeast's market. A larger, more modern, enclosed shopping center—Oakhill, a 15–20 minutes' drive from Northeast—began operation on a major highway. Furthermore, the downtown development committee was actively trying to increase downtown business by attracting suburban shoppers. The committee's efforts had been enhanced by two large federal grants. Sales at Northeast were not keeping up with inflation. Only a few stores did not suffer to some extent; a grocery store, liquor store, and nationally known hardware store held their own.

Northeast's management felt a major renovation was necessary. Northeast had experienced several previous "facelifts," but more improvements were needed. Gerald Slaten, the manager of Northeast, had several ideas: (1) modernize the storefronts with a colonial facade, (2) design a new logo and color scheme, (3) build a "tot lot" for children, (4) launch a major advertising campaign, and (5) redesign the parking lot.

Slaten discussed the problem with the chief executive officer of Mitroff on a visit to the home office. He mentioned his belief that the proposed modernization and advertising campaign would boost sales temporarily, but in the long run he felt the center could decline further. Selling the center after the advertising increased revenues was proposed. But the corporate management was reluctant to sell because it felt anyone with sufficient resources to purchase the center would have the savvy to realize the underlying problems. At that point, enclosing the center was suggested. No one knew whether or not it would be a good idea. Everyone agreed that the proposal warranted examination.

Slaten suggested the enclosure to several of Northeast's major tenants. He mentioned that some shared cost arrangement would be necessary, although no details were mentioned. Support was not unanimous, but it was generally favorable. The larger tenants, who had long-term leases, were strongly supportive, whereas a few of the smaller establishments indicated indifference or opposition. The general attitude of the tenants led the center management to hire consultants to analyze the prospects.

THE MARKET STUDY

Two consulting firms were hired to make market studies of the enclosure. This dual choice represented the conviction that a single study might be subject to large errors. By commissioning two market studies, the shopping center owners reserved the right to weigh and balance alternative perspectives. The decision also indicated a healthy degree of skepticism regarding the ability of market studies to be purely scientific. In the words of the manager of Northeast, "The market analysis was to us an investment tool, not an answer that is black or white."

One of the consulting jobs was given to a small local partnership composed of an architect and a part-time commercial broker. While they had handled other projects, this represented their largest project thus far. Since they would be competing against, or at least compared with, another firm, which, they were told, had a national reputation, they wanted to present a creditable report. Their proposal emphasized the following six steps involved in the market and feasibility studies.

Market Study
1. Determine and describe the current market area
2. Present the results of a survey of shopping market trends
3. Evaluate current and future competition and market trends

Feasibility Analysis
4. Develop a feasible enclosure sketch, including an analysis of possible implementation problems such as government regulation and neighborhood objections.
5. Estimate costs and benefits of enclosure
6. Make recommendations about whether or not to enclose, actions that may enhance enclosure, and alternatives to enclosure

Determining the Market Area

The first step was to estimate the market area. The technique, used frequently in retail analysis, was to define the market in terms of approximate driving time. The zone within a 5-minute drive of Northeast was considered the primary market area. Areas requiring a 5–15 minute drive were classified as the secondary zone. A river just outside the secondary zone significantly diminished the southern market area.

The report explained that the driving-time technique is most frequently used to estimate *potential markets* for yet-to-be-established centers. An alternative technique might be to estimate the area in which over 50% of the residents' shopping trips are to the center. Since Northeast was an existing facility, a survey would be possible to determine market zones. However, since the anticipated enclosure would increase the market penetration of the center, the driving-time definition was determined to be most appropriate. The survey, described later, was used to check the reliability of the time-distance definition.

After establishing the boundaries of the trade area, the focus was turned to describing the size of the market area in terms of population and buying power. In order to estimate populations and population distributions, the trade zone map was superimposed on a census tract map. The population of each census tract was allocated to the trade zone in which it was located. If a census tract had about 25% of its geographical area in the primary zone, then 25% of its population was allocated to the primary zone.

Population counts for each census tract were taken from the 1980 *Census of Population* and updated based upon building permits. The age composition of the area was assumed to be the same as it was in 1980. Table 9–1 shows the population distribution. The total primary and secondary market area was 326,700. This is a substantial market, reflecting the high density of the area.

The primary and secondary trade areas were noted for the higher than average affluence of the residents. Houses were generally valued from $65,000 to $85,000, and median incomes were above average for the metropolitan area. Total effective buying income is defined as personal income minus taxes and miscellaneous governmental payments such as fees and penalties. In Table 9–2, "Effective Buying Income" for the metropolitan area was derived from *Sales and Marketing Management: Survey of Buying Power*. Comparable figures for the primary and secondary zones were estimated as follows. First, median household income for each census tract and portion of a tract was taken from the 1980 *Census of Population* census tract estimates. The information was updated to reflect the same average annual increase that existed for the nation. *Sales and Marketing Management* provided separate estimates for the nearby county as well as the metropolitan area. These separate estimates were used as a check on the estimates shown in Table 9–2.

The distribution of income is also shown in Table 9–2. The fact that the majority of the families were in the upper two income brackets explains the high median effective buying income. The low percentage of households in the lower income bracket is important because it suggests that there was little potential for certain types of merchandise

Table 9–1. Population

Area	Total Popula- tion	Median Age	% of Population by Age Group				House- holds (1,000s)
			18–24	*25–34*	*35–49*	*50+*	
Metropolitan	1,106.9	29.2	12.5	16.4	16.5	27.6	412.2
Secondary zone	273.0	29.5	13.9	16.7	18.5	22.2	85.3
Primary zone	53.7	30.6	13.5	16.5	18.7	20.7	16.8

Table 9–2. Effective Buying Income
1980

Area	Total Effective Buying Income (1,000s)	Median Household Effective Buying Income	% of Households by EBI[a]			
			$10,000–14,999	$15,000–24,999	$25,000–49,999	Over $50,000
Metropolitan area	7,697,111	23,076	9.9	28.9	38.7	5.4
Secondary trade zone	1,767,899	25,389	8.0	26.3	46.0	6.4
Primary trade zone	344,133	26,087	7.2	24.8	49.0	9.3

[a] EBI = effective buying income.

in the primary and secondary areas. The areas to the north and west were generally about equal to the primary and secondary zone in terms of income. The areas to the east and, particularly, the south had significantly lower incomes.

Table 9–3 shows estimates of the expenditures by residents of the metropolitan area, the secondary trade zone, and the primary trade zone. They were developed by combining U.S. Department of Commerce data on expenditures by income group with the total effective buying income. For instance, the estimate that upper-income households spent about 15.7% of their income on "Food at Home" was combined with the total effective buying income figure for the primary zone to estimate the "Food at Home" expenditures.

The static picture of the market area that emerged was consistent with the socioeconomic picture of the merchants and the shopping center management. However, the relatively high income of area residents created a slight dilemma. Should the center evolve in such a way as to expand its market area into the lower-income areas located in the south and east, or should it attempt to increase its share in the (current) upper-income market area? Each strategy implies a different type of tenant mix and a different type of product line for the major tenants. For instance, an attempt to expand the market area would suggest that the stores should carry lower-cost items and that management should try to attract "discount"-type stores. The issue was analyzed in detail

Table 9–3. Estimated Expenditures
1,000s

Area	All Commodities	Food at Home	Apparel and Shoes	Restaurants	Services (Minus Rent)	Other Nondurables	Household Durables
Metropolitan area	48,108,363	1,345,452	689,107	384,392	24,909,255	1,111,725	367,011
Primary trade zone	193,135	54,013	27,663	15,431	100,006	19,558	14,732
Secondary trade zone	1,104,968	309,027	158,276	88,287	572,145	111,905	84,296

in the report, but the problem has its roots in the income and demography of the area.

Shopping Market Trends

A survey was conducted for two purposes: (1) to determine how actual shoppers compared with the demographic description and (2) to provide additional insight into developing trends and how they might be affected by enclosure. The survey was conducted in June between 2:00–4:00 p.m. on a Wednesday and between 6:30–9:00 p.m. on a Friday. A total of 1,562 shoppers responded. The times represent a normal shopping period and a peak period, respectively. The combined results are assumed to be a representative sample of nonholiday shopping at Northeast.

The questionnaire was designed to take about 3 minutes. It was cleared by the mall management and the president of the Merchants' Association. They wanted to be certain they didn't irritate customers, and so no income questions were asked because they might be offensive to some. In addition, many shoppers do not accurately know their incomes.

Table 9–4 was derived from the customer survey. It confirmed the driving-time description of the market area. About 45% of the customers were from the driving-time area that constituted the primary market zone. The secondary zone included about 38% of the customers. The primary and secondary zones combined accounted for about 83% of the total shopping visits. Also, the daytime weekday

Table 9–4. Reported Residence Zone of Northeast Shoppers

Place of Residence	Shoppers Interviewed		
	Number	Percent	Cumulative Percent
0–5.0 minute zone	682	45.1	45.1
5.1–10.0 minute zone	379	25.1	70.2
10.1–15.0 minute zone	201	13.3	83.5
15.1 minutes or more	247	16.3	100.0[a]

[a] Will not add to 100% because of rounding.
Not all responses to this question were usable.

survey showed that a higher percentage of the customers were from the primary market area than was indicated in Table 9–4. On the other hand, the Friday evening survey revealed a slightly higher percentage of customers from the 5.1–15.0 minute range. The survey also established that nearby customers made more frequent trips to Northeast than distant customers.

The customers were also asked what stores they were visiting during their shopping trips. Table 9–5 shows the results. For example, Table 9–5 shows that 56.7% of individuals visiting the supermarket were from the 0–5.0 minute area. The pattern for each type of establishment was similar to the distribution of mall customers previously described. Generally, the closer the residence, the greater the percentage of customers. The answers also show that the establishments that sell items for which comparison shopping was not customary had higher percentages of customers from the primary trade area than other establishments. For example, the supermarket, specialty goods and liquor, and services—such as repair shops and personal services—all had over 50% of their customers from the primary market area.

When asked whether they were increasing or decreasing their shopping visits, only a small minority of those interviewed (about 10%) were increasing their trips to Northeast. The percentages in the "remain the same" and "decreased" categories were roughly equal at 30%. The largest category consisted of those who didn't know whether

Table 9–5. Distribution of Shopping Visits by Zone of Residence

Type of Establishments	Zone of Residence[a]				
	0–5.0	5.1–10.0	10.1–15.0	Over 15.1	All Zones
Supermarket	56.7	24.5	6.8	11.9	100.0
Specialty goods, liquor, tobacco	51.2	48.8	0.0	2.1	100.0
Restaurants	49.9	14.9	10.6	25.5	100.0
Clothing and shoe	38.5	28.0	16.1	17.5	100.0
Department store	41.2	31.6	13.6	15.5	100.0
Drug/variety	44.2	26.6	13.6	15.5	100.0
Other retail	40.0	27.7	15.0	17.3	100.0
Services	55.6	25.9	9.3	9.3	
Snacks	N/A	N/A	N/A	N/A	N/A
Total	42.4	27.0	13.8	16.8	

[a] The columns will not sum to 100% because multiple answers were accepted.

their trips were increasing or not. The trends were not cause for encouragement regarding the prospects for the mall. However, it was pointed out that neither gross sales nor rents were decreasing as rapidly as would be expected from the survey. Perhaps the decreases in trips reported by customers were small and affected nonbuying trips more than actual purchase trips.

On the basis of the cross-tabulation, the consulting team concluded that while the exact decline in customer patronage could not be determined from survey data, it was apparent that Northeast was losing its share of the regional market. If present trends continued, Northeast's share of the market would continue to fall. The sales in the past several years reinforced this conclusion.

If, as shown, customers were decreasing their trips to Northeast, where were they going? A direct answer to this question was not possible, given the nature of the questionnaire. However, a good approximation was possible by cross-tabulating the two questions: (1) Where do you currently do most of your shopping? and (2) During the last few months how have the number of your trips to Northeast changed? Table 9–6 shows the results.

Two points stood out regarding Table 9–6. First, Northeast was attracting some customers from the downtown area. Of those who were increasing their shopping at Northeast, 21% considered the downtown area as their primary shopping area. Second, Oakhill, the enclosed mall nearby, was considered a primary shopping area for 38% of those who claimed their visits to Northeast were decreasing. This is consistent with the belief among many that the rise of Oakhill was responsible for Northeast's stagnation.

Table 9–6. Primary Shopping Area by Northeast Shopping Trends

| | Trends in Northeast Shopping | | |
Primary Shopping Area	Increase	Decrease	About the Same
Northeast	17.3	9.6	37.2
Downtown	21.3	8.4	15.3
Oakhill	13.2	38.1	13.1
Riverside	14.1	17.7	5.2
Other or no primary area	34.2	26.5	29.3

Would enclosure help increase sales? In order to help answer this question, shoppers were asked to select the improvements that would encourage more trips to Northeast. Multiple answers were allowed. It was felt that asking customers to rank which improvements they would like most would be too complicated to administer. Allowing each interviewee to select only one improvement would be too restrictive. The results are shown in Table 9–7.

As with most opinion polls, caution in interpreting the results of Table 9–7 was essential. For instance, the fact that about 70% of the respondents claim they would shop at Northeast more frequently if it had an enclosed mall does not necessarily mean that they would make a specific number of additional trips per period. Because intentions often differ from actual behavior, some of them may not increase their trips at all and some of those that do may spend only a few dollars per trip. Nevertheless, several important conclusions were drawn from Table 9–7:

1. Generally, individuals from different distances ranked similarly the improvements they would like to see. The differences in responses did not appear to be related to distance from the center.
2. There was no significant preference for parking or public/community facilities.
3. There was a preference for more specialty stores, a movie theater, and a restaurant. (The research team mentioned that they

Table 9–7. Improvements That Would Encourage Shopping at Northeast

	Time Distance in Minutes			
Improvement	*0–5.0*	*5.1–10.0*	*10.1–15.0*	*Over 15.1*
More specialty stores	45.3	40.8	42.1	45.3
"Tot lot"	10.5	12.2	13.8	10.7
Community room	5.0	4.0	3.0	0.0
Public events	15.2	32.3	17.2	17.1
More parking	5.3	6.2	7.1	7.3
Enclosed mall	72.1	63.7	71.5	75.0
Movie theater	52.4	60.0	45.3	35.5
More restaurants	47.3	63.2	25.1	31.2
More department stores	20.9	31.3	32.2	42.3

did not believe there was a sufficient market for another movie theater in the area.)
4. There was significant desire for enclosure. It was the most preferred item among all time-distance groups.

Determining the Competitive Environment

The third step in the market study was to estimate market trends and describe the competitive environment. Several of the questionnaire responses had implications for the description of the market environment, and they were described. In addition, population forecasts to 2005 were developed based upon benchmark estimates from the state's Department of Labor. The Department of Labor forecast a 1.5% growth rate for the metropolitan area for a 10-year period. A higher rate of growth was projected for the exurban counties, however. The metropolitan area's growth rate was a combination of population declines in the central city, moderate growth in the outer city and close-by suburbs, and substantial growth in outlying areas. Population forecasts of 1.7% for the primary zone and 3% for the secondary zone were made. The population forecasts were higher than is typical, and in retrospect proved to be too large. The population forecasts were combined with an informed assumption that real incomes would grow annually at 1.5% to estimate increases in buying power. On the basis of the population and income data, the consultants concluded that the market was expanding enough to absorb extra commercial space. Table 9–8 summarizes the market prospects.

The competitive environment of the area was stiff. The three major sources of competition were the CBD to the south, a major enclosed mall to the northwest, and two small local shopping strips. The CBD was the largest but was the least threatening of the three sources of competition. The report concluded that the

> CBD was not a source of significant future competition with Northeast. It would not grow significantly during the next few years. Furthermore, the CBD was not oriented toward the same market as Northeast. The CBD served special goods purchasers, business-oriented customers, and low-income populations that live nearby . . .

The commercial strips were described as significant, but "constant competitors." There was little prospect for major expansion in most of the commercial strips because the neighborhoods in which they were

Table 9–8. Annual Anticipated Market Increases

Area[a]	Population	Real Income Growth	Inflation	Estimated Total Growth[b]
Metropolitan area (16.3)	1.5	1.5	5	8.2
Secondary area (38.4)	3.0	1.5	5	9.8
Primary area (45.3)	1.7	1.5	5	8.4
Northeast	2.2	1.5	5	8.9

[a] ( ) = proportion of individuals visiting Northeast from the market areas. See Table 9–4.
[b] $(1 + 0.15)(1 + .015)(1 + .05) = 1.082$ or a change of 8.2%. The approach is more accurate than simply adding together the population, real income growth, and inflation factors because the multiplicity approach includes interactive effects.

located were primarily residential and the long-range plans did not include significant commercial expansion. A strip located on Rock Road near Northeast had some growth potential, but it had not been expanding. It was a strip composed primarily of fast-food restaurants, gas stations, offices, and auto, electronics, and similar shops. Furthermore, because of the proximity of Northeast to Rock Road, their relationship was symbiotic, not competitive. Although no specific questions regarding trip combinations were asked on the survey, it was the analysts' belief that many customers combined trips so that the slight growth that might occur on Rock Road would have some benefits as well as costs to Northeast.

The major source of future competition was Oakhill, which was only about 3 years old. Oakhill had about 670,000 square feet of gross leasable area. It was nearly twice the size of Northeast. In addition, major development was occurring around Oakhill, so the attraction of the area would continue to grow. The survey results also indicated that Oakhill was cutting into Northeast's market area. As Table 9–6 indicated, Oakhill was the primary shopping area among those who claimed their trips to Northeast were decreasing. The development of Oakhill undoubtedly explains the small market penetration in the northwest uncovered by an examination of customer addresses.

The problems created by the Oakhill agglomeration were not diminishing. The area was continuing to grow. Plans to build a freestanding discount department store one-half of a mile from Oakhill were reported. This would further aggravate the problem of declining market shares. In addition, the consulting team suspected that alternative shopping patterns were still developing that would increase the pull of Oakhill.

Three primary conclusions emerged from the analysis of market trends:

1. The market area was growing at a rate sufficient to warrant additional commercial space. The growth was large enough to consider enclosure.
2. The major increases in competition would be from the Oakhill complex. The CBD and commercial strips would not make significant inroads into Northeast's market share.
3. If current trends continued, it was highly unlikely that Northeast would increase its market share. On the contrary, its growth rate would be much slower than the growth of the market.

FEASIBILITY ANALYSIS

Sketch Plan and Cost Estimates

The development of an enclosure sketch was intended to be a first assessment of feasibility and cost. Its purpose was not to present architectural and mechanical details such as the location of electrical outlets or heating ducts. Figure 9–1 is a copy of the enclosure sketch.

The principle of the design was to enclose the shopping area while minimizing the costs of creating additional commercial space. The western side was enclosed by a hallway with large windows. The grocery store maintained a separate outside entrance as well as a mall entrance into the western hall. The separate entrance was believed necessary because the customer survey showed that most food customers were not multiple shoppers. In addition, it was believed that even the customers who purchased items in addition to food usually purchased their groceries last. They normally left directly from the supermarket (with their groceries) to their cars. The enclosure took no parking from the grocery area, where parking was most needed. The total amount of parking lost would be insignificant. The lot was seldom near full, so the lost spaces would make the center appear busier. The look of popularity was desirable.

It was essential to bring the third freestanding department store into the enclosure. Otherwise the store would not be viable. In order to add the store to the enclosure, it was necessary to enclose additional space.

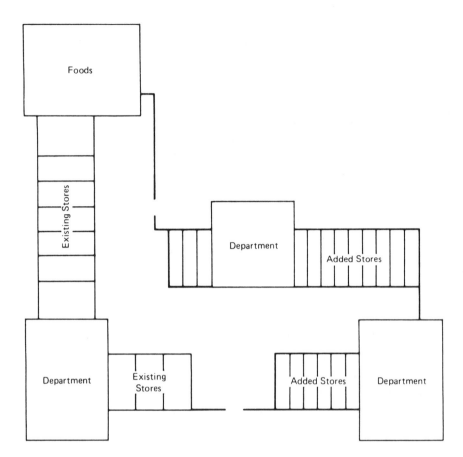

Figure 9–1. Enclosure sketch.

Consequently, some additional retail space could be created without significantly increasing cost. The new stores were intended to be small specialty establishments with 15–30 foot fronts. Thus 10–12 stores could be added to the mall as part of the enclosure. The types of shops envisioned included a health food shop, a book store, and so forth. The shops were types that would appeal to the higher-income residents of the market area, and create a recreational shopping area. Thus the consulting team decided that it would not be advisable to expand by attracting low-income customers located south of Northwest.

The enclosure would not create any significant implementation problems in the opinion of the market analysts. No major zoning changes would be required. Furthermore, the traffic pattern was such that most cars entered and exited on a major commercial road. Consequently, an increase in traffic would have practically no effect on the nearby residential neighborhood. Stores on the commercial strips would be enhanced by the extra traffic. In addition, the manager of the center claimed Northeast had "excellent" relations with residents in the surrounding neighborhood. Thus no major political problems were anticipated.

Determination of Cost

The estimation of costs and benefits was central to the actual decision. If the benefits of enclosure outweighed the costs, then the presumption would be that enclosure would be beneficial.

The costs could be most accurately estimated. The sketch plan, if adopted, would require an enclosure of 66,500 square feet. Slightly more than one-half of the total, 35,800 square feet, would be enclosed leasable area. The leasable area would be slightly more expensive to construct because of heating, electrical, and other operating needs. The total construction cost of enclosure in 1983 was estimated at $6.1 million. Annual extra operating costs were estimated at $138,000.

The cost of construction to Mitroff, the mall owners, could be less than the $6.1 million estimate. The analysts believed that $1,000,000 of the costs could be shifted to the individual tenants. The market researchers did not negotiate with particular tenants about their contributions because they felt it would be inappropriate to broach such a question in a hypothetical manner and without the authority to bargain. The management agreed. However, all of the major tenants had long-term leases. Thus they had substantial financial interest in the mall. Furthermore, there had been other cases in which tenants contributed to enclosure costs. As a result of potential tenant contributions, the cost to Mitroff was estimated at $5.1 million. The research team concluded that enclosure would have three important impacts on revenues. First, during the construction period rents would fall. People would be reluctant to shop at the mall because of dirt, noise, and inconvenience. It was anticipated that several marginal tenants would vacate their stores during this period. New tenants would be reluctant to rent space during the construction period. Second, after completion there would be more square feet to rent. However, the space would be different from the typical shopping center. Because the tenants would be small independent or franchised stores, rents and vacancy rates should be higher. A 10% vacancy rate for the new space was deemed appropriate. Finally, the enclosure should increase the ability of the mall to charge higher rents to other tenants. In the absence of enclosure the consultants doubted that rents could keep pace with the rate of general price increases. If the theory behind enclosure was correct, both annual square-foot rents and income due to percentage-of-gross-receipts clauses would increase total rental income.

The alternative to enclosure was considered to be a "facelift," including major facade work, advertising, a secure "tot lot," and redesign of the parking area. The cost of the facelift was set at $400,000.

Cash Flow Analysis

The methodology used to estimate the net benefits of enclosure was somewhat complicated. The fundamental idea was to determine whether the discounted value of the NOI after enclosure would be greater than the comparable value without enclosure by enough to warrant the $5.1 million expenditure. Furthermore, two estimates of income were developed for the mall in the absence of enclosure, and two estimates were made assuming the mall were enclosed. Each projection of what would happen in the absence of enclosure was compared with the enclosure case to determine net benefits of enclosure.

Even assuming enclosure, the market analysis team did not believe that net operating income would increase at the same rate as the market growth estimates shown in Table 9–8. There was ample land for commercial expansion in many strategic places throughout the market area. Thus, much of the market's growth would be absorbed by new enterprises. In other words, Northeast's market share was anticipated to decline, but the sales growth and net operating incentive would be positive. An important difference, however, is that the decline in market share would be smaller if the center were enclosed than if it had a "facelift."

Four scenarios were projected, two assuming enclosure and two without. For each decision—to enclose or not—both an optimistic or high scenario and a pessimistic or low projection of gross operating income were made. The optimistic-scenario enclosure assumes an 8.5% growth in gross income throughout most of the 1980s. Since the market as a whole was anticipated to grow at 8.9% (see Table 9–8), the loss of market share was assumed to be small. Market share loss was assumed to be greatest in the low, nonenclosure scenario.

On the basis of the gross income assumptions (see Table 9–9), four

**Table 9–9. Growth Rates of Gross Income:
Alternative Scenarios**

	Enclosure[a]		Nonenclosure	
	High	Low	High	Low
1984	−.025	−.025	0	0
1985	.034	.034	.06	.05
1986–1989	.085	.07	.06	.05
1990–1995	.07	.055	.05	.04
1996–2008	.06	.06	.05	.04

[a] The growth in 1984 was assumed to be affected by renovation expenses of the enclosure. The 1985 enclosure growth rate reflects a rebound from the construction-induced decline in 1984.

cash flow models were estimated. The cash flow projections are shown in Tables 9–10 and 9–11. In addition to the previously discussed income assumptions, all four models assume: (1) operating costs increasing at 5% (the same inflation rate shown in Table 9–8) and (2) a 10% discount rate. The enclosure scenarios assume that the additional leasable square footage will add to gross income and operating expenses.

As one would expect, the enclosure scenarios provided higher cumulative net present values than the nonenclosure cases, and the optimistic scenarios provided higher results than the low forecasts. The "Cumulative P.V. Net Income" does not by itself represent the value of enclosure. The value of enclosure is the difference between the present value with enclosure and the present value without enclosure. The value of enclosure would depend upon whether the high or low scenario occurred.

In order to estimate net benefits from enclosure, the estimated discounted present value of Northeast assuming enclosure was compared with the comparable scenario without enclosure. The present value of the net operating income without enclosure was adjusted to account for the cost of a "facelift" that would be needed. The difference between the enclosure and nonenclosure estimates was the benefits from enclosure. The costs of enclosure were subtracted from the benefits to generate the net benefits from enclosure (see Table 9–12). Thus, assuming the high scenario, the difference between the present value of the project with enclosure and without enclosure (adjusted for facelift) is $5,796,070. Since the cost of enclosure to the center management was estimated at $5,100,000, the net benefits were $696,070.

Table 9–10. Projections without Enclosure

		High Scenario		
Year	*Gross Income*	*Net Income*	*Present Value Net Income*	*Cumulative P.V. Net Income*
1984	1,413,619	789,037	789,037	789,037
1985	1,498,436	836,379	760,344	1,549,381
.	.	.	.	.
.	.	.	.	.
.	.	.	.	.
1990	1,986,328	1,100,347	392,672	9,277,556
1991	2,085,645	1,146,504	—	—
.	.	.	.	.
.	.	.	.	.
.	.	.	.	.
2007	4,552,701	2,423,455	270,647	11,840,089
2008	4,780,336	2,544,628	258,345	12,098,434

		Low Scenario		
Year	*Gross Income*	*Net Income*	*Present Value Net Income*	*Cumulative P.V. Net Income*
1984	1,413,619	789,037	789,037	789,037
1985	1,484,300	822,243	747,493	1,536,531
.	.	.	.	.
.	.	.	.	.
.	.	.	.	.
1990	1,876,343	990,361	559,033	4,710,489
1991	1,951,397	1,012,256	519,447	5,229,937
.	.	.	.	.
.	.	.	.	.
.	.	.	.	.
2007	3,654,929	1,525,684	170,385	10,020,155
2008	3,801,126	1,565,419	158,930	10,179,085

The analysis pointed out that regardless of whether the environment created conditions for the high or low scenario, the management company would be better off if it enclosed. However, the difference would be much greater under the high than the low scenario. Since the advisability of enclosure under the low scenario was so problematic, the analysts did not make a clear recommendation to enclose.

A qualitative discussion suggested that the actual outcome would more likely be toward the high rather than the low end of the estimate. Reasons for the opinion included:

Table 9–11. Projections with Enclosure[a]

		High Scenario		
Year	Gross Income	Net Income	Present Value Net Income	Cumulative P.V. Net Income
1984	1,060,214	366,234	366,234	366,234
1985	1,563,887	828,268	752,971	1,119,205
.	.	.	.	.
.	.	.	.	.
.	.	.	.	.
1990	2,498,115	1,513,691	854,439	5,453,152
1991	2,672,983	1,629,494	836,188	6,289,340
.	.	.	.	.
.	.	.	.	.
.	.	.	.	.
2007	7,050,205	4,684,377	523,142	16,987,982
2008	7,473,217	4,989,098	506,521	17,494,504
		Low Scenario		
Year	Gross Income	Net Income	Present Value Net Income	Cumulative P.V. Net Income
1984	1,060,214	366,234	366,234	366,234
1985	1,563,887	828,268	752,971	1,119,205
.	.	.	.	.
.	.	.	.	.
.	.	.	.	.
1990	2,334,803	1,350,379	762,253	5,173,097
1991	2,463,217	1,419,728	728,545	5,901,642
.	.	.	.	.
.	.	.	.	.
.	.	.	.	.
2007	6,140,205	3,774,378	421,515	14,530,018
2008	1,031,847	4,024,499	408,589	14,938,607

[a] One-half of the 35,801 square feet of newly created space is assumed to lease at $8 per year during 1985, and the other half is assumed to lease in 1986. Thus, the gross income is increased accordingly.

1. The estimates of inflation, while consistent with conservative practice, were possibly too low. High real interest rates and several economic forecasts indicated an inflation rate greater than 5%. The lower rate of inflation biased the projections against enclosure because if NOI increased by the same percentage for both enclosure and nonenclosure, the difference between the two (the net benefit of enclosure) would also increase by the same percentage.

Table 9–12. Net Benefits of Alternative Choices

	High Scenario	Low Scenario
1. P.V. of NOI enclosure	17,494,504	14,938,607
2. Less P.V. of NOI nonenclosure (less cost of facelift, $400,000)	12,098,434 −400,000	10,179,085 −400,000
	11,698,434	9,779,085
3. Equals benefits from enclosure	5,796,070	5,159,522
4. Less cost of enclosure (excluding tenant costs)	5,100,000	5,100,000
5. Equals net benefits to mall management	696,070	59,522

2. Growth in the market would lead new commercial development by a year or so. Thus, Northeast might capture a greater share of the market in the short run than indicated in Table 9–9.

3. The analysis did not reflect the dynamics or snowball effect of shopping behavior. An extremely successful enclosure could increase revenues much more than projected as establishments compete for space in a successful mall. Nearby space could be developed, creating a mutually beneficial agglomeration.

Of course, the normal caveats that are perennial in most market studies were also listed. Sharp changes in the aggregate economy, international or social disruptions, and national disasters were all noted as other factors that would invalidate the projections.

PROJECT DECISION

Mitroff decided to enclose the mall. Most of the construction was undertaken during 1984. The mall's management was pleased with the market study. They were even more pleased, however, with the results of the enclosure. The NOI did not decline during the construction of the mall. Many merchants claimed that individuals visited Northeast in order to see the construction. The new leasable area was 85% occupied before construction was completed—at rents about $2 per square foot greater than anticipated. Sales of tenants increased almost immediately after enclosure. Two years after construction was completed, the NOI was over 15% higher than projected in the high-enclosure forecast.

SUMMARY AND ANALYSIS

But was the enclosure decision really correct? Might not rent have increased in the absence of enclosure? Possibly, but there were no changes in the neighborhood, regional, or national economic environment that could have caused the reversal in Northeast's prospects. The problems faced by Northeast were experienced by many shopping centers throughout the United States. The responses varied from enclosure to other types of revitalization to no change. None of the approaches were universally successful. The appropriate response depended upon the local environment. In this case, the affluent local market was conducive to successful enclosure.

Even if we agree that enclosure was the key to revitalizing the center, was the market and feasibility study successful? It was well received by the owners of Northeast, and it provided information that was useful to the owners of the center. Yet the report did not reach a definitive conclusion.

The development of "scenarios" rather than presentation of straightforward recommendations is both a strength and a weakness. It is a strength because it provides the client with more information than would have been transmitted by a single "most probable" scenario. The scenario type of forecast is most definitive when all of the reasonable cases point to the same conclusion. Unfortunately, in the enclosure instance, the presentation of scenarios could have left the clients as uncertain as they were before reading the report. Furthermore, a scenario can be developed that will support almost any outcome. As one developer quipped, "If you placed all the economists in the world side by side they wouldn't reach a conclusion."

The scenario approach would have been enhanced if the consultants had devoted more effort to describing, in qualitative terms, the outcome they believed was most likely. The analysts who prepared the report should have been most able to make judgmental conclusions. The report would have been better if an opinion had been clearly stated.

Although the authors were hesitant to make definitive statements about the enclosure, "leaps of logic" were required in several phases of the research. In particular, the analyses of current market trends, customer responses to the survey, and nearby competition were used to inform the consultant's judgment regarding the center's gross operating income, and they did not provide strictly scientific predictions. Even though two estimates were given, there were still judgments. Among the explicit and implicit assumptions included in the estimate were: (1) the growth of rival centers would not be great, (2) the national and local economies would remain healthy, (3) the neighborhood in which the center is located—particularly the primary market area— will remain stable, and (4) consumer preferences for large-scale shopping centers will continue. In light of the numerous, albeit necessary, judgments, why not make a recommendation regarding whether or not to proceed with enclosure? Sophisticated developers are aware of the limitations of consulting reports, so the consultants would not be misleading their clients by making a recommendation.

The strongest part of the report should also be noted. The analysts were helped because the enclosure study was an incremental rather than discontinuous change. Therefore, they were able to place more confidence in elements of the report such as the market area, driving time, and market pull of competitors than would have been the case if the entire project were new. The ability to interview the shopping center customers before enclosure was an advantage that the researchers exploited. Most good market and feasibility studies include unique aspects that show the analysis is not a routine undertaking.

SELECTED BIBLIOGRAPHY

"Big Investors Still Love Retail Centers for Their Potential," *National Real Estate Investor,* vol. 21 (August 1979), pp. 20+.

Davies, J. M., and Wyndelts, R. W., "Component Depreciation for a Shopping Center," *Appraisal Journal,* vol. 47 (April 1979), pp. 204–217.

Harriman, S., "Greening of Bridgewater: Mill Converted to Shopping Mall," *Blair and Ketchums,* vol. 5 (January 1978), pp. 64–66+.

Howell, Brent F., "Under New Ownership," *Urban Land,* vol. 45, no. 6 (June 1986).

Mason, J. Barry, and Mayer, Morris L., *Modern Retailing,* 3rd ed., Business Publications Inc., Plano, Tex., 1984, ch. 17.

Patricios, N. N., "Human Aspects of Planning Shopping Centers," *Environment and Behavior* (December 1979), pp. 511–538.

10

Case Study: Luxury High-Rise Residential Development

In the mid-1960s most large cities acquired tracts of deteriorating "slum" property under federally financed urban renewal programs. A Northern city successfully redeveloped part of a redevelopment area with a high-rise apartment complex that later attracted a small convenience shopping center. The combined development is known as Manhattan East. However, two blocks remained undeveloped. Consequently, the Redevelopment Authority of the city decided to hire a consulting firm to do a market and feasibility study of the vacant land.

IDENTIFICATION OF PROBLEMS AND OBJECTIVES

The Redevelopment Authority asked for bids from firms interested in undertaking the project. William Kenny, the Director of the Redevelopment Authority, was impressed by the proposal submitted by Land Planning Research (LPR), a nationally known real estate consulting firm. There were several reasons for the selection of LPR. First, although the cost of LPR's proposal was higher than that of several other proposals, it was clearly written and oriented toward high-rise residential development—the land use many city officials intuitively felt was best suited to the area—and the overall development goals of the city. In their proposal, LPR indicated an interest in and knowledge of condominium development. Second, since the city hoped to use the study to attract private developers, the reputation of the group that undertook the market study was a consideration.

Also important in the choice of LPR was the belief that the staff had the technical capabilities to deliver what they promised. Finally, the city had worked with LPR on other occasions and was satisfied with its work. Kenny had a good working and personal relationship with Wilt Kermmal, the senior partner who would direct the project.

Scope of the Project

The contract involved two major stages. Stage 1 was primarily an analysis of the market potential for high-rise rental and condominium residences in the downtown area as well as demand at the site. Stage 2 was a profit feasibility analysis. A sketch of the proposal will give the details presented in the market and feasibility study.

Stage 1, the market study, consisted of four steps:

1. The first step was to generate projections and analyze demographic trends. Components of this step included:

- Projection of population for the SMSA, the city, and groups that would most likely be attracted to relatively expensive downtown residences.
- Estimation of locational preferences, marketable unit sizes, amenities, and building services.
- Determination of residential requirements by socioeconomic group.
- Estimation of annual absorption rates by type of unit. At this stage the analysis would disregard price and the competitive environment.

2. The second step was a site analysis of the subject property. The site analysis was to include:

- Description and analysis of the physical characteristics of the site and its environs.
- Analysis of the environs' attractiveness as a residential site.
- Design suggestions to ameliorate unfavorable locational characteristics and enhance the favorable aspects of the site.

3. The third step was to study the competitive environment and document potential effective demand. Components include:

- Conduction of an inventory of existing multifamily units to determine rents or purchase prices, unit size, vacancy rates, building amenities, services, and whatever extra fees were applicable.
- Personal interviews with owners and managers of middle- and upper-income residential units. Particular emphasis was to be placed upon condominium units.

- Development of socioeconomic profiles of potential condominium owners who would be attracted to the site.

4. Provision of recommendations was the final step of the market analysis. Recommendations were to focus on the suitability of the site for condominium development, number and mix of units, price range, actions to enhance the attractiveness of the site for development, a development timetable, and marketing strategies.

Stage 2, the profitability study, would be undertaken at the option of the city if Stage 1 was satisfactory and indicated that a potential market existed for high-rise residential property. The Stage 2 research contained three components:

1. The first component was a description of the land development parameters involved, including:

- A rough description of the number of units, nature of amenities, and auxiliary structures.
- Development of an illustrative site plan.
- Estimation of overall development costs.

2. The next component was the construction of a phasing plan for land and structure development.
3. The final component was the development of a cash flow model that would incorporate the conclusions and assumptions made in the previous stage.

THE MARKET STUDY

Several parts of the market study were initiated simultaneously under the direction of Wilt Kermmal. As he formulated the work schedule, Kermmal wanted to minimize the amount of time spent away from the home office and at the same time fulfill the terms of the contract and the expectations of local officials. Much of the demographic and financial analysis could be done in the home office, but interviews, map development, and contact maintenance with local officials required that some staff time be spent in the field.

Demographic Projections and Analysis

Population estimates were developed for both the SMSA and the city. The reason that both geographical areas were used was the belief that the market for high-rise units would be regionwide and not confined to those who are currently attracted to the city. In the interests of space, however, this case study will detail only the SMSA analysis.

Kermmal knew that the attraction of the as yet opaquely visualized development would vary among socioeconomic groups. Therefore, he instructed that demographic estimates were to be made separately for the nine socioeconomic groups shown in Table 10–1.

The current city and SMSA population income distributions were derived from census data regarding the distribution of families by demographic composition and income. The socioeconomic matrix for the SMSA and its components is shown in Table 10–2. By cross-multiplying family distribution percentages by income distribution percentages, the LPR analysts were able to approximate the percentage of persons in each socioeconomic group. A similar tabulation for the city was also made.

In order to generate an estimate of housing units, the average number of residents per household was estimated using national census data modified by local conditions. The average number of residents per

Table 10–1. Population Groups
Income

   I. High income
       Annual income over 130% of median family income for families; over 100% of median family income for singles and childless couples
       a. Single persons and childless couples under 65
       b. Families
       c. Single persons and childless couples over 65
  II. Middle income
       Annual income between 129–90% of median family income for families; between 99–85% for single persons and childless couples
       a. Single persons and childless couples under 65
       b. Families
       c. Single persons and childless couples over 65
 III. Low income
       Annual income under 90% of median family income for families; under 85% for single persons and childless couples
       a. Single persons and childless couples under 65
       b. Families
       c. Single persons and childless couples over 65

Table 10–2. SMSA Population

		Income				
		Low	*Middle*	*High*	*Totals*	
	Nonfamily under 65	5.8% (81,000)	19.7% (277,000)	3.5% (49,000)	29.0%	(407,000)
Family Composition	*Family*	12.6% (177,000)	42.8% (601,000)	7.6% (107,000)	63.0%	(885,000)
	Nonfamily over 65	1.6% (23,000)	5.5% (77,000)	0.9% (12,000)	8.0%	(112,000)
Totals		20.0% (281,000)	68.0% (955,000)	12.0% (168,000)		(1,404,000)

household was divided into the corresponding cell in the "Family Composition"/"Income" cell of Table 10–2 to estimate the housing units.

Until this point the study had focused upon current population conditions, but it had not been looking forward. In forecasting the population of the SMSA, Kermmal relied upon a recently published study by the state. The study, based upon revised national fertility/mortality rates, estimated that the area's population would increase 8.3%, or by 117,000 persons. Since the report not only was useful, but was recommended by Kenny, who clearly thought it was a good study, the report served as the benchmark for the projections. Estimates of family status and income distribution for new residents were more difficult to forecast, but were supported by the following qualitative reasoning.

New SMSA residents were expected to have a slightly higher income because: (1) migration into the area by low-income groups would diminish, (2) higher-income service jobs would increase, (3) corporate offices would probably expand due to the aggressive efforts of the Redevelopment Authority, and (4) the proportion of working women would increase.

Household size would decrease because: (1) birth rates would decline, (2) increased desire of individuals to live with only the nuclear family would reduce household size, and (3) increased life expectancy due to improved health would increase the number of older persons able to live on their own.

The family size was also expected to decrease, so that the number of households per thousand population should increase. Consequently, the SMSA household increase was estimated as presented in Table 10–3.

On the basis of the population and household data, plus some reasonable and fairly standardized assumptions regarding vacancy rates and demolition, Table 10–4 was derived.

The aggregate demographic analysis provided an overall picture of housing requirements, but it did not focus upon residential demand in the central business district. What percentage of the 65,570 new households were likely to be attracted to the CBD? Land Planning Research had developed a set of characteristics describing individuals who would be attracted to the CBD. The information was collected (at

Table 10–3. Projected SMSA Household Increase 1970–1980

		Income				
		Low	*Middle*	*High*	*Totals*	
Family Composition	*Nonfamily under 65*	6.8% (3,000)	26.4% (10,000)	6.8% (3,000)	40.0%	(16,000)
	Family	7.8% (3,000)	30.4% (13,000)	7.8% (3,000)	46.0%	(19,000)
	Nonfamily over 65	2.4% (1,000)	9.2% (4,000)	2.4% (1,000)	14.0%	(6,000)
Totals		17.0% (7,000)	66.0% (27,000)	17.0% (7,000)		(41,000)

Table 10–4. Residential Growth of the SMSA

	1970	1980
a. SMSA population	1,403,688	1,520,688
b. Pop. per occupied dwelling unit	3.24	3.21
c. Number of households	432,678	473,678
d. Vacancy rate	3.7%	3.5%
e. Number of vacant units	16,009	16,578
f. Household increases 1970–1980		41,000
g. Additional vacancies 1970–1980		570
h. Structures demolished or abandoned [.055 of 1970 (current) stock]		24,000
i. Total addition dwellings required in SMSA		65,570

significant expense) from a nationally selected sample of urban families. The analysis of various socioeconomic groups compared with the characteristics of the proposed site led to the conclusion that:

1. Families with children prefer single-family units in low-density areas with good educational facilities. Therefore, families with children would not be attracted to the CBD.

2. If the project is to be profitable, rents will not be affordable to low-income households.

3. Young and old, upper- and middle-income, nonchild households could be attracted to a project of single-family units, duplexes, townhouses, and high-rise condominium units. But an attractive neighborhood of recognized status and amenities would be required.

On the basis of data and hunch, the analysts decided that of the new housing units constructed between 1970 and 1980, the CBD would capture 3.3% of the metropolitan area market. Thus the CBD would capture approximately 2,164 housing units. However, two major socioeconomic groups would account for a very small fraction of the CBD future housing market: families with children and low-income groups.

Families with children would not be attracted to the CBD. They were and would continue to be concentrated in lower-density outlying areas. Low-income nonchild households would not be able to afford the higher rents associated with new CBD construction. Low-income households normally locate in housing that has filtered down and is located in the periphery of the CBD. Table 10–5 presents a summary of the size of the relevant potential market for the residential units.

Table 10–5. CBD Housing Demand Forecast for 1980

	Low	*Middle*	*High*	*Total*
Nonfamily under 65	N	930 (43)	180 (08)	1,110 (51)
Family	N	N	N	N
Nonfamily over 65	N	415 (19)	90 (04)	505 (23)
Total	N	1,345	270	1,615 (74)

N means that the share of market for the proposed project is assumed to be negligible

Percent of CBD requirements $= \dfrac{1,615}{2,164} = 74\%$

Percent of SMSA requirements $= 1,615 \div 65,570 = 2.4\%$

( ) = percent of CBD requirements

Next, the dominant housing unit preferences for each of the four target groups were examined in detail. There would be a market for both sales and rental units. The rental market was believed to be strongest among the middle-income group.

The similarity of amenities for the middle- and upper-income age groups was cited as evidence that a development directed to both income groups was feasible. The age groups required different amenities, but given the envisioned large scale of the project, the analysts felt both groups could be satisfied.

Table 10–6 presents the distribution of units for middle- and upper-income nonfamily households in the CBD. It also shows the distribution that would result if the projected 450-unit development tapped the CBD market in proportion to the expected housing mix in the CBD as a whole. For instance, since the 450 units account for 28% of the CBD requirements and since 560 of the middle-income, nonfamily, under-65 households will be in the rental market, then 156 (560 × .28) rental units should be allocated to the nonfamily under-65 middle-income category.

If the 1,615-unit requirement was to be satisfied in 10 years, then approximately 160 additional units per year should be constructed. Assuming a development of 450 units, which absorbs 50% of the total

Table 10–6. Size Cost Distribution of CBD and Proposed 450-Unit Development Upper and Middle Income

| | CBD | | | | Proposed Project | | | |
| | Middle Income | | High Income | | Middle Income | | High Income | |
	Rental	Sales	Rental	Sales	Rental	Sales	Rental	Sales
Nonfamily under 65	560	370	90	90	156	103	25	25	309
Nonfamily over 65	40	375	0	90	12	104	0	25	140
Total	600	745	90	180	168	207	25	50	449[a]

[a] Did not add to 450 due to rounding.

incremental CBD demand each year (80 units), the project could be expected to reach peak occupancy in slightly less than 6 years. However, the analysts concluded that because of the tight local housing market, the rent-up period could be reduced to 3–5 years. The more rapid absorption period, however, was based upon the assumption of a "vigorous and sophisticated marketing strategy."

Potential for Upgrading

Additional evidence for the strong upper-income housing market was based upon census data. The analysts pointed out that approximately 63,000 households in the SMSA earned more than $17,000 annually. However, only about 15,000 rental units were in the rental price range that one would expect from this group. There was a deficit in upper-income units. Consequently, the analysis team concluded that a review of the statistics indicated that the city had a large deficiency in units serving high-income residents.

The size of the deficit in upper-income housing was quantified, and the results are shown in Table 10–7.

These figures indicated a significant potential for high-income unit development. They could justify a change in the previous unit-mix projections to roughly two-thirds middle income and one-third high income.

Site Analysis

The previous analysis demonstrated the potential market for the project. Simultaneously a land planner was examining the site to determine its adequacy as a residential development. Since the young planner was unfamiliar with the city and could devote only 3 days to this

Table 10–7. Income and Unit Costs

	City	SMSA	Suburbs
Families with incomes in excess of $15,000	33,932	90,382	56,450
Rental units over $250 per month	791	1,621	830
Houses over $25,000	9,429	69,044	59,615
Deficiency in comparable units	−23,712	−19,717	+3,995

portion of the study, he relied upon knowledgeable persons in the local development agency. The site was examined along criteria developed previously by Land Planning Research. A grid analysis was employed to evaluate the site according to four general characteristics: (1) location, (2) neighborhood, (3) housing unit, and (4) competition. Each major category was made up of numerous subcharacteristics, which were assigned points according to quality.

The total site score was 306 out of 350 possible points. The 87.4% rating was highly encouraging. The excellent access to jobs and amenities contributed to the rating. Also, since the project was yet to be designed, the planner assumed it would be constructed according to the best architectural standards. Therefore, the "characteristics of housing" received a 90% score even though the project was yet to be designed.

Numerous pictures and maps helped to clarify and illustrate many of the qualitative judgments that were necessarily part of site studies.

While the site was generally viewed as favorable, several major impediments to luxury residential development were isolated:

1. The undistinguished design of low- and moderate-income residential developments north of the site inhibits high-income development. The land uses are not compatible.

2. In general, the area lacks any unifying qualities. Each building has no relationship to other buildings. Plazas and pedestrian walkways are not developed.

3. The street pattern prevents the assemblage of one large residential site.

4. The area lacks significant social activity. Streets are deserted, especially at night. There are few activity generators in the area.

5. Security is a concern, although not a substantial threat. The belief that the area is unsafe needs to be overcome.

6. The area has an urban renewal stigma. This appears to be a stigma most highly correlated with vacant parcels rather than the new development. Possibly, new development would counter the poor image.

7. Traffic on Bornekell Avenue is too heavy at peak hours for a good residential site. It should be buffered or diverted from proposed development.

8. A significant lack of trees, shrubs, and developed open space is characteristic of the area's lack of "greenery" and is a particularly negative feature in the current market.

The planner suggested several measures that could counter most of the environmental problems:

1. Orient the new development away from the industrial area to the north and northwest. Windows and balconies should focus on the building's own interior plaza and on the lakefront.

2. A link with the nearby shopping center should be established. Perhaps Manhattan East could be included in the link via a vacant site south of the shopping center. This strip could be improved with small shops and recreational facilities. A health club would be ideal. The roof of the facility could be used to overcome the disjointed nature of the area. Outdoor tennis courts, putting greens, and a sun deck could be constructed and connected by a small pedestrian bridge to the residential plaza level of the site.

3. The two lots that constitute the subject site should be physically connected by a plaza across the intervening street. A one- and two-level parking garage beneath the entire two-block development could also be built to link the towers.

4. Buchanan Street between Station Avenue and Bornekell Avenue should be rededicated to the site developer, or its use should be changed. A buffer strip should be built if the street is not rededicated to the site developer.

5. The city should try to encourage activity in the area. For example, small shops, restaurants, and recreational facilities (such as tennis courts or theaters) could be incorporated into the site.

6. Twenty-four-hour activities would do much to reduce concerns about security in this area. An all-night coffee shop, a late-night theater, or a small grocery shop would help. The construction of the apartments on a higher level than the street, such as over the garage structure, would tend to decrease the project's perceived vulnerability to crime.

7. The development should be oriented toward an appealing landmark. The lakefront would be a good focus, as would a nearby church square. The authority should be particularly sensitive to what is permitted on nearby parcels. The way they are used is crucial to the successful development of the subject site. The development of the nearby parcels should be of a very high quality.

8. The adverse effects of traffic on Bornekell Avenue can be minimized by constructing the residential quarters over the two-level parking structure.

9. Amenities, which are closely associated with the residential units, are required in the area. Among the amenities that should be considered are swimming pools, tennis courts, a putting green, a sun deck, party rooms, storage spaces, bicycle rooms and outdoor racks, exercise rooms, and a sauna. Other sophisticated facilities that could improve the prospects for successful development include restaurants, boutiques, a theater, and so forth.

Potential Effective Demand

Given the housing requirements of the SMSA and the likely CBD share, it remained to be seen whether the proposed project would be marketable. Would individuals be willing to pay for the kind of units envisioned? Simultaneously with the site analysis, a team of two researchers were developing an inventory of existing multiunit developments in the area. Effective demand is used to estimate what prices the market would support. The distinction between effective demand and requirements (the subjects of the first section of the report) is a critical distinction in almost all market studies. The examination of effective demand required systematic collection of key data on representative rental and condominium units. A total of 13 rental and 11 condominium projects were examined. Data on some representative units are shown in Table 10–8.

A second part of the analysis required the staff members to interview several apartment managers, developers, rental agents, and realtors in the area. The purpose of the interviews was to develop a qualitative as well as quantitative assessment of the city's high-rise market. Among the significant findings of the interviews were:

1. Upper-income high-rise apartments were operating at occupancy levels of slightly over 95%.

2. Of the units most representative of the proposed development, average rent for a one-bedroom unit was $206.75. Average rent for a two-bedroom unit was $294.25.

3. Rents were increasing at about 7% per year.

4. Apartment managers listed the most sought-after amenities as a lake view (where applicable), security systems, swimming pools, and party rooms. Security was an especially important concern in Manhattan East, an apartment complex adjacent to the proposed development.

Table 10–8. Representative Rental Apartment Developments in SMSA

Name	Year Opened	Number of Structures	Number of Stories	Type of Unit	Number of Units	Rental Range
1. Towers of the Lake	1963	1	11	Efficiency	30	$130–$150
				1-BR	80	$175–$185
				2-BR	70	$205–$215
				2-BR, 2-Story	29	$215–$220
					209	
2. Lincoln Towers	1965	1	23	Efficiency	40	$150–$170
				1-BR	120	$210–$260
				2-BR	40	$375–$415
					200	
3. Hilltop Terrace	1967	1	17	1-BR	30	$165–$207
				2-BR	30	$250–$300
				3-BR	15	$340–$385
					75	
4. Manhattan East	1966	1	28	Efficiency	52	$148–$185
		2	14	Studio	156	$171–$188
		3		1-BR	312	$188–$247
				2-BR	78	$275–$325
					598	

5. High-rise apartment dwellers generally desire small but spacious-appearing units, modern conveniences, and good accessibility to activities and amenities.

6. Many managers reported that a sizable number of their tenants were mature couples who returned to the city from suburban homes after raising families.

7. With regard to condominium development, the vast majority of the city's condominiums were garden apartments or townhouses. They therefore appealed to traditional single-family residents, not to individuals who prefer high-rise apartments.

8. The condominium market in the area was considered weak by many real estate observers. However, this did not appear to apply to all units. There were only two high-rise condominium units in the city. The older of the two units was fully occupied. Two-bedroom, two-bath

Table 10–8. Continued

Area (in Square Feet)	Rent per Square Foot per Month	Vacan-cies	Parking		Comments
			Indoor	Outdoor	
425	$.31–$.35	1	—	20 free	Individual air conditioning,
650	$.27–$.28	—		spaces	outdoor swimming pool,
850	$.24–$.25	—			commissary, party rooms,
850	$.25–$.26	—			laundry, storage, TV-moni-
		1			tored security system, and
					dishwasher in two-bedroom
					units
435	$.34–$.39	—	200 @ $30	—	Sun deck, individual air con-
657–747	$.32–$.35	—	per space		ditioning, beauty and barber
900–990	$.42–$.42	—			shops, security, outdoor
					pool, storage, and laundry
502–636	$.33–$.33	1	46 @ $25	29 @ $15	Lounge and sun deck, individ-
94–1,015	$.27–$.30	2	per space	per space	ual air conditioning, carpet-
1,212					ing, dishwasher, disposal,
					storage, and laundry
480	$.31–$.39	1	350 @ $20	—	Individual air conditioning,
540–560	$.32–$.34	2	per space		sun deck, outdoor pool,
680–750	$.28–$.33	2			party room, putting green,
1,200	$.23–$.27	1			concierge, gym, bicycle
		6			room, laundry, and storage

units of 1,600–2,200 square feet sold for $50,000–$75,000. The Zenith House, which only recently opened, was selling units briskly.

9. Except for innovative and large projects, developments in the city included little in the way of amenities or innovative design. The few successes, however, led to the conclusion that there was a considerable latent market for quality design and imaginative development, including semiprivate amenities.

10. It usually takes 3–4 years for condos to be accepted in an area. The city was in the second year of large-scale condominium development. Therefore, they should catch on in the next 1–2 years.

The report concluded that a market did exist for the proposed development of a high-rise with ample amenities for primarily childless couples.

Table 10–8. (Continued). Representative Condominium Apartment Developments in SMSA

Development Name	Year Opened	Number of Structures	Number of Stories	Type of Unit	Number of Units	Price Range
1. Newton Place[a]	10 years	1	14	2-BR (2 baths)	81	$50,000 $60,000 $75,000
2. Wilson Place[b]	7 years	1	12	1-BR 2-BR 3-BR Penthouse	10 20 20 _3_ 53	$23,000–$27,500 $39,000–$43,500 $50,000–$54,500 $87,500+
3. Camelot Village	3 years	10	1½ and 2	2-BR (1½ baths)	66	$26,900
4. Dillman Heights	1 year	27	11½	2-BR (2 baths)	54	$50,000

[a] Cooperative form of ownership.
[b] Recent conversion from rental to condominium.

The Recommendations

The recommendations were written by the senior partner. He was well aware that this section would be read more carefully than others by major policymakers. The conclusion should have intuitive appeal. It was therefore essential to be clear and to equivocate only when necessary. The section began with a strong sentence: "It is the opinion of Land Planning Research that there exists in the City considerable potential for downtown, high-rise condominium residences for middle- and upper-income individuals, primarily couples without children."

Several of the disadvantages of the site were reiterated, but the advantages and experiences of similar developments were similarly restated. "The advantages are substantial," and "It is for this reason that we recommend a development of 450 dwelling units, 400 in high-rise towers and 50 in townhouse and terrace units. The units should be above a 1½-level parking garage and a plaza which bridges Buchanan

Table 10–8. Continued

Square Foot Area	Price per Square Foot	Units Sold to Date	Parking			Comments
			Total	Indoor	Out-door	
1,600	$31.25	81	—	—	—	Elevator building construction, central air conditioning, dish-washer, disposal, doorman, all two-bathroom units
1,700	$35.29+					
2,200	$34.09+					
607	$37.89–$45.30		—	—	—	Elevator building construction, solarium, sundeck, dishwasher, laundry, storage, doorman, TV, security, individual air condition-ers
1,026	$38.01–$42.40	25+				
1,332	$37.54–$40.98	8				
626–2,343	$53.81+					
1,450	$18.55	66	138	102	36	Townhouse construction, range, refrigerator, and disposal in-cluded, recent resales up to $33,900, $23.38 per square foot
1,680	$29.76	54	108	108	—	Two units per structure, range, disposal, and dishwasher, first phase of 54 units sold out, second phase of 51 units starting, poten-tial of 200 units with 10-acre lake

Street.'' The unit distribution that was recommended is shown in Table 10–9.

The senior partner was quick to include the caveat "These figures are highly preliminary and will be adjusted during the financial feasibil-ity phase of the study." It was also pointed out that the combined rental-sales approach would appeal to a larger market. Thus there was less of a chance that the market would be glutted by one or the other type. Overbuilding is always a danger when developments are as large as the proposed project. Furthermore, each type of units would en-hance the other; professionals who are frequently transferred would be attracted to the project, and the rental units would allow a testing of the condominium market before actual commitment.

Table 10–9 summarizes the unit distribution. The mix of the number of bedrooms reflects the focus on childless couples. The unit prices are consistent with rents paid in comparable units throughout the area. The comparable adjustment techniques were not used. The range is slightly

Table 10–9. Unit Distribution of 450-Unit Development

Unit Type	Unit Price (1973 Dollars)	Number
Rental	$250–$345	170
Rental	Over $345	30
		200
Sales	$28,750–$48,000	
		200
Sales	Over $46,000	50
		250

Unit Sizes and Prices

Unit Type	Unit Price (Current)	Area, Square Feet	Num-ber	Price per Square Foot
1BR–1B	$250–$280	750	85	$00.33–$00.37
2BR–1B	$300–$350	1,000	85	$00.30–$00.35
2BR–2B	$350–$400	1,150	30	$00.30–$00.35
1BR–1B	$28,750–$32,500	750	60	$38.00–$43.00
2BR–1B	$32,500–$40,000	1,000	70	$33.00–$40.00
2BR–2B	$35,000–$46,000	1,150	70	$30.00–$40.00
Townhouse 2BR–2B	$50,000–$55,000	1,300	20	$38.00–$42.00
Terrace 2BR–2B	$46,000–$50,000	1,200	30	$38.00–$42.00

higher than one would expect from the comparables because of the anticipated high quality of the site and structure. The condominium sales prices exhibit a wide range. This reflects some uncertainty, caused primarily by a lack of comparable properties.

Finally, ten specific suggestions to achieve marketability were reiterated.

1. The complex must be oriented away from Manhattan East. Lakeshore focus is necessary.

2. An architectural firm with a respected national reputation should be commissioned. This will help provide a real alternative to existing developments in the SMSA and help to improve the image of the area.

3. Activity generators such as a theater/restaurant complex should be located near or incorporated into the development. A vacant lot

adjacent to the subject site could conceivably be developed as an extension of commercial/recreational activities.

4. The plaza should be visually interesting and provide a sense of activity and motion. Green space should be combined with swings, tennis, or putting activity.

5. A superior security system that reassures residents but does not create the appearance of siege must be developed and promoted.

6. The combined site has great potential. It should not be split under any but the most pressing circumstances. Adjacent proposed developments should be scrutinized in view of their impact on the subject size.

7. The interiors of individual apartments or condominium units should be well designed and spacious. Substantial balconies should be provided. Terrace units should be no more than three stories. The design should reflect the lifestyle of the targeted market—singles and childless couples.

8. Consideration should be given to providing duplex apartments.

9. All units should be designed for ultimate conversion to condominiums.

10. The project should be developed in two phases in order to avoid glutting the market in one period. The first phase would include one tower, the parking garage, the plaza, townhouses, and terrace houses. The second tower would be constructed in Phase 2.

FINANCIAL FEASIBILITY

City officials were impressed with the study. In fact, the developmental director was so impressed with the general argument that downtown residential development should focus upon nonchild households that many future aspects of housing policy were affected. In light of the marketability, the city exercised its option to commission Stage 2 of the study—financial feasibility.

Because the feasibility section of the report could be completed in LPR's home office, it was less expensive than the market study. The same planner who was responsible for the site analysis was responsible for the development of a land use plan.

The land use plan conformed closely to the general parameters that were set forth at the start of the market study. The project was described as consisting of two 205-unit towers (31 stories + penthouses), 20 townhouses, and 30 terraced houses. The total of 460 units was slightly more than the 450 envisioned in the market study. The physical design convinced the planner that the extra 10 units would be possible without diminishing the aesthetic appeal of the project. A 700-space 1½-level parking garage and plaza were also included for reasons cited in the market study. Of course, it would be greatly modified in the architectural design stage. But the site plan could help potential developers form a picture of the site's potential.

Overall development costs were estimated from standard cost manuals such as *Building Construction Cost Data* (Robert Snow Means Company, Inc., Duxbury, Massachusetts) and the *Dodge-Building Cost Calculator and Valuation Guide* (McGraw-Hill, Inc., New York, New York). The figures shown in Table 10–10 were adjusted to reflect current area business conditions.

Table 10–10. Overall Development Costs

Component Costs	Cost/Sq. Ft.	Total Cost
Residential Tower 1	$24.48	5,486,200
Residential Tower 2	25.44	6,164,120
Townhouses	19.07	1,230,100
Tenant houses	19.07	
Parking garage	8.50	1,933,750
Land	2.00	366,000
Plaza (including amenities)		375,000
Promotion		85,000
Leasing		35,000
Administrative costs		60,000
Miscellaneous		7,000

Plus: architectural fees = 5% of building costs and improvements
Sales commission = 3% of sales price

Operating Costs on Rental Tower and Garage	Percent of Gross Revenue
Rental tower	
Property taxes	30.5
Insurance	1.0
Maintenance	12.0
Utilities	7.2
Management	4.8
Garage	$120/space

The services and facilities included in the residential development provide for major appliances (including dishwasher and garbage disposal), security system, receiving room with valet service, individual air conditioning, laundry facilities, and storage rooms. Amenities include swimming pool, sun deck, putting green, tennis courts, and party and exercise rooms. A $125 per year membership fee for selected amenities is assumed in the average rent estimates for 60% of the tenants.

A development phasing plan was drawn up with the purposes of minimizing spent capital that would not be generating revenues. Rapid development of the plaza was also important in order to project a positive image from the outset. During the first two years, the parking garage, plaza, pool, 205-unit rental tower, and 25 units of low-rise condominiums were to be constructed. Additional parking and plaza development would be initiated in the third year. Also, during the third and fourth years, 25 additional low-rise condominiums and a 205-unit condominium tower would be built.

Financial Analysis

Each of the development's components underwent a preliminary analysis. They were intended only as approximations. The analysts assumed a 95% occupancy level for the rental properties and interim and long-term mortgages at 85% of actual cost. Construction loans would require 13% interest; a 30-year, 9%, long-term mortgage would be available.

The most surprising and challenging finding was that the high-rise rental tower would generate an NOI of $337,453 in a typical rental year from a capital investment of $6,275,000 (construction cost plus prorated share of other costs). The rate of return before financing would therefore be 5.4%. This return was much below the prevailing equity investor return, which was about 12%, and well below the 9% current financing rates. Because the equity return was below the mortgage interest rate, mortgage financing would further reduce the return to the equity investor. Borrowing assuming the mortgage terms described above would result in a negative cash flow of $182,547.

The condominium portions of the project were much more promising. The townhouse and terrace room condominiums were projected to generate a net income (net of construction and allocated costs), after final sales, of $1,051,000 from a capital investment of $1,499,000, resulting in a return of 70%. After financing, the rate of return (ROR) rose to 227%! The high-rise condominium tower resulted in a prefinancing rate of return of 13.3%. This was viewed as adequate although not outstanding.

Finally, the parking garage provided a negative ROR. After financing, an annual negative cash flow (loss) of $20,250 was projected.

The results of the component analysis were shown to the senior partner. There was a general feeling of disappointment among the planning team. They felt disappointed not, as is often the case, because they wanted to secure additional work for the firm, but because they thought that they had identified a viable combination. They wanted the personal satisfaction.

The senior partner studied the two problem components, the rental tower and the parking garage. He concluded that the parking garage loss was slight and was necessary to the success of the total development. The small loss should not, however, negate the overall project. The high-rise rental tower was more difficult to rectify. Increased rental rates would improve the profitability, but could not be applied since they were based on actual current market conditions. Likewise, decreased costs were not likely for two reasons. First, high-quality design was believed to be essential to the overall concept. Second, the construction costs were assumed to be competitive.

The viability of Tower 2 suggested that there were more profits in condominium development. Two other options for the rental tower were accelerated conversion to condominiums and initial development as a condominium without a rental phase. The latter alternative, however, carried with it the probability that the condominium market would be saturated because the two towers would appeal to the same market.

Two cash flow models were simulated. They varied only in treatment of Tower 1. Alternative A considered accelerated conversion of rental apartments to condominiums over a 5-year period for Tower 1; Alternative B simulated initial offering of the units in Tower 1 as condominiums without a rental period. The townhouse-terrace homes, Tower 2, and the parking garage are the same in both models. The combined project totals are shown in Tables 10–11 and 10–12. The 2% appreciation reflects *real* appreciation as opposed to purely inflationary increases.

The accelerated conversion model shows a sharp jump in gross sales income and a modest decline in gross rental income in Year 4. This is the year that Tower 2 comes "on line" and many of the rental units in Tower 1 are being converted to condominiums. Appreciation of 2% per year was incorporated into the rent and sales figures for both models. The discount rate of return for the total project is 12.67%. This represented a satisfactory return, although not outstanding; cash flow is negative through Year 3, but significantly positive in Years 4 and 5.

Alternative B assumed that the units in Tower 1 initially were to be built as condominiums. The rental income is composed only of the parking fees. Not only is the total (cumulative) cash flow greater, but the cash flow is positive in Year 2. These two factors combine to provide a discounted rate of return of 25.27%—an outstanding return even given the prevailing high interest rates.

The senior analyst concluded that Alternative B was a superior project from a purely financial perspective. However, he held unequivocal support for the sales-only option in abeyance because he feared saturating the market with condominiums. High vacancy rates with unsold units could contribute to the poor "redevelopment" image. Consequently, the report concluded that Alternative B was preferable. Final strategy decisions, however, must be based upon this analysis along with determinations of future condominium market conditions without an initial rental transition period.

SUMMARY AND ANALYSIS

The luxury high-rise residential case study represents a thorough market and feasibility study. Consequently, the weak links in this study are particularly important to recognize because they are likely to be found in almost all residential market studies. (1) The analysis of past and present population distributions is accurate. (2) Forecasts of future distributions are less accurate, but since these variables change slowly over time, the past is a good guide to the future. (3) Estimates of a particular project's share of a future market are most precarious because there is little "past" to serve as a guide. Lack of historical precedent is particularly significant in light of the uncertainty of the potential for condominiums. (4) Construction estimates are normally accurate at the time they are made. Given the rapid inflationary construction cost increases, the estimates would have been low by the time the project was initiated. (5) Design issues such as number of square feet, proper combination of bedrooms/baths, and exterior design are largely judgments, although they are an important part of a market study.

Table 10–11. Total Project Combined Summary
Alternative A
(With Tower 1 Rental With Conversion to Condominiums)

				Year			
	0	1	2	3	4	5	Total
Revenue							
Gross rental income—95% occupancy	$ 0	$ 0	$ 383,229	$ 983,084	$ 857,289	$ 258,163	$ 2,481,765
Gross sale income	0	0	523,000	1,072,000	6,556,400	11,713,600	19,865,000
Recreational income	0	0	5,266	19,035	27,324	38,916	90,541
Total revenue	$ 0	$ 0	$ 911,495	$2,074,119	$7,441,013	$12,010,679	$22,437,306
Development Cost							
Land—$2 per square foot	$366,000	$ 0	$ 0	$ 0	$ 0	0	$ 366,000
Plaza allocation	144,000	231,000	0	0	0	0	375,000
Building and improvements	0	5,608,910	1,888,590	5,752,624	1,664,038	0	14,914,162
Architectural fees	0	280,438	94,427	287,631	83,202	0	745,698
Promotion	0	55,000	0	30,000	0	0	85,000
Leasing expense	0	5,000	15,000	15,000	0	0	35,000
Selling expense	0	0	15,690	32,160	196,692	351,408	595,950
Administration and overhead	0	15,000	10,000	20,000	10,000	5,000	60,000
Miscellaneous operating expense	0	1,000	1,000	2,000	2,000	1,000	7,000

Conversion—legal and miscellaneous	0	0	0	0	2,850	7,400	10,250
Conversion remodeling	0	0	0	0	5,700	14,800	20,500
Total development cost	$510,000	$6,196,348	$2,024,707	$6,139,415	$1,964,482	379,608	$17,214,560
Operating Expenses for Rental Property							
Total operating expenses	$ 0	$ 0	$ 187,959	$ 534,468	$ 433,138	84,000	$ 1,239,565
Financing at 85% Cost							
Interim loan amounts	$ 0	$5,586,896	$1,721,001	$5,331,579	$1,669,811	322,667	$14,631,954
Mortgage loan amounts	0	0	1,161,154	0	573,219	0	1,734,373
Interim loan repayment	0	0	1,416,487	510,665	4,845,994	7,858,808	14,631,954
Mortgage debt service (principal and interest)	0	0	113,027	113,027	168,824	168,824	563,702
Interim interest	0	367,503	670,614	1,079,244	1,148,891	489,849	3,756,101
Mortgage loan fee	0	0	11,612	0	5,732	0	17,344
Cash Flow after Financing							
Cash flow	($510,000)	($ 976,955)	($ 630,756)	($ 971,121)	$1,116,982	$ 3,352,257	$ 1,380,407
Cumulative cash flow	($510,000)	($1,486,955)	($2,117,711)	($3,088,832)	($1,971,850)	1,380,407	—
Discounted rate of return	—	—	—	—	—	12.67%	12.67%

Table 10–12. Total Project Combined Summary
Alternative B
(With Tower 1 Built as a Condominium)

				Year			
	0	1	2	3	4	5	Total
Revenue							
Gross rental income—95% occupancy	$ 0	0	$ 160,997	$ 165,134	$ 251,584	$ 258,163	$ 835,878
Gross sale income	0	2,700,400	6,873,600	4,265,000	5,616,000	19,455,000
Recreational income	0	0	5,266	19,035	27,324	38,916	90,541
Total revenue	$ 0	$ 0	$2,866,663	$7,057,769	$4,543,908	$5,913,079	$20,381,419
Development Cost							
Land—$2 per square foot	$366,000	0	0	0	0	0	$ 366,000
Plaza allocation	$144,000	231,000	0	0	0	0	375,000
Building and improvements	0	5,608,910	1,888,590	5,752,624	1,644,038	0	14,914,162
Architectural fee	0	280,438	94,427	287,631	83,202	0	745,698
Promotion	0	55,000	0	30,000	0	0	85,000
Leasing expense	0	0	0	0	0	0	0
Selling expense	0	0	81,012	206,208	127,950	168,480	583,650
Administration and overhead	0	15,000	10,000	20,000	10,000	5,000	60,000

Miscellaneous operating expense	0	1,000	1,000	2,000	2,000	1,000	7,000
Conversion—legal and miscellaneous	0	0	0	0	0	0	0
Conversion remodeling	0	0	0	0	0	0	0
Total development cost	$510,000	$6,191,348	$2,075,029	$6,298,463	$1,887,190	$174,480	$17,136,510
Operating Expenses for Rental Parking Spaces							
Total operating expenses	$ 0	$ 0	$ 56,400	$ 56,400	$ 84,000	$ 84,000	$ 280,800
Financing at 85% Cost							
Interim loan amounts	$ 0	$5,582,646	$1,763,774	$5,314,579	$1,604,112	$ 148,308	$14,413,419
Mortgage loan amounts	0	0	1,161,154	0	573,219	0	1,734,373
Interim loan repayment	0	0	2,905,632	4,377,218	3,296,086	3,834,483	14,413,419
Mortgage debt service (principal and interest)	0	0	113,027	113,027	168,824	168,824	563,702
Interim interest	0	367,227	576,048	638,232	551,922	239,601	2,373,030
Mortgage loan fee	0	0	11,612	0	5,732	0	17,344
Cash Flow after Financing							
Cash flow	($510,000)	($ 975,929)	$ 53,843	$ 889,008	$ 727,485	$1,559,999	$ 1,744,406
Cumulative cash flow	($510,000)	($1,485,929)	($1,432,086)	($ 543,078)	$ 184,407	$1,744,406	—
Discounted rate of return	—	—	—	—	4.40%	25.27%	25.27%

Was the market and feasibility study a success? The question requires a simple answer, but none can be given. It was a good, technically competent study; yet it did not result in development of the tract. No developer was interested. The ability to attract developers, however, should not be a criterion for a good study. Such thinking is likely to lead to pressures to provide biased analysis and could lead to the kinds of shortcomings discussed previously. The city did receive some benefits from the project, however. Because of the focus on the potential for middle- and upper-income childless families in the city, the Department of Urban Development was better able to focus its development planning in other areas. Since the study, the city has focused its residential development efforts on this group.

Urban Revitalization

In recent years there has been evidence that middle-income families are reentering the city. Neighborhoods are going through a process of "gentrification"—a return of the affluent, driving prices up, out of the range affordable to previous residents. In late 1978, Allman argued that the urban crisis had left town and moved to the suburbs.[1] The projected increase in the central city's share of new metropolitan housing was correct. However, while the analysts may have correctly perceived a trend, few developers are willing to anticipate or be in the vanguard of individuals investing in new trends. The bulk of investors prefer to imitate proven projects. The fact that the area had no recent examples of similar developments may have hurt its prospects for implementation. The market study did, however, describe the success of condominium developments elsewhere in the nation.

The Plaza and Generation of Activity

The need to affect the environs of the site, to make it more appealing both visually and socially, was a significant theme in both the marketing and design study. The suggested solutions were: encourage street-level activity and the development of a garage-top plaza/recreation area and a restaurant/theater. Urban design in which individuals venture outside only to pass from one structure to another was implicit in many early developments, but is currently in disfavor. Planners have been increasingly recognizing the importance of "human-scale" structures and activities in the midst of downtown high-rise development.

Raquel Ramata, Director of Urban Design for New York City, commented on the importance of architectural techniques.[2]

> The emergence of the skyscraper in downtown areas has fostered the destruction of traditional street activities. Although planners were aware of the light/air relationship between buildings, the environment at street level and the relationship of buildings to one another on the ground was ignored. Isolated, windy leftover spaces between buildings, often used as parking lots, are common sights replacing the once vital streetscape. The physical reality of these leftover spaces is one of the causal factors in the deterioration of the quality of downtown life.
>
> All across the country, there has recently been a new effort to revitalize the streetscape, fostered by the need for a "sense of place," the reintroduction of vital commercial and social activities, and the requirement of places for people to sit, watch, and enjoy the city. It is the beginning of a movement to reintroduce the human dimension to cities.

Another advantage of generating pedestrian traffic, particularly evening activities as suggested by the restaurant/theater proposal, is that crime tends to decrease when there is a lot of activity. In light of the perceived safety concerns among residents of Manhattan East (based upon interviews with the manager and the importance of a security system), the creation of an active environment is important.

The importance of open communities explains why the plaza was considered essential to the whole project even though it was an unprofitable component when viewed in isolation. The project could have been expanded to include other activity generators, but enlarging the complex would reduce the number of developers interested in pursuing it. Alternatively, a larger development could have been designed as an option or additional stage. Unfortunately, the market and feasibility study's costs would also have increased accordingly.

SELECTED BIBLIOGRAPHY

Asabere, Paul K., and Bauie, Harvey, "Factors Influencing the Value of Urban Land," *American Real Estate and Urban Economic Association Journal* (Winter 1985), pp. 361–377.

Brimmer, A., "Homeownership and Condominium Conversion," *Black Enterprise,* vol. 10 (August 1979), p. 55.

Burchell, R. W., and Sternlieb, G., "Multi-family Housing Demand: 1980–

2000," *American Real Estate and Urban Economic Association Journal,* vol. 7 (Spring 1979), pp. 1–38 and 123–130.

Cutsinger, S. L., "Valuing Apartments with the Unit Mix Adjustment Technique," *Real Estate Appraiser and Analyst,* vol. 45 (May 1979), pp. 16–19.

Dertina, D. C., *Condominium Conversions: The Newest Way to Strike It Rich,* Burke-Ives Pub. Co., Denver, 1980.

Downs, A., *Rental Housing in the 1980's,* The Brookings Institution, Washington, D.C., 1983.

Eggbeer, W., "New Rental Apartments Can Be a Good Investment but It Will Require the Changing of Many Conventionally-Held Concepts," *Mortgage Banker,* vol. 39 (May 1979), pp. 7–8+.

Kawater, I. G., "Macroeconomic Determinants of Multi-family Housing Starts: A Descriptive Analysis," *American Real Estate and Urban Economic Association Journal,* vol. 7 (Spring 1979), pp. 45–62.

Robert A. McNeil Corporation, *The American Housing Market: A National View,* Robert A. McNeil Corporation, San Mateo, Calif., 1979.

Rosen, K. T., "Regional Model of Multi-family Housing Starts," *American Real Estate and Urban Economic Association Journal,* vol. 7 (Spring 1979), pp. 63–76.

Stegman, M. A., "Multi-family Distress: A Case for National Action," *American Real Estate and Urban Economic Association Journal,* vol. 7 (Spring 1979), pp. 77–94.

Turner, M. G., and Struyk, R., *Urban Housing in the 1980's,* The Urban Institute, Washington, D.C., 1984.

U.S. Department of Housing and Urban Development, *The President's National Urban Policy Report,* Department of Housing and Urban Development, Washington, D.C., 1982.

11

Case Study: Office Space Development

The techniques of analysis used in real estate market feasibility studies can be adapted to a variety of uses that were not envisioned when the techniques were initially developed. In fact, almost all market and feasibility projects present new wrinkles that require innovative solutions. In this case, the analysis had two relatively new twists to consider: (1) the declining school-age population and (2) the concern for historic preservation. Specifically, a medium-size Midwestern suburb was concerned about an abandoned school building in a designated historical district. City officials felt that the property had development potential, but they were uncertain about how to proceed.

IDENTIFICATION OF PROBLEMS AND OBJECTIVES

A real estate analyst, Jay Darth, was approached by the city manager of Birthfair. The city manager explained that the local school district had given (actually sold for $1) the city an abandoned school building, Birthfair Elementary School. The city intended to relocate part of its office staff into the building, but 16,000 square feet and a gym would still remain vacant. The city had created a Citizens' Task Force to determine how the remaining 16,000 square feet should be used. Many of the original ideas—a community center, expanded public service use—were considered too expensive. Birthfair, as was true of many other cities, was under pressure to keep taxes low. At the same time, there was strong community sentiment that the property should not be abandoned or fall into disrepair. Birthfair Elementary was a landmark in the community. Several members of the Citizens' Task Force had attended the school. Thus, a use that was not a tax drain and that was in keeping with the historical character of the property and neighborhood was necessary.

Before committing to the project, the analyst was interviewed by the Citizens' Task Force. At that meeting, the political dilemma faced by the city manager became clear. Some of the more vocal members of the task force had believed a community center was the most feasible idea. Others thought a small mall could be developed. Nevertheless, there was enough openness so that Jay Darth felt he would be free to make the recommendation he felt was appropriate, subject to the dual constraints of (1) minimizing the cost to the city and (2) maintaining the architectural integrity of the property. Consequently, he submitted a 2-page, semiformal proposal and received the commission.

Scope of the Project

The project consisted of four stages:

Stage 1:   Review the alternative uses of Birthfair Elementary, and determine the appropriate use given the constraints.

Stage 2:   Examine the competitive market for the land use suggested in Stage 1, including (1) a presentation of qualitative findings about the market environment and (2) an analysis of rent levels of the most comparable office sites.

Stage 3:   Forecast the supply and demand for the suggested land use in both the metropolitan market and the immediate Birthfair market area. Both the short-term and long-term projects were to be undertaken to ensure underlying demand.

Stage 4:   Determine profit feasibility. This section was to include advice on structuring the project, a static appraisal, and a dynamic cash flow. The purpose was to ensure that the project would not be a tax drain.

REVIEW OF SITE USES

The review of alternative site uses was not extensive. It included an examination of how other communities had used abandoned schools and a discussion of several options. The analyst concluded that rental office space was the most appropriate use. He based his conclusion upon three factors:

1. A partial use of the building will be office space for governmental offices, and it is important to maintain homogeneity throughout the complex.
2. The building is a historic landmark and has significant charisma associated with it. If marketed correctly, the building could possibly be perceived as having a prestigious status. This would enhance the marketability of the Birthfair Elementary School project as an office site.
3. The location is good for office space. Birthfair Elementary School is only a few blocks from a major military research base, Williams Air Force Base (WAFB). The base contracts with many private R&D and engineering firms, and they want to be close to the base and other major access points. The location of Birthfair Elementary School will be important to the outside contractors working in this area of the base.

Office space use had been suggested previously by the city manager and by members of the Citizens' Task Force. It was further recommended that the office space be targeted toward basic, high-tech tenants rather than local service tenants (doctors, insurance agents, etc.) for several reasons. First, if the space is absorbed by local service tenants, the likely effect will be movement rather than improvement. If local businesses moved to Birthfair Elementary, it would cause other vacancies throughout Birthfair. The net effect of the relocation could leave local service space in other buildings empty. This potential problem is compounded by the fact that downtown Birthfair currently has ample vacant space suitable for local service tenants. Furthermore, the demand for local service space depends on the local population, so increasing the available local service space will not directly attract new enterprises to use the space. Adding the proposed 16,000 square feet of local service space would intensify the high vacancy rate in the nonbasic rental market.

If the city is able to attract basic tenants new to the area to the Birthfair site, the results could be an increase in employment and the municipal tax base. Also, there would be a multiplier effect that would facilitate further growth in the local service sector.

A developer could capitalize on the location by finding a contractor who deals extensively with WAFB. It was suggested that contractors currently in the area were often provided offices on the base. If the developer could not locate a client from the private sector, the Air Force should not be ignored as a possible tenant or at least a source of leads. Depending on the availability of space within WAFB, the Air Force might wish to rent office space, and Birthfair Elementary would be a good site. In any event, Air Force purchasing and operations officers should be important contacts in attempting to market space.

COMPETITIVE MARKET ANALYSIS

This part of the report examined the competitive market in which the Birthfair School project would operate. Two aspects of the competitive market analysis were described. The first section presented qualitative findings about the market environment. It stressed particular features that would be relevant in the development of the renovation plans. The second section analyzed rent levels of the most comparable office sites in the market area.

Qualitative Considerations

Could Birthfair School be renovated in a way that would be appropriate for the needs of basic tenants, or do qualitative factors make the property more suitable to local service uses? The analyst believed that there could be a good match between the needs of basic tenants and the renovated section of Birthfair. A grid of office site characteristics was used to support the qualitative considerations. Specific reasons and factors to be considered during renovation included:

1. After interior renovation, the site could be as efficient and look as attractive as almost any of the sites in the suburban market area. Quality renovation that took advantage of historical architectural features had great promise.
2. Basic tenants did not generally require separate utilities, but many local service users did. Separation of utilities (electricity, heat, water) for the elementary wing would increase costs. Failure to separate utilities would not be a major deterrent to the basic tenants envisioned in Part I.
3. Escalator clauses appear to be acceptable to basic tenants and should not present a marketing problem if basic tenants were targeted.

4. A generous supply of free parking is usually available to basic tenants in suburban locations. The survey results indicated that one parking place per 135 square feet is ample. This would mean that a minimum of 119 spaces would be necessary to service the elementary wing. However, basic tenants require fewer spaces since there is less need for customer parking.
5. Basic users desire flexibility in the area of wall treatment, carpet selection, room layout (partitions, new doorways, etc.).
6. Many tenants in defense, sales, and high-technology enterprises are security-conscious. Although the owner normally provides maintenance in the buildings we examined, there may be some tenants who prefer to provide their own janitorial service within the space they rent. It could be a reason for rent variations.

   The need for security reinforces the need to separate the private rental space from the traffic flow of governmental offices (see point 7).
7. The sharing of Birthfair Elementary with governmental offices constitutes a potential negative marketing feature because many office complexes have distinct identities that are important marketing tools. In order to minimize potential problems, the report suggested:

   • Keeping the government offices separate and distinct from the private offices.
   • Avoiding governmental uses that would generate a high level of traffic, particularly governmental business where casual attire is appropriate.
   • Giving governmental offices separate entrances and restricting their space to the ground floor.
   • Designing the parking-pedestrian traffic flow so as to facilitate the use of the front entrance of the elementary wing solely for the private clients.
   • Installing elevators to allow easy access to the private space.
   • Using interior colors to give the private portion of the project a separate identity. A logo may be particularly useful in developing an appropriate image and identity.

8. The gym should be spruced up and the locker room redone for exclusive use by employees of the tenants. In many new projects (including a proposed local project), areas have been set aside for jogging tracks, exercising, and other recreational uses which his-

torically haven't been considered appropriate for an office complex.

The qualitative review indicated that renovation could make the site competitive compared with other quality space. However, some potential problems were noted, specifically, the need to develop a separate identity and differentiate traffic flows. But these potential problems could be overcome. The Birthfair Elementary site appeared to be suitable for conversion to office space intended for basic tenants.

Potential Rents

Assuming Birthfair School were renovated in the manner indicated in the qualitative section, what rents could it command? In order to answer the question, three comparable sites that appealed to high-tech tenants were analyzed in detail.

The three properties used as comparables are:

• The Hudgin Building
• Catcrow Office Center
• 1010 Wood Avenue

Table 11–1 shows the rental levels of the three comparable properties and the salient features that have an important bearing on rent. The annual rents per square foot were adjusted to make them comparable to the envisioned Birthfair School project. When one of the features of a comparable unit was superior to Birthfair School, the rents of the comparable site were adjusted downward to reflect that difference. When a comparable was less desirable than the subject property in a particular dimension, rents were adjusted upward.

The indicated rents ranged between $7.25 and $9.50. The average indicated rent was about $8.50. That represented a conservative estimate because the analyst believed that some tenants at 1010 Wood paid more than $8.09 per square foot. Nevertheless, it was a reasonable base from which to make a conservative profit feasibility projection.

Rent variations among tenants in the same building did exist in the market area. However, the floor a tenant occupies was not a significant factor in causing rent variations. Some allowances had been made to entice larger square-foot commitments or longer lease terms. However, this did not appear to be a universally followed practice in the market area.

Table 11–1. Comparative Rent Analysis

	Birthfair Central Office Park	Hudgin Building	Catcrow Office Center	1010 Wood
		$9	$10.50	$8
Condition	Good	Better (−.25)	Best (−.50)	Good
Age of building	Older	Older	New (−.25)	New (−.25)
Class of space	A	A− (+.25)	A+ (−.25)	A+ (−.25)
Time of leasing	Present	Past (+.25)	Present	Present
Quality of construction	Good	Fair (+.25)	Best (−.25)	Best (−.25)
Visibility and image	Good	Good	Good	Good
Utilities	Owner pays	Owner pays	Owner pays	Owner pays
Parking	Ample—included in rent	Ample—included in rent	Ample—included in rent	Ample—included in rent
Net adjustments		(+.50)	(−1.25)	(−.75)
Indicated price		$9.00	$9.25	$7.25[a]
Subject rent	$8.50			

[a] Quoted rate was $8 and up.

FORECAST OF OFFICE DEMAND AND SUPPLY

The feasibility of an office development depends upon future as well as present market conditions. Consequently, the supply and demand conditions in both the metropolitan area and the Birthfair area were examined.

The Metropolitan Market

The metropolitan area had a relatively low occupancy rate. The most recent data, supplied by the Metro Development Council, indicated that the overall occupancy rate in major metropolitan offices was about 90%. In other words, the vacancy rate was about 10%. However, compared with previous studies, the occupancy rate had increased. Perhaps this increase indicated recent growth.

The data on key metropolitan buildings also indicated that the highest vacancy rates are in older, lower-quality office space. This finding implied that as newer offices have been constructed and leased, their tenants have left lower-quality (and less expensive) sites. The conclusion that Birthfair School planners should concentrate on developing a high-quality site was supported by the metropolitan area finding.

On the basis of the area vacancy data, the amount of known vacant office space was estimated at 10%, or

$$3,856,000 \text{ sq. ft.} \times .10 = 285,600 \text{ sq. ft.}$$

The above represents only known vacancies in established office buildings. It was not feasible to calculate the vacant space that existed in small, freestanding structures, storefronts, and offices mixed with residential users.

The high vacancy rates in the metropolitan area were matched by relatively high vacancy rates in the Birthfair market area. Also, the high metropolitan vacancy rates indicated that the Birthfair project would not receive significant "spillover" from tenants whose first preference might have been for a downtown location but who might otherwise have been unable to find an adequate downtown site.

The Long-Term Outlook

Like many older urban regions, the SMSA was not growing as rapidly as it had in the past. The SMSA had been adversely affected by spatial shifts among its major industrial employers, the nationwide problems in heavy manufacturing activities, and the national business recession. However, several facts suggested that the employment history was brighter for the market area relevant to Birthfair.

- Growth in the Birthfair School area was greater than that in the SMSA as a whole.
- Greene County's growth may be more indicative of growth in the Birthfair School market area. Greene County accounts for about 35% of the metropolitan area's growth.
- The growth of the SMSA indicates that Birthfair School is located near a significant metropolitan growth axis.
- Birthfair occupies a strategic location in the metropolitan area. It has access to suppliers and to major industrial and consumer markets. It has four interchanges on Interstate 775, allowing excellent access to a larger market of the region and excellent development capabilities.
- Birthfair is flanked by three growing and dynamic metropolitan centers.

Quantitative Analysis

This section presented a short-run quantitative analysis of the demand for office space in the Birthfair market area. There were six steps in the analysis:

1. Estimate office space using employment increases in the SMSA.
2. Estimate the market area's share of metropolitan SMSA employment growth, and calculate employment growth in the Birthfair market area.
3. Estimate space requirements for office space per employee.
4. Use Steps 2 and 3 to estimate total increase in space needs.
5. Estimate office space under construction.
6. Compare Steps 4 and 5.

The six steps are summarized in Table 11–2.

Conclusion

The amount of current excess space was larger than normal for most markets and confirmed the opinion of many local experts that the general market area of Birthfair would grow more rapidly than previously, perhaps absorbing the space in less than 3.5 years. The qualitative

**Table 11–2. Space/Requirements Forecast to 1986
Birthfair Elementary School Market Area**

1. Office space using employment increases, SMSA[a]	17,581
2. Estimated share for Birthfair School market area[b]	$\times$ .25
	4,395
3. Average number of square feet per employee using office space[c]	$\times$ 200 sq. ft.
	879,000 sq. ft.
4. Total projected increase per year to 1986 ÷ 3	÷ 3
	293,000 (say, 300,000)
5. Space under construction and excess vacancies[d]	1,043,640
	÷ 300,000
6. Years to absorb current excess vacancies and planned increases	3.5 years

[a] Based upon a separate employment forecast provided by a local university researcher.
[b] Based upon past growth and a subjective assessment of growth potential.
[c] Based upon International Building Owners and Managers Association annual survey.
[d] Based upon building permits.

analysis suggested that this is possible. However, the prospect of developing an office complex in an already overbuilt market was a negative factor.

The forecast indicated that the development would be running against the wind. The prospect of stiff competition means that the project would have to be well conceived and managed to be successful. However, the project could still be successful in the face of competition.

PROFIT FEASIBILITY

The previous analysis indicated that the project was marketable, but it would face stiff competition. The profit feasibility section was intended to determine whether the development could be profitable or whether public monies would be required to subsidize the proposed office complex. The first section described general assumptions about the way we believe the project should be structured. The second section presented a more sophisticated, dynamic cash flow analysis that included the impact of tax benefits associated with the project.

The conclusion of the financial analysis was that the renovation could be profitable.

Structuring the Project

Jay Darth believed the best way to structure the renovation was for the city of Birthfair to lease the elementary wing on a long-term basis to a private developer or, more realistically, to a limited partnership formed by the developer. The private developer and associates would agree to renovate, market, and manage the project. The developer would sublease the office space to tenants.

One principal advantage of the proposed structure was that the developer would take full advantage of tax credits and depreciation. If the city controlled the project, the tax benefits would be lost, since the city does not have taxable income, which is needed to exploit the tax writeoffs. A second principal advantage is that a private developer would be in a better position to manage the project due to experience and might have more flexibility than if the project were run by the city.

Dynamic Cash Flow

The financial analysis of the dynamic cash flow assumed the structure described above. Further:

- The developer and his associates were treated as a single entity.
- The city was primarily interested in renovating and leasing the structure. The cash flow analysis assumes the developer will pay no rent to the city, or, alternatively, that rents will equal property tax payments. Later this assumption should be modified after affordable rents can be projected.
- The developer would attract private investors who might be interested in the ability to shelter other income from federal taxes. Later in this report it was shown that the income tax factors were critical.
- Birthfair will retain reversionary rights to the property.
- A 30-year 12% mortgage loan was available. The city of Birthfair was willing to subordinate its fee simple interest so that the developer and associates could obtain the mortgage loan and the mortgagee could obtain a priority loan.

Three tax advantages would be available to investors due to the historical nature of the site. First, it was assumed that the elementary wing will qualify to receive a 25% investment tax credit. An additional advantage of the historical nature of the site is that the rehabilitation will qualify for accelerated depreciation. The costs of the renovation could be written off over a 15-year period. This allows tax benefits to accrue more quickly than under the traditional forms of depreciation, and consequently the tax benefits have a higher present value. Third, the basis (depreciable tax base) need not be adjusted for the 25% tax credit. Clearly, the tax advantages were an important part of the profit potential picture.

The cash flow model is shown in Table 11–3. The analysis showed that an investor could earn an adequate return on investment (12%) and still earn additional revenues (including tax savings) over a 30-year period. The higher the required rate of return, the lower the value of the project will be. If the required return on investment were to increase, the present value of future returns (line 33) would decrease.

Explanation of Table 11–3

Line 1: Gross (Income) Revenue.   Initially gross income was set at $8.50 per square foot times 16,000 square feet, or $136,000 annually. Beginning in 1987, rents are adjusted upward by 5% per year. This reflects the consensus forecast for moderate inflation.

Line 2: Vacancy (and Collection) Loss.   This line shows reductions in gross income due to vacancies. The model assumes a 50% vacancy rate in 1985, a 25% vacancy rate in 1986, and a 5% vacancy rate for the rest of the project's simulation period. The 5% rate is slightly below average for the area.

Line 3: Effective Gross (Income) Rent.   This line is gross revenue less vacancies.

Line 4: Operating Expenses.   Operating expenses represent costs of operating the project. Projections of operating expenses are based on numerous sources. Gas, electric, and heating oil costs are based on figures provided by Birthfair officials. Elevator maintenance and insurance were based on conversations with Test Elevator and an independent insurance agency. All figures are based on a percentage of effective gross rents. Cost figures not provided were projected from various sources, including Lloyd D. Hanford, *Analysis and Management of Investment Property*, and *Income/Expense Analysis: Suburban Office Buildings,* published by the Institute for Real Estate Management.

The estimate of expenses as 48% of income is slightly above the national average and provides a good, conservative standard with which to calculate income pro forma.

Table 11–3. Birthfair Office Complex Total Return on Investment 30-Year Pro Forma (000 omitted).

		1985	1986	1987	1990	1995	2000	2005	2010	2014
1. Gross revenue		136.0	136.0	142.8	165.3	211.1	269.4	343.8	438.8	533.3
2. Less vacancy		68.0	34.0	7.1	8.2	10.5	13.4	17.1	21.8	26.5
3. Effective gross rent		68.0	102.0	135.7	157.1	200.6	256.0	326.7	417.0	506.8
4. Less operating expenses		32.6	57.6	65.0	75.4	96.3	122.9	156.9	200.2	243.3
5. Net operating income		35.4	44.4	70.7	81.7	104.3	133.1	169.8	216.8	263.5
7. Less interest		84.0	83.6	83.3	81.8	77.9	71.0	58.9	37.6	9.3
8. Less depreciation		98.8	85.3	75.4	51.9	38.7	—	—	—	—
9. Net taxable income		(147.7)	(124.5)	(88.0)	(52.0)	(12.3)	62.1	110.9	179.2	254.2
11. Debt service		86.9	86.9	86.9	86.9	86.9	86.9	86.9	86.9	86.9
12. Cash throw-off		(51.5)	(42.5)	(16.2)	(5.2)	17.4	46.2	82.9	129.9	176.6
14. Principal payments		2.9	3.2	3.6	5.1	9.0	15.9	28.0	49.3	77.6
Return on investors' shares										
17. Cash throw-off		(51.5)	(42.5)	(16.2)	(5.2)	17.4	46.2	82.9	129.9	176.6
18. Tax benefits @ 40% bracket		59.1	49.8	35.2	20.8	4.9	(24.8)	(44.4)	(71.7)	(101.7)
19. Principal payments		2.9	3.2	3.6	5.1	9.0	15.9	28.0	49.3	77.6
20. P.V. investment tax credit, original investment	(130.0)									
Present value of returns										
25. Annual investment	(130.0)	(51.5)	(42.5)	(16.2)	(5.2)	—	(74.8)	(44.4)	(71.7)	(101.7)
26. Annual returns		269.5	53.0	38.8	25.9	31.3	62.1	110.9	179.2	254.2
27. Total	(130.0)	218.0	10.5	22.6	20.7	31.3	37.3	66.5	107.5	152.5
30. Present value interest factors @ 12%		.8929	.7972	.7118	.5066	.2875	.1631	.0916	.0525	.0334
33. Present value annual returns	(130.0)	194.7	8.4	16.1	10.5	9.0	6.1	6.2	5.6	5.1
34. Cumulative returns	(130.0)	64.7	73.0	89.1	124.9	170.0	211.6	242.5	271.9	293.1

Variable operating expenses are based on a percentage of effective gross rents as follows:

Electric	7.4%
Gas	.4
Heating oil	17.5
Janitorial	11.0
Supplies	.9
Management	.5
Legal	.75
Miscellaneous	.75

Fixed expenses were estimated as follows:

Elevator maintenance	$1,200 annually, with inflation (.05 in 1987)
Insurance	$1,000
Real estate taxes	

Line 5: Net Operating Income.   This line represents income from operations that would accrue to an owner. It is used in estimating value in traditional appraisal methodologies.

Lines 7–9:   These lines represent the calculation of taxable income.

Line 7: Interest.   A $700,000 loan at 12% interest rate for 30 years is assumed. The loan constant is .124144. Therefore, annual payments are .124144 × 700,000 = $86,900. A mortgage at reasonable rates should be attainable, especially if Birthfair subordinates its interest in the property as security for the loan.

Line 8: Depreciation.   The depreciation technique assumes a 175% declining balance until 1993. A switch to straight line is allowable under the ACRS, and the profit maximizing point occurs in 1993.

Line 9: Net Taxable Income.   Net taxable income is NOI less interest payments and depreciation.

Line 11: Debt Service.   See line 7 for explanation.

Line 12: Cash Throw-off.   Cash throw-off indicates the money that will accrue to the developer before taxes. A negative cash throw-off indicates payments that the developer will have to put into the project.

$$\text{Cash throw-off} = \text{NOI (line 5)} - \text{debt service (line 11)}$$

No replacement revenue is assumed.

Line 14: Principal Payments. Principal payments represent wealth that accrues to the developer by virtue of the decline in debt. See line 7.

$$\text{Principal payment} = \text{line 11} - \text{line 7}$$

Line 17: Cash Throw-off. See line 12.

Line 18: Tax Benefits. Depreciation is an accounting cost that is not an actual loss. It has value to an investor because it can be used to reduce the amount of other income subject to tax. The same logic applies to interest payments, although, unlike depreciation, interest payments are a real, out-of-pocket cost. The value of the tax loss was determined by:

$$\text{Value} = \text{tax loss} \times \text{marginal tax rate}$$

We assumed the investor would be in the 40% marginal tax bracket. Therefore:

$$\text{Line 18} = \text{line 9} \times .40$$

Line 19: Principal payments. See line 14.

Line 20: P.V. Investment Tax Credit. The investment tax credit is a direct tax savings equal to the investment tax credit.

$$\text{Line 20} = \$830,000 \times .25$$

Line 25: Annual Investment. Since cash throw-off is negative for the first 7 years of operation, the total investment will increase until cash throw-off is positive. Also, by 1997, revenues increase, so that taxes on operating income will be due.

Line 26: Annual Returns. This line is the annual sum of positive benefits which occur due to cash throw-off, tax benefits, principal payments, and the investment tax credit.

Line 27: Total

$$\text{Line } 27 = \text{line } 25 + \text{line } 26$$

Line 30: Present Value Interest Factors. The present value interest factor represents the value of $1 at 12% for ($n$) periods.

Line 33: Present Value Annual Returns

$$\text{Line } 33 = \text{line } 27 \times \text{line } 30$$

Line 34: Cumulative Returns. This line represents the cumulative income calculated in line 33. This line allows us to view returns for alternative time horizons. For instance:

> Present value over 10 years = $161,000
> Present value over 20 years = $326,400
> Present value over 30 years = $293,100

Profitability Analysis

The cash flow analysis indicates that the Birthfair School renovation project can be profitable. In fact, the project appears to be able to maintain profitable prospects even if effective gross revenues are off substantially, or if Birthfair decided to charge rent equal to some fraction of effective gross rents.

The key factor that causes the project to appear profitable is the 25% tax credit and the value of the depreciation. In the absence of these factors, the project would be marginal. But once the project is initiated, the tax benefits will accrue to the investor with a high degree of certainty.

Rent Recommendation

The static and dynamic both excluded rent payments to Birthfair. The reason for doing so was to determine how much rent a developer could afford to pay before setting a rent level for tenants who will sublet. Property taxes, however, were included.

The cash flow model indicates that one of the potential problems of the project is that the cash throw-off is negative. High rent levels would accentuate this problem. Consequently, a rent structure is recommended that is low but provides the kickers, or high rents in the out years, when the project generates a positive cash flow. The fact that the mortgagee will have a lien on the elementary wing reinforces Birthfair's ability to bargain for a kicker in the lease payments.

Conclusion

This section reviewed profit potential. It showed that the renovation can be very profitable. However, the project's profitability depends upon the value of the tax writeoffs more than the cash flow.

SUMMARY AND ANALYSIS

Since a developer could earn an adequate return and still earn about $300,000, Darth concluded that the city could charge a modest rent and still have a venture that would appeal to developers. Several additional versions of Table 11–3 were produced in response to requests about alternatives.

Darth presented the findings to the Citizens' Task Force. He stressed the favorable feasibility finding, although he also made it clear that the project would have to compete in a competitive environment. He suggested that the next step was to interest a developer.

The market and feasibility study was well received by the Citizens' Task Force, and the city manager had only minor questions about details of the report. He was particularly concerned about whether the gym might be better used for citizens' recreation rather than for the private use of tenants. He was also concerned that tax laws might change in a way that would be detrimental to the project. This in fact happened, and the project was never completed.

The City Council became concerned that the cost of moving some city offices to the school was too high. As more groups were brought into the decision-making process, numerous small changes were made and impediments were created. Ultimately, the City Council voted a modest appropriation to temporarily "mothball" the building. The project was never initiated.

SELECTED BIBLIOGRAPHY

Black, J. Thomas, Roark, Kelly, and Schwartz, Lisa S., *The Changing Office Workplace,* ULI, Washington, D.C., 1986.

Pygman, James, and Kateley, Richard, *Tall Office Buildings in the United States,* ULI, Washington, D.C., 1985.

Reynolds, Judith, *Historic Properties: Preservation and the Valuation Process,* American Institute of Real Estate Appraisers, Chicago, 1982.

Seymore, Charles F., "Market Value vs. Syndication Price," *The Appraisers Journal,* vol. LIV, no. 3 (1986), pp. 438–442.

Chapter Notes

CHAPTER 1

1. Chapter 4 expands upon the weaknesses which have plagued most market and feasibility studies.

2. Council on Environmental Quality, *The Third Annual Report,* U.S. Government Printing Office, Washington, D.C., August 1972.

CHAPTER 2

1. Portions of this chapter have been adapted from, "Appraisal Should Be Market Study: Techniques of Analysis," by G. Vincent Barrett, *Appraisal Journal* (October 1979). Reprinted with the permission of and copyrighted by the American Institute of Real Estate Appraisers of the National Association of Realtors, 1979.

The options expressed herein are those of the author(s) and do not necessarily carry the endorsement of the American Institute of Real Estate Appraisers.

CHAPTER 3

1. A reader interested in prior tax law and its impact on investment analysis is referred to the first edition of this text.

2. See Leon W. Ellwood, *Ellwood Tables for Real Estate Appraising and Financing,* 2nd ed., American Institute of Real Estate Appraisers, Chicago, 1967, ch. 1, pp. 3–5.

3. L. W. Ellwood, MAI, *The Appraisal Journal,* "All Rights to Future Benefits" (January 1974), pp. 38–44.

4. Changes take place in stages through 1989 and are indexed for inflation thereafter.

5. An in-depth discussion of the rational and methods of "sensitivity" analysis is beyond the scope of this text. However, for the interested, a reasonable discussion of this topic may be found in "Evaluating Risk of Investment Real Estate," by Michael S. Young, *The Real Estate Appraiser,* vol. 43 (September/October 1977), pp. 39–45. Also see Austin J. Jaffe and C. F. Sirmans, *Real Estate Investment Decision Making,* Prentice-Hall, Inc., Englewood Cliffs, N.J., 1982, pp. 431–457.

6. For a review of some criticisms of the IRR, see Austin J. Jaffee and C. F. Sirmans, *Real Estate Investment Decision Making,* Prentice-Hall, Inc., Englewood Cliffs, N.J., 1982, pp. 419–428.

CHAPTER 4

1. There are many individual consultants who work independently of the larger firms, but, even so, many if not all of the weaknesses identified here are commonplace in their studies. We are using the larger firms for explanatory purposes since their actions encompass all of the problems alluded to.

2. The lesson was not easily learned; there was pressure from various sources to produce a feasibility study substantiating the original design. Fortunately this pressure did not manifest itself in the market study, where the project *should* have begun.

CHAPTER 5

1. Oliver P. Williams, *Metropolitan Political Analysis: A Social Access Approach,* The Free Press, New York, 1971, p. 30.

2. Bruce Lindeman, "Anatomy of Land Speculation," *Journal of the American Institute of Planners* (April 1976), pp. 142–153. Also see H. J. Brown, R. S. Phillips, and N. A. Roberts, "Land Markets at the Urban Fringe," *Journal of American Planners* (April 1981), pp. 131–43.

3. T. Lee, "The Urban Neighborhood as a Socio-Spatial Schema," *Human Relations,* vol. 21 (1968), pp. 241–268.

4. American Institute of Real Estate Appraisers, *The Appraisal of Real Estate,* 8th ed., American Institute of Real Estate Appraisers, Chicago, 1983.

5. Anthony Downs, *Urban Problems and Prospects,* Markham, Chicago, 1970.

6. J. Barry Mason and Morris L. Mayer, *Modern Retailing,* Business Publications, Plano, Tex. (1984).

7. David L. Huff, "A Probabilistic Analysis of Shopping Center Trade Areas," *Land Economics,* vol. 39 (1963). Also see John R. Nevin and Ruth Smith, "The Predictive Accuracy of a Retail Gravitation Model," in *The Changing Market Environment,* K. Bernhardt et al., Eds., American Marketing Association, Chicago, 1981.

8. Mason and Morris, *op. cit.,* pp. 793–794.

CHAPTER 6

1. Robert Plattner, "Regional Migration," *The Real Estate Appraiser and Analyst* (Summer 1983), pp. 5–12.

2. U.S. Bureau of the Census, *Current Population Reports: Population Characteristics,* Series p. 20, no. 154, Government Printing Office, Washington, D.C., August 22, 1966.

3. Charles M. Tiebout, *The Community Economic Base Study,* Committee for Economic Development, Washington, D.C., 1962.

4. Throughout the rest of this chapter a dot over the symbols indicates that the variable is forecast.

5. Benjamin Chinitz, "Contrasts in Agglomeration: New York and Pittsburgh," *American Economic Review* (May 1961), pp. 259–279.

6. U.S. Department of Housing and Urban Development, *Urban Housing Market Analysis,* U.S. Government Printing Office, Washington, D.C., 1967.

7. Norton J. Schussheim, "The Impact of Demographic Change on Housing and Community Development," *The Appraisal Journal* (July 1984), pp. 375–381.

8. Joel Bergsman, Peter Greenstan, and Robert Healy, "Agglomeration Process in Urban Growth," *Urban Studies,* vol. 9 (October 1972), p. 263.

9. Edgar M. Hoover, *Location Theory and the Shoe and Leather Industries,* Harvard University Press, Cambridge, Mass., 1937, pp. 90–91.

10. John P. Blair and Robert Premus, "Determinants of Locational Factors," *Urban Development Quarterly* (forthcoming).

11. Wilber Thompson, *Preface to Urban Economics,* Johns Hopkins, Baltimore, Md., 1968, p. 53.

CHAPTER 7

1. Neil A. Stevens, "Housing: A Cyclical Industry on the Upswing," *Federal Reserve Bank of St. Louis Review* (August 1976), pp. 16–20.

2. C. Lowell Harris, "National Economic Fluctuations and Property Values," *International Property Assessment Administration Proceedings,* International Association of Assessing Officers, Chicago, 1974, pp. 316–324.

3. Wesley C. Mitchell, *What Happens during Business Cycles,* National Bureau of Economic Research, Inc., New York, 1951, p. 6.

4. Clayton P. Pritchett, "Forecasting the Impact of Real Estate Cycle on Investments," *Real Estate Review,* Winter 1984, pp. 85–89.

5. Gordon T. Brown, "Real Estate Cycles Alter the Valuation Perspective," *The Appraisal Journal* (October, 1984), pp. 539–547.

6. Donald M. Manson, Marie Howland, and George Peterson, "The Effects of Business Cycle on Metropolitan Suburbanization," *Economic Geography,* 1985.

7. Gary Fromm, "Econometric Models of the Residential Construction Sector: A Comparison," in *National Housing Models,* R. Bruce Ricks, Ed., Lexington Books, Lexington, Mass., 1977, pp. 125–153.

8. Kenneth D. Wilson, "Forecasting Futures," *Society* (January/February 1978), p. 108.

9. Francisco Arcelus and Allen H. Meltzer, "Markets for Housing and Housing Services," *Journal of Money Credit and Banking* (February 1973), pp. 78–99.

10. Neil A. Stevens, "Housing: A Cyclical Industry on the Upswing," *Federal Reserve Bank of St. Louis Review* (August 1976), pp. 16–20.

11. On rare occasions the rates may actually move in opposite directions. However, these instances tend to be temporary deviations.

12. A. N. Causing and K. N. Esliger, Jr., "The Remarkable Rise of One Person Household," *Real Estate Review* (Spring 1983), pp. 89–91.

13. Eric Smart, "With a Maturing Population, Age Is Only Part of the Picture," *Urban Land* (May 1983), pp. 32–34.

14. B. Robey, "Demographic Myths," *Urban Land* (June 1983), pp. 38–42.

15. "Outlook 87 and Beyond," *The Futurist* (November–December 1986), pp. 54–60.

16. The equation includes the terms (GI) and (SP), which represent the interaction of the general price effect with the specific factor. If we ignore the interaction effect, the problem can be solved by simply subtracting the base price plus the inflation effect from the actual market price:

$$P_n = P_1(1 + GI)^n + P_1(SP)$$

In this case, SP is the specific price increase for the entire n years, not an annual rate.

17. If the capitalization rate increased by 6% (.08 × 1.06 = .0848), then the value would remain $53,000 in spite of the higher net return to land.

18. James E. Gibbons, "Cost-Push Variety of Inflation Threatens Economic Feasibility of Real Estate Development," *The Appraisal Journal* (October 1974), pp. 485–493.

19. R. Bruce Ricks, "Managing the Best Financial Asset," *California Management Review* (Spring 1976), pp. 79–84.

20. The monetary and real rates of return were calculated as follows: Let the initial property value equal V. Appreciation, then, is .06 times V. The initial 10% down payment is equal to .10 times V. Thus the appreciation rate based on equity is $.06V/.10V = .60$. However, because of inflation, the dollar's purchasing power diminishes to 1.00/1.10 or .909 at the end of the period. Therefore, we must multiply the monetary value by the price deflator to get the real or base-year dollar increase.

21. David K. Gillogly, "Housing and Inflation—Victim or Villain?" *Business Economics* (January 1975), pp. 23–30.

CHAPTER 8

1. For a brief review of these factors see "The Plant Site Preferences of Industry, and the Factors of Selection," a *Business Week* Research Report (August 1958). Also "New Light on Site Seeking," *Dun's Review and Modern Industry* (March 1959), pp. 90–91, 104–111.

2. There are publications, too numerous to mention here, which are of invaluable assistance in analyzing industrial trends. However, one of the best overall approaches is direct contact by either telephone, personal interviews, or letters with knowledgeable leaders within each industrial sector. An excellent source for the names and locations of these people is: Craig Colgate, Jr., Ed., *Combined Insurance Companies of America, National Trade and Professional Associations of the United States,* Columbia Books, Inc., Washington, D.C., 1970.

3. The Clearfield facilities were originally government buildings which were sold at a very low cost to private interests. Consequently, warehouse space was available from 3 to 6.5 cents per square foot per month, whereas in Reno, the rates were 17–18 cents in public facilities.

4. This factor became so significant in the movement of firms from central California to Nevada that a study of the situation was made. Robert E. Warren, *An Examination of the Extent and Impact of Tax-Exempt Warehousing and Assembly in Nevada under Provisions of the Free Port Law,* transmitted to Hon. Casper W. Weinberger, Dir., Department of Finance, State of California, Sacramento, California, Economic Development Agency, State of California, June 15, 1968.

5. Data developed from personal interviews and materials supplied by members of Freeport Center Associates, Clearfield, Utah, and the Business and Industrial Development Department, Reno, Nevada, February 1971.

6. The following firms were locating or planning on doing so in the planning area, while planning studies were ongoing.
    a. Four trucking firms, requiring a minimum of 25 acres each.
    b. One modular home manufacturer, requiring a minimum of 10 acres.
    c. One mobile home manufacturer, requiring a minimum of 10 acres.
    d. One ski equipment manufacturer, requiring a minimum of 10 acres.
    e. One prefab concrete form manufacturer, requiring a minimum of 13 acres.
    f. One construction company, requiring a minimum of 22 acres.

7. Nearly 100 industrial districts across the United States were surveyed by mail and telephone. All industrial districts in Colorado and Wyoming were surveyed.

8. There was considerable discussion between the client and his consultants on this point. Recent sales of undeveloped property in the area were above

$3,000 an acre. The client, however, did not wish the return on equity to appear low as a result of raising the land values to recent prices. He was not interested in return on equity as such, but only on reasonable debt coverage and a positive net bank balance.

9. If the equity investment had been raised to $3,000 per acre, the project would not have passed this index of profitability.

CHAPTER 10

1. T. D. Allman, "The Urban Crisis Leaves Town and Moves to the Suburbs," *Harpers* (December 1978).

2. Raquel Ramata, "The Plaza as an Amenity," *Urban Land* (February 1979), pp. 9–12.

Index